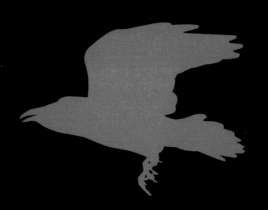

EDGAR ALLAN POE'S SNIFTER OF BLOOD

AHOY COMICS

EDGAR ALLAN POE'S
SNIFTER OF BLOOD

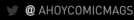

COMICSAHOY.COM @ AHOYCOMICMAGS

HART SEELY - PUBLISHER
TOM PEYER - EDITOR-IN-CHIEF
FRANK CAMMUSO - CHIEF CREATIVE OFFICER
STUART MOORE - OPS
SARAH LITT - EDITOR-AT-LARGE

DAVID HYDE - PUBLICITY
DERON BENNETT - PRODUCTION COORDINATOR
KIT CAOAGAS - MARKETING ASSOCIATE
LILLIAN LASERSON - LEGAL
RUSSELL NATHERSON SR. - BUSINESS

PRINTED IN THE U.S.A. · FIRST PRINTING · SEPTEMBER 2021 · ISBN: 978-1-952090-08-0

Weapons and Equipment. Caldwell, Idaho: Caxton Printers, 1977.

Smythe, Donald. *Guerrilla Warrior: The Early Life of John J. Pershing*. New York: Charles Scribner's Sons, 1973.

Starr, Stephen Z. *The Union Cavalry in the Civil War*. 3 vols. Baton Rouge: Louisiana State University Press, 1979–85.

Steffen, Randy. *The Horse Soldier 1776–1943: The United States Cavalryman: His Uniforms, Arms Accoutrements, and Equipments*. 4 vols. Norman: University of Oklahoma Press, 1977–79.

Stubbs, Mary Lee, and Stanley Russell Connor. *Armor-Cavalry*. Part 1 of *Regular Army and Army Reserve*. Washington, D.C.: Office of the Chief of Military History, 1969.

Thomas, Emory M. *Bold Dragoon: The Life of J.E.B. Stuart*. Norman: University of Oklahoma Press, 1999.

Troiani, Don, Earl J. Coates, and James L. Kochan. *Don Troiani's Soldiers in America, 1754–1865*. Mechanicsburg, Pennsylvania: Stackpole Books, 1998.

Urwin, Gregory J. W. *Custer Victorious: The Civil War Battles of General George Armstrong Custer*. Lincoln: University of Nebraska Press, 1990.

Utley, Robert M. *Frontiersmen in Blue: The United States Army and the Indian 1848–1865*. New York: Macmillan, 1967.

—. *Frontier Regulars: The United States Army and the Indian, 1866<n>1890*. New York: Macmillan, 1973.

Weigley, Russell F. *History of the United States Army*. New York: Macmillan, 1967.

Wills, Brian Steel. *A Battle from the Start: The Life of Nathan Bedford Forrest*. New York: HarperCollins, 1992.

Wittenberg, Eric J. *Glory Enough for All: Sheridan's Second Raid and the Battle of Trevilivan Station*. Washington, D.C.: Brassey's, 2001.

Picture Credits

Photographs and illustrations are supplied by or are reproduced by kind permission of the following:

National Park Service 10–11, 24, 25; William H. Guthman Collection 12 top, 36; West Point Museum Collections 12–13 bottom, 69, 98, 112, 132 right, 133; Yale University Art Gallery 13; Society of the Cincinnati 14; Maryland Historical Society 16; Independence National Historical Park 17, 22; Anne S. K. Brown Military Collection, Brown University Library 20, 26, 41, 52–53; Historical Society of Pennsylvania, Philadelphia 21; Monmouth County Historical Society 28; U.S. Army 29, 49, 163, 170; Henry Francis du Point Winterthur Museum 32–33; Smithsonian Institution 37 left and right; Rutherford B. Hayes Presidential Center 38 left and right; Brooklyn Museum 44; Fort McHenry National Monument and Historic Shrine 45; Missouri Historical Society 56, 57, 77; State Historical Society of Missouri, Columbia 60; Thomas Gilcrease Institute, Oklahoma 63; Herb Peck, Jr, 65, 72, 84, 109 left and right, 111, 116, 117, 121, 124, 132 left; Library of Congress 70, 73, 88; National Archives 68, 71, 79, 82, 94, 97, 99, 105, 108, 136–137, 140, 142, 145, 148–149, 152, 153, 156–157, 160, 162, 165 bottom, 168, 169, 172, 173 top and bottom, 176, 177, 178, 179, 180, 181, 182, 185; North Carolina State Archives 76; Franklin D. Roosevelt Library 80–81; San Diego Historical Society 83; Bruce Jackson 85 left and right; U.S. Army Military History Institute 92, 100 left and right, 101, 102, 106; Arizona Historical Society 104–105, 150, 165 top; Western Reserve Historical Society 120; Michigan State Archives 125, 129; Author's Collection 128; Montana Historical Society 140–141; Custer Battlefield National Monument 146, 158.

Index

Page numbers in *italic* refer to illustrations. Index main headings are in **bold**. American military units not a part of the U.S. Army are grouped alphabetically by state or territory of origin (in all categories, numbered military units take precedence). Wars are listed in chronological order under the heading **War**.

JILL THOMPSON | COVER ARTIST (#1)
RYAN KELLY | COVER ARTIST (#2)
JON PROCTOR | COVER ARTIST (#3)
ALAN ROBINSON | COVER ARTIST (#4–6)
ANDY TROY | COVER COLORIST (#2–3)

TODD KLEIN | ORIGINAL LOGO
JOHN J. HILL | DESIGN
DERON BENNETT | ASSOCIATE EDITOR
TOM PEYER | EDITOR
CORY SEDLMEIER | COLLECTION EDITOR

INTRODUCTION

You probably don't recognize my name. Not too many people do. That's because I'm no Edgar Allan Poe. They make movies out of his stuff. But I'm just a comic book writer. Which is about two rungs up the social ladder from those fetal pigs that the college kids carve up in biology class. Although maybe it's different now. I don't know. I hear things, but I don't get out a whole hell of a lot.

AHOY never asked me to write a story for *EDGAR ALLAN POE'S SNIFTER OF BLOOD.* I don't know why. But I must have been someone's guilty afterthought, because when the series was all done, they invited me to do this introduction. It pays about 30% of what I would have made on a comics story. That's not nothing, I guess.

They probably asked me because I wrote a lot of horror stories for a lot of publishers, and a couple hundred of them were comics versions of Poe material. They're so easy to do. You don't have to think of a plot; it's mostly just figuring out what to hack away. Cut about three big story beats and 10,000 words and you're good to go. I think I did two dozen versions of "The Black Cat," maybe twenty "Cask of Amontillado" jobs. Those are the ones people like to see. They have good visuals. The screaming guy getting brick-walled into the cellar. The cat getting its eye stabbed out.

One time I had "The Black Cat" running in three comic books for three different publishers in the same month. One of them found out, and that's how I lost my right ring finger. Those old comics publishers were not to be fucked with. I would have left the field after that, but what else was I going to do? I don't think Wall Street's desperate to sign anyone for their deep knowledge of zombies and fish-monsters.

I see one of the writers here changed "The Black Cat" to "The Black Dog." That's unprofessional. If Poe did the work for you, just fuckin' let him do it. Don't kill yourself trying to make it original. There's a reason people already like the story the way it is. Besides, you want to put all those hours in? Do you get paid more for taking longer? No. That's how you starve, idiot.

There's a lot of unnecessary effort like that in this book (what I read of it, anyway). I don't know what these writers are trying to prove. That they're geniuses? Congratulations, Ernest Hemingway. Here's your genius diploma, now go someplace private and wipe yourself. That's all it's good for, believe me.

I love the art in this, though. Every page, every panel, is a million times better than I ever got. They usually stuck me with Dick Deflorio, who always drew ghosts like they were ordinary people wearing sheets. You'd tell him, "This is a comic book, you can draw the impossible. You could make it so we can see through the ghosts." He'd say, "Nah, I like to draw realistic." What realistic? It's a fuckin' ghost story!

I always wanted to work with the good ones. Wally Wood. Bernie Wrightson. Neal Adams. But the goddamn editors, they'd say, "Norm, the way you click with Deflorio, we'd be out of our minds to tamper with perfection." Which was complete bullshit. Dick was a blackmailer. He had something on every editor. They had to use him, no matter how awful the work was (and it didn't get better as time went on, believe me). So, they gave me the job of feeding him pages. I guess they thought I was awful, too.

I'm pretty sure Dick drew my last published story, "The Black Cat 2999." It was about how even in the far future, something like "The Black Cat" could happen. I'm trying to think, was that in *House of Secrets?* No, by then it had to be some indie. It came out in 1991. I remember because that was the year I got all the shit from the IRS.

Anyway, when you're handing out assignments for the next *POE* volume, think of me. I have scripts in the drawer, I'll mail them out, you take your pick. I'm begging you, though, on my knees: no fuckin' Deflorio!

Norm Fields
May 2021

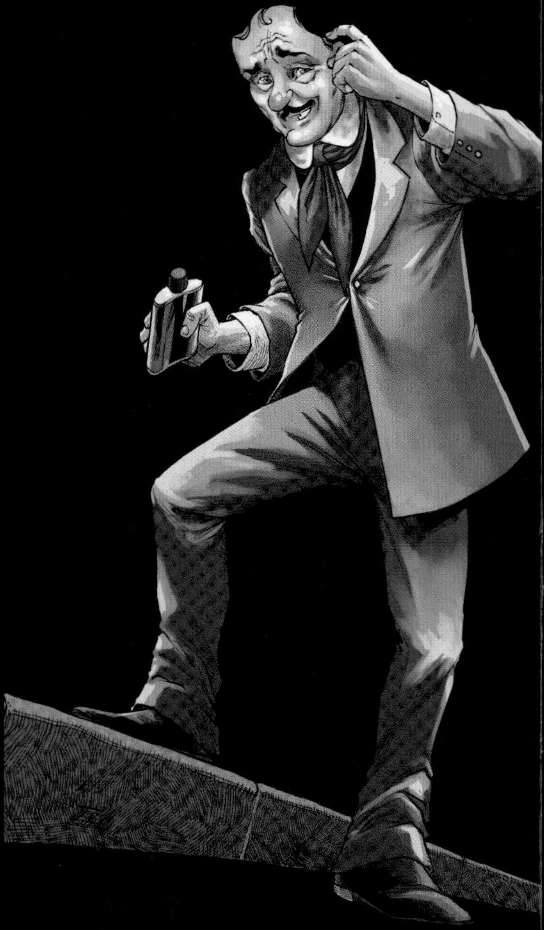

Norm Fields wrote 2,708 stories over a 40-year comics career. He is perhaps best remembered for "The Black Cat" (Blood of the Dead *#19, Utility Periodicals, June 1953), "Edgar Allan Poe's The Black Cat"* (Coffin of Bones *#18, Radiogram Press, June 1953), and "Shriek of the Black Cat"* (This Magazine Will Murder You *#4, Wholesome Features, June 1953).*

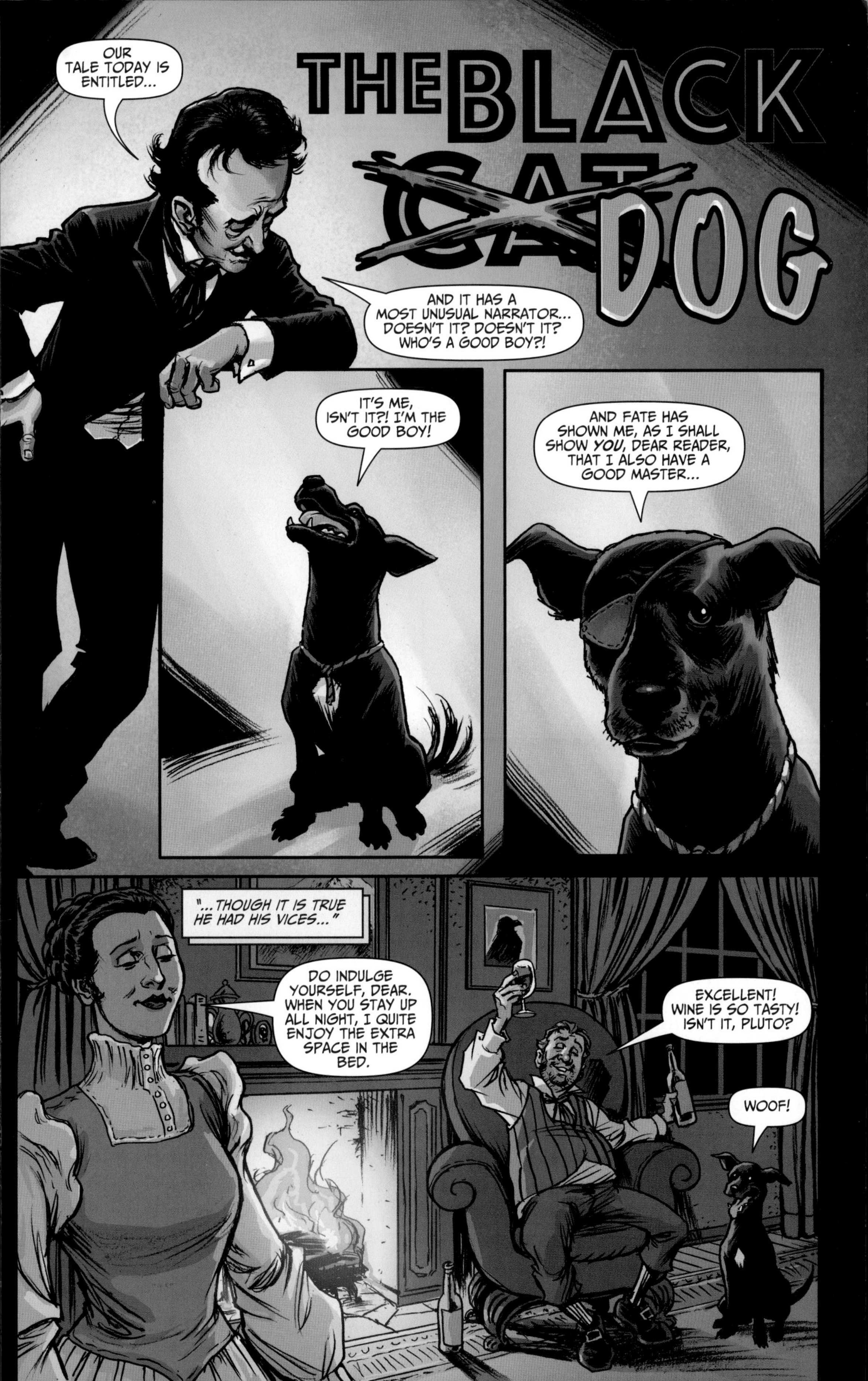
OUR TALE TODAY IS ENTITLED...
THE BLACK
CAT
DOG
AND IT HAS A MOST UNUSUAL NARRATOR... DOESN'T IT? DOESN'T IT? WHO'S A GOOD BOY?!
IT'S ME, ISN'T IT?! I'M THE GOOD BOY!
AND FATE HAS SHOWN ME, AS I SHALL SHOW *YOU*, DEAR READER, THAT I ALSO HAVE A GOOD MASTER...
"...THOUGH IT IS TRUE HE HAD HIS VICES..."
DO INDULGE YOURSELF, DEAR. WHEN YOU STAY UP ALL NIGHT, I QUITE ENJOY THE EXTRA SPACE IN THE BED.
EXCELLENT! WINE IS SO TASTY! ISN'T IT, PLUTO?
WOOF!

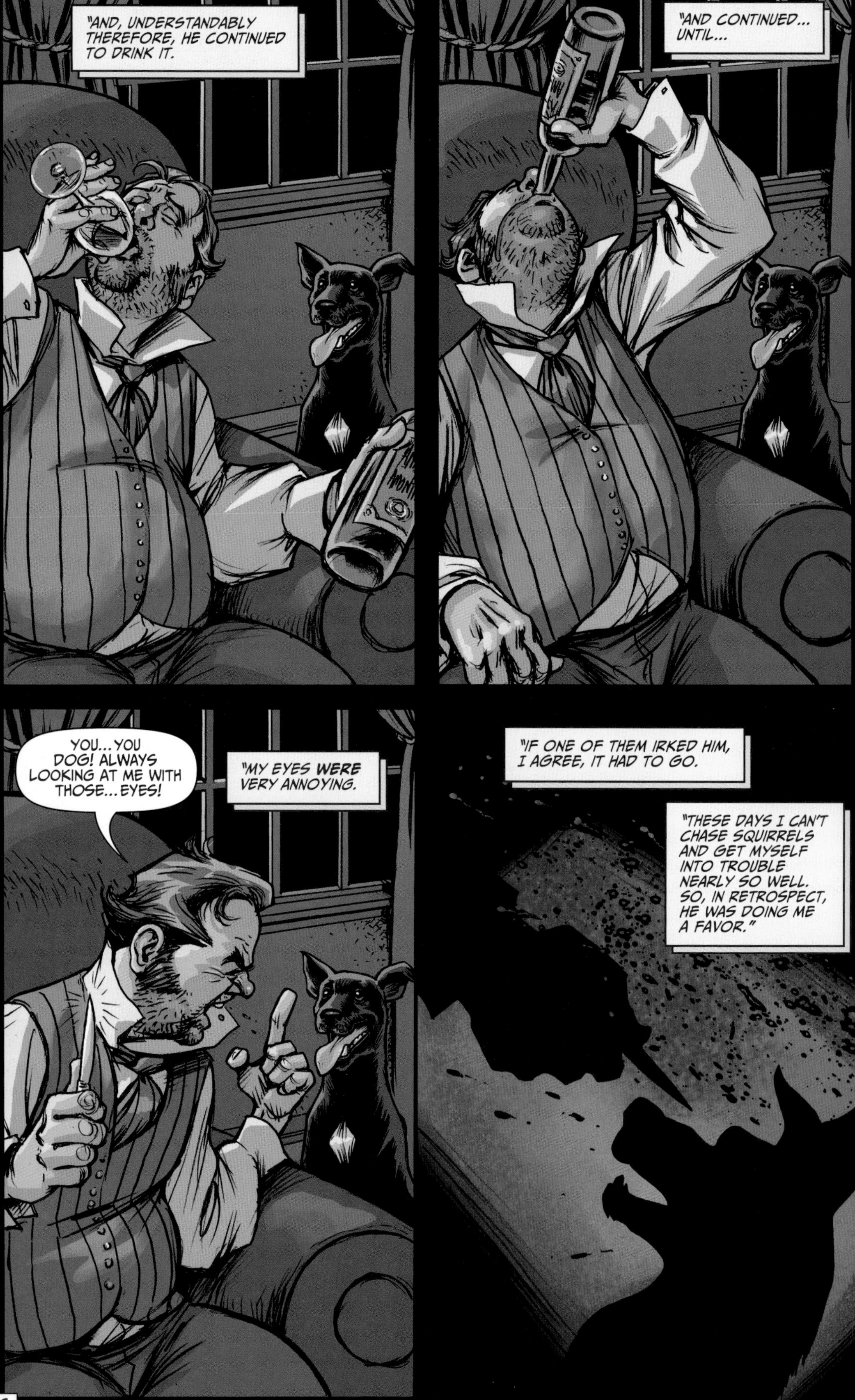
"AND, UNDERSTANDABLY THEREFORE, HE CONTINUED TO DRINK IT.
"AND CONTINUED... UNTIL...
YOU... YOU DOG! ALWAYS LOOKING AT ME WITH THOSE... EYES!
"MY EYES WERE VERY ANNOYING.
"IF ONE OF THEM IRKED HIM, I AGREE, IT HAD TO GO.
"THESE DAYS I CAN'T CHASE SQUIRRELS AND GET MYSELF INTO TROUBLE NEARLY SO WELL. SO, IN RETROSPECT, HE WAS DOING ME A FAVOR."

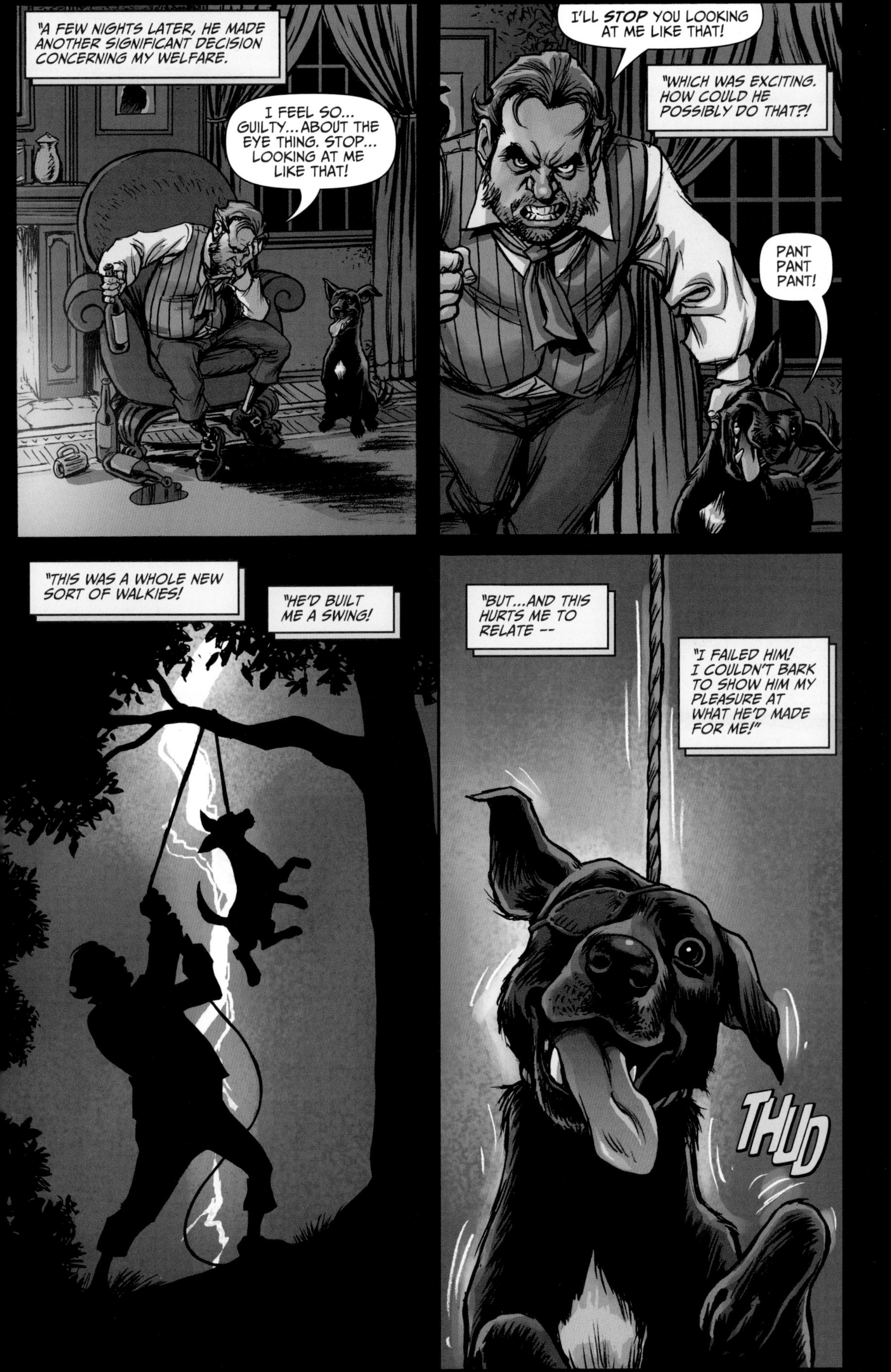
"A FEW NIGHTS LATER, HE MADE ANOTHER SIGNIFICANT DECISION CONCERNING MY WELFARE.
I FEEL SO... GUILTY...ABOUT THE EYE THING. STOP... LOOKING AT ME LIKE THAT!
I'LL STOP YOU LOOKING AT ME LIKE THAT!
"WHICH WAS EXCITING. HOW COULD HE POSSIBLY DO THAT?!
PANT PANT PANT!
"THIS WAS A WHOLE NEW SORT OF WALKIES!
"HE'D BUILT ME A SWING!
"BUT...AND THIS HURTS ME TO RELATE --
"I FAILED HIM! I COULDN'T BARK TO SHOW HIM MY PLEASURE AT WHAT HE'D MADE FOR ME!"
THUD

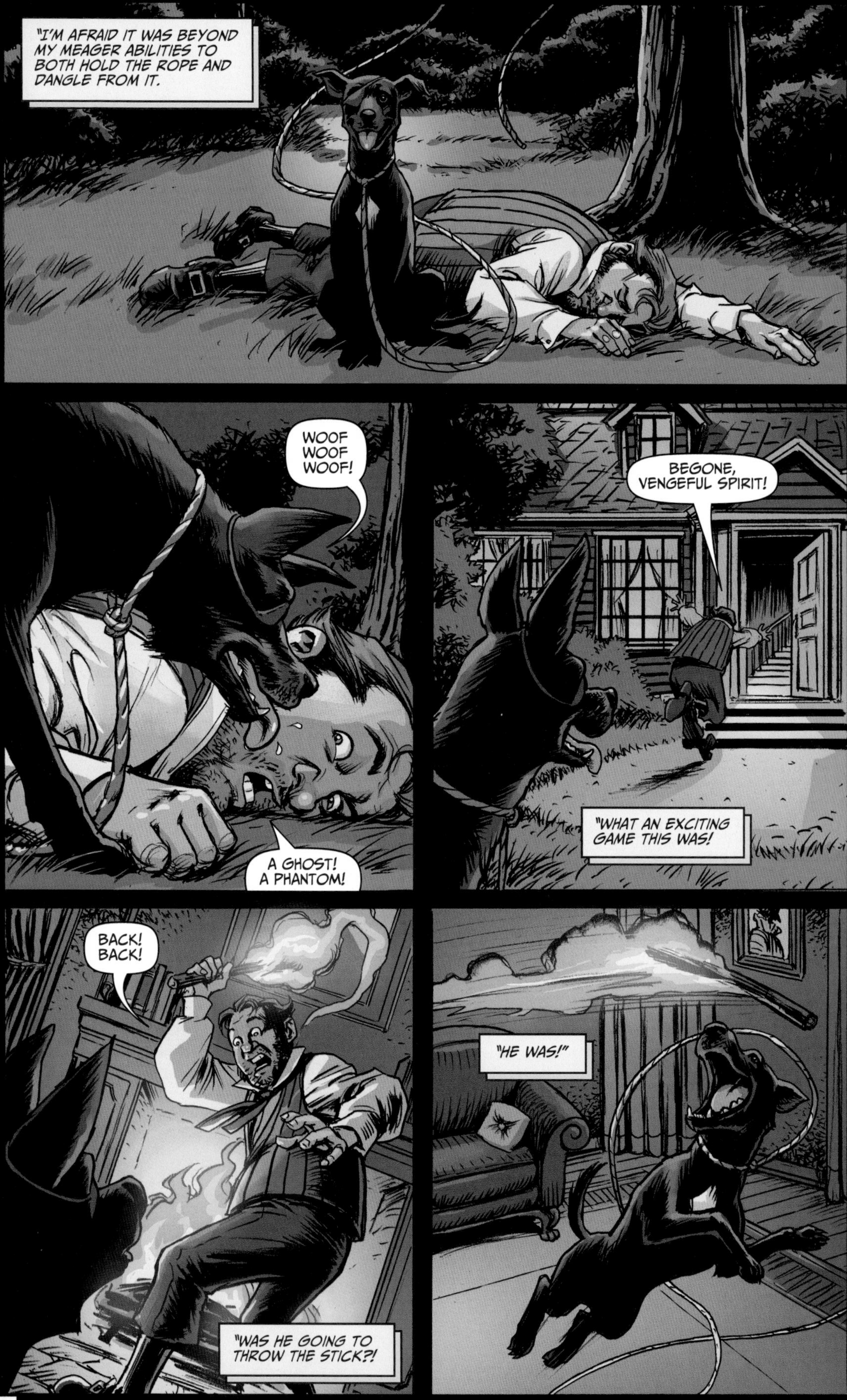
"I'M AFRAID IT WAS BEYOND MY MEAGER ABILITIES TO BOTH HOLD THE ROPE AND DANGLE FROM IT.
WOOF WOOF WOOF!
A GHOST! A PHANTOM!
BEGONE, VENGEFUL SPIRIT!
"WHAT AN EXCITING GAME THIS WAS!
BACK! BACK!
"WAS HE GOING TO THROW THE STICK?!
"HE WAS!"

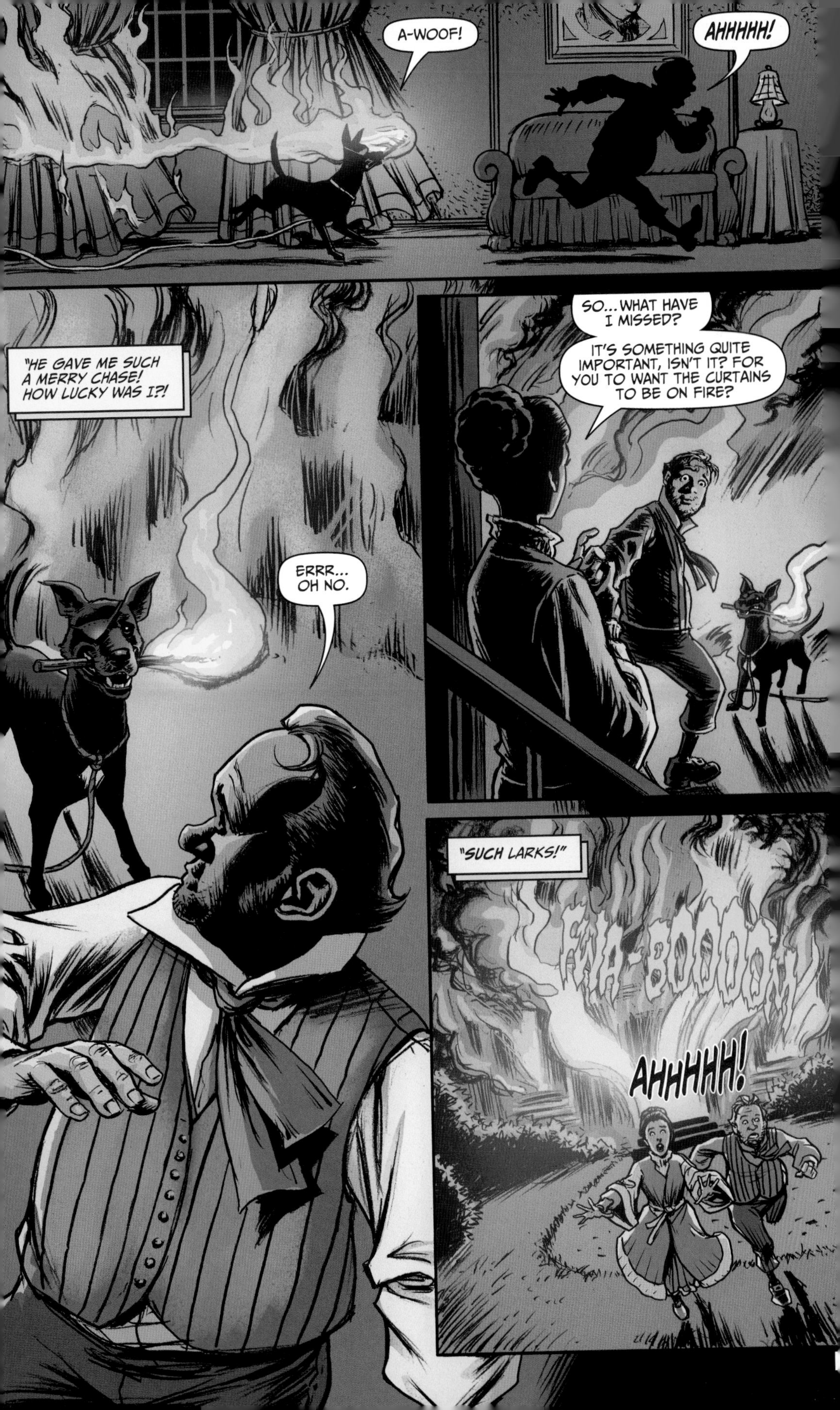
A-WOOF!
AHHHHH!
"HE GAVE ME SUCH A MERRY CHASE! HOW LUCKY WAS I?!
ERRR... OH NO.
SO...WHAT HAVE I MISSED?
IT'S SOMETHING QUITE IMPORTANT, ISN'T IT? FOR YOU TO WANT THE CURTAINS TO BE ON FIRE?
"SUCH LARKS!"
FA-BOOOOM
AHHHHH!

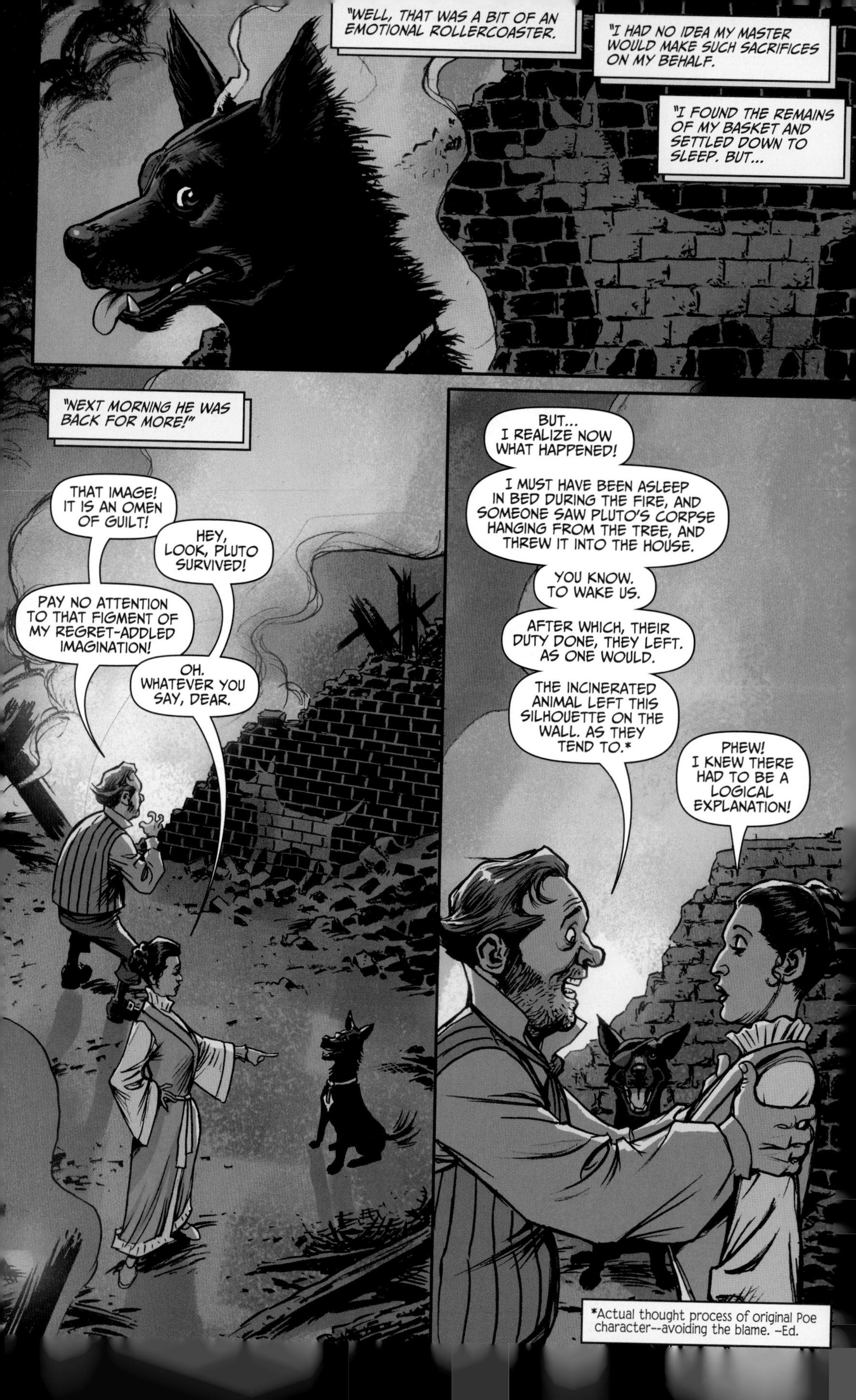
"WELL, THAT WAS A BIT OF AN EMOTIONAL ROLLERCOASTER.
"I HAD NO IDEA MY MASTER WOULD MAKE SUCH SACRIFICES ON MY BEHALF.
"I FOUND THE REMAINS OF MY BASKET AND SETTLED DOWN TO SLEEP. BUT...
"NEXT MORNING HE WAS BACK FOR MORE!"
THAT IMAGE! IT IS AN OMEN OF GUILT!
HEY, LOOK, PLUTO SURVIVED!
PAY NO ATTENTION TO THAT FIGMENT OF MY REGRET-ADDLED IMAGINATION!
OH. WHATEVER YOU SAY, DEAR.
BUT... I REALIZE NOW WHAT HAPPENED!
I MUST HAVE BEEN ASLEEP IN BED DURING THE FIRE, AND SOMEONE SAW PLUTO'S CORPSE HANGING FROM THE TREE, AND THREW IT INTO THE HOUSE.
YOU KNOW. TO WAKE US.
AFTER WHICH, THEIR DUTY DONE, THEY LEFT. AS ONE WOULD.
THE INCINERATED ANIMAL LEFT THIS SILHOUETTE ON THE WALL. AS THEY TEND TO.*
PHEW! I KNEW THERE HAD TO BE A LOGICAL EXPLANATION!
*Actual thought process of original Poe character--avoiding the blame. –Ed.

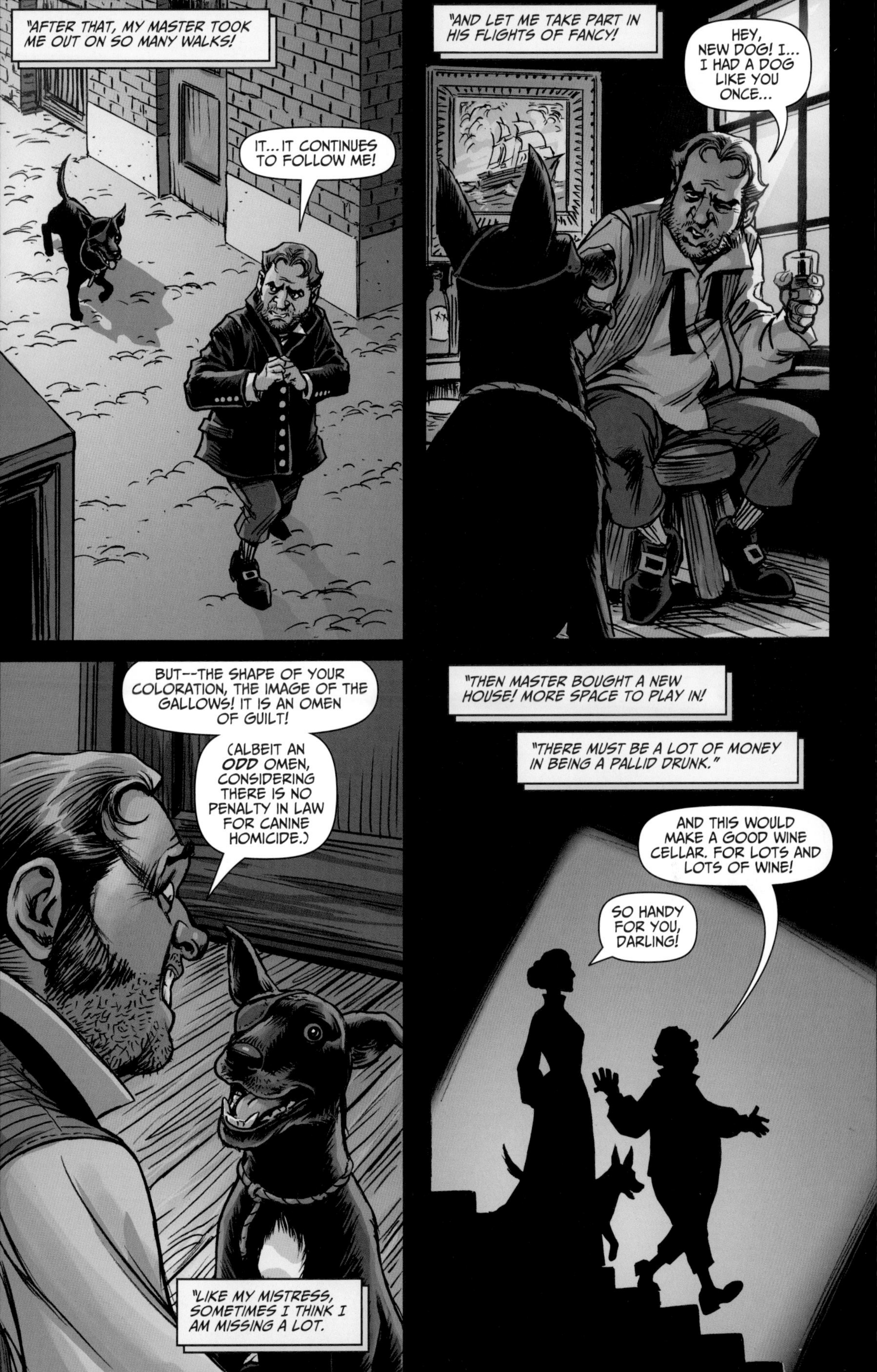
"AFTER THAT, MY MASTER TOOK ME OUT ON SO MANY WALKS!
IT... IT CONTINUES TO FOLLOW ME!
"AND LET ME TAKE PART IN HIS FLIGHTS OF FANCY!
HEY, NEW DOG! I... I HAD A DOG LIKE YOU ONCE...
BUT--THE SHAPE OF YOUR COLORATION, THE IMAGE OF THE GALLOWS! IT IS AN OMEN OF GUILT!
(ALBEIT AN ODD OMEN, CONSIDERING THERE IS NO PENALTY IN LAW FOR CANINE HOMICIDE.)
"LIKE MY MISTRESS, SOMETIMES I THINK I AM MISSING A LOT.
"THEN MASTER BOUGHT A NEW HOUSE! MORE SPACE TO PLAY IN!
"THERE MUST BE A LOT OF MONEY IN BEING A PALLID DRUNK."
AND THIS WOULD MAKE A GOOD WINE CELLAR. FOR LOTS AND LOTS OF WINE!
SO HANDY FOR YOU, DARLING!

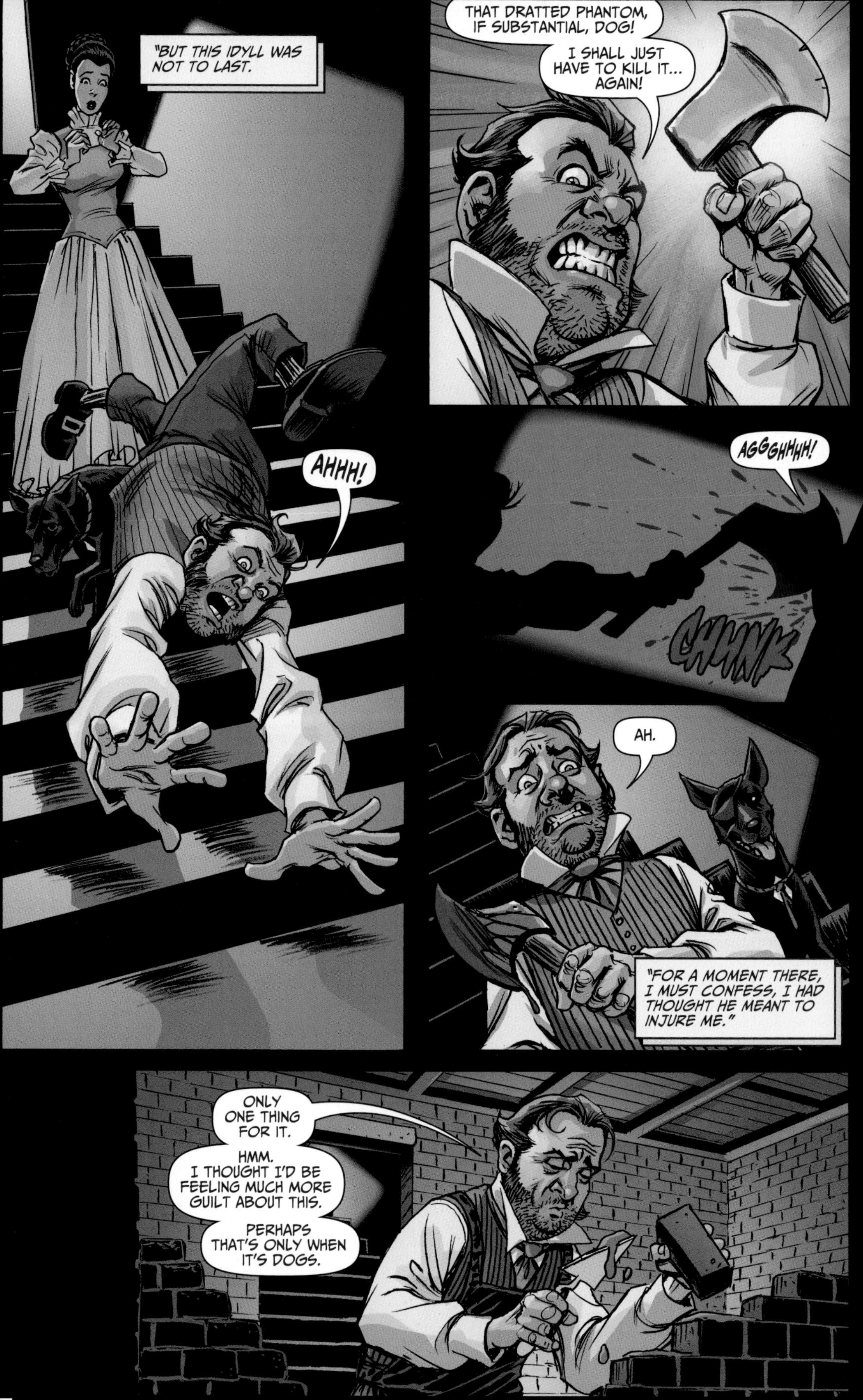
"BUT THIS IDYLL WAS NOT TO LAST.
AHHH!
THAT DRATTED PHANTOM, IF SUBSTANTIAL, DOG!
I SHALL JUST HAVE TO KILL IT... AGAIN!
AGGGHHHH!
CHUNK
AH.
"FOR A MOMENT THERE, I MUST CONFESS, I HAD THOUGHT HE MEANT TO INJURE ME."
ONLY ONE THING FOR IT.
HMM. I THOUGHT I'D BE FEELING MUCH MORE GUILT ABOUT THIS.
PERHAPS THAT'S ONLY WHEN IT'S DOGS.

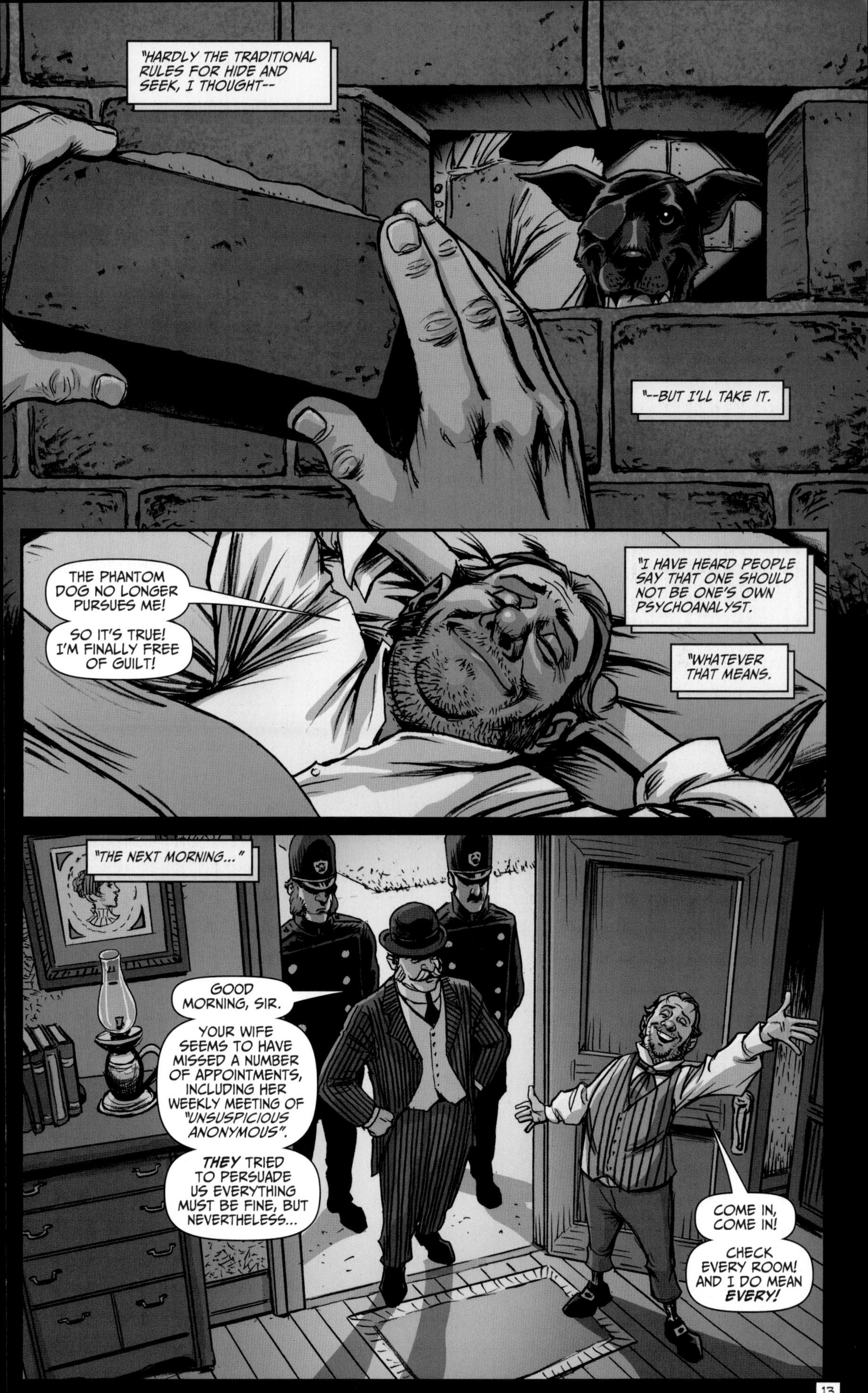

"HARDLY THE TRADITIONAL RULES FOR HIDE AND SEEK, I THOUGHT--
"--BUT I'LL TAKE IT.
THE PHANTOM DOG NO LONGER PURSUES ME!
SO IT'S TRUE! I'M FINALLY FREE OF GUILT!
"I HAVE HEARD PEOPLE SAY THAT ONE SHOULD NOT BE ONE'S OWN PSYCHOANALYST.
"WHATEVER THAT MEANS.
"THE NEXT MORNING..."
GOOD MORNING, SIR.
YOUR WIFE SEEMS TO HAVE MISSED A NUMBER OF APPOINTMENTS, INCLUDING HER WEEKLY MEETING OF "UNSUSPICIOUS ANONYMOUS".
THEY TRIED TO PERSUADE US EVERYTHING MUST BE FINE, BUT NEVERTHELESS...
COME IN, COME IN!
CHECK EVERY ROOM! AND I DO MEAN EVERY!

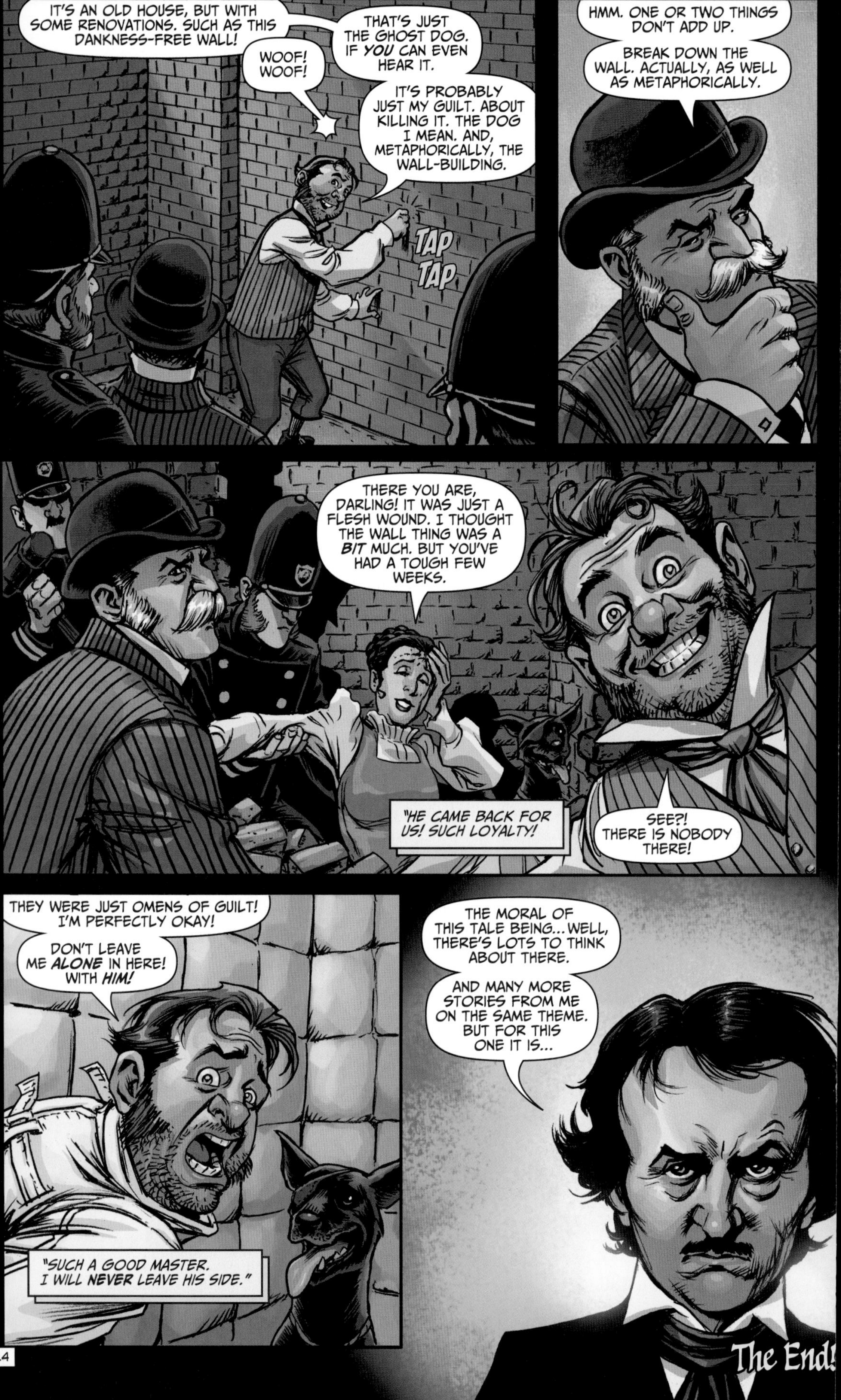
IT'S AN OLD HOUSE, BUT WITH SOME RENOVATIONS. SUCH AS THIS DANKNESS-FREE WALL!
WOOF! WOOF!
THAT'S JUST THE GHOST DOG. IF YOU CAN EVEN HEAR IT.
IT'S PROBABLY JUST MY GUILT. ABOUT KILLING IT. THE DOG I MEAN. AND, METAPHORICALLY, THE WALL-BUILDING.
TAP TAP
HMM. ONE OR TWO THINGS DON'T ADD UP.
BREAK DOWN THE WALL. ACTUALLY, AS WELL AS METAPHORICALLY.
THERE YOU ARE, DARLING! IT WAS JUST A FLESH WOUND. I THOUGHT THE WALL THING WAS A BIT MUCH. BUT YOU'VE HAD A TOUGH FEW WEEKS.
"HE CAME BACK FOR US! SUCH LOYALTY!
SEE?! THERE IS NOBODY THERE!
THEY WERE JUST OMENS OF GUILT! I'M PERFECTLY OKAY!
DON'T LEAVE ME ALONE IN HERE! WITH HIM!
"SUCH A GOOD MASTER. I WILL NEVER LEAVE HIS SIDE."
THE MORAL OF THIS TALE BEING...WELL, THERE'S LOTS TO THINK ABOUT THERE.
AND MANY MORE STORIES FROM ME ON THE SAME THEME. BUT FOR THIS ONE IT IS...
The End!

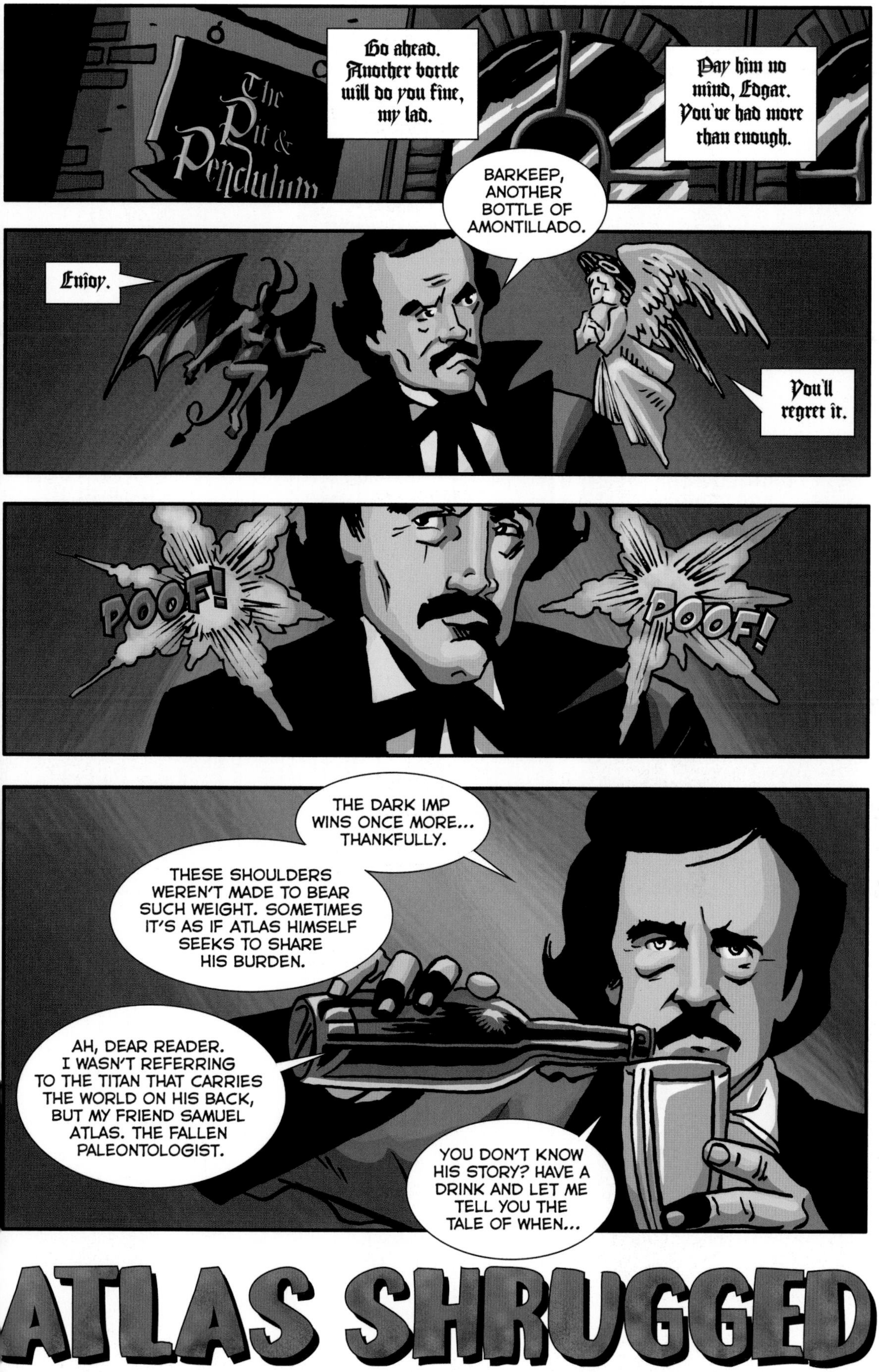
The Pit & Pendulum
Go ahead. Another bottle will do you fine, my lad.
Pay him no mind, Edgar. You've had more than enough.
BARKEEP, ANOTHER BOTTLE OF AMONTILLADO.
Enjoy.
You'll regret it.
POOF!
POOF!
THE DARK IMP WINS ONCE MORE... THANKFULLY.
THESE SHOULDERS WEREN'T MADE TO BEAR SUCH WEIGHT. SOMETIMES IT'S AS IF ATLAS HIMSELF SEEKS TO SHARE HIS BURDEN.
AH, DEAR READER. I WASN'T REFERRING TO THE TITAN THAT CARRIES THE WORLD ON HIS BACK, BUT MY FRIEND SAMUEL ATLAS. THE FALLEN PALEONTOLOGIST.
YOU DON'T KNOW HIS STORY? HAVE A DRINK AND LET ME TELL YOU THE TALE OF WHEN...
ATLAS SHRUGGED

IT WAS DURING MY TRAVELS WESTWARD WHEN I FIRST MET HIM FACE TO FACE. WE HAD CORRESPONDED, AS I HAD FOLLOWED HIS EXPLORATIONS IN THE JOURNALS.

ATLAS? GOOD LORD, MAN! WHAT HAS HAPPENED?

I HAVE SEEN IT. WITH MY OWN EYES. I HAVE DISCOVERED THE IRREFUTABLE SIGNPOSTS OF HEAVEN AND HELL.

IT COMES AT THE COST OF MY SOUL. I HAVE BLOOD ON MY HANDS.

PRAYTELL. CALM YOURSELF WITH DRINK AND TELL ME.

"IT TOOK PLACE NOT FAR FROM HERE. IN GALT'S GULCH THERE IS A RAVINE THAT WAS, IN PREHISTORIC TIMES, A LARGE PEAT BOG. THE STEDFIELD BOG.

"MANY CREATURES HAD FALLEN INTO THIS PIT, AND THEIR FOSSILIZED REMAINS ARE REMARKABLY WELL PRESERVED. I HAVE BEEN EXCAVATING SPECTACULAR SAMPLES FOR SOME TIME NOW. I'M SURE YOU HAVE READ MY ACCOUNTS OF SOME OF THESE. BUT I WASN'T PREPARED FOR WHAT I HAD FOUND MOST RECENTLY.

"THE JAWBONE OF NEPHILIMICUS.

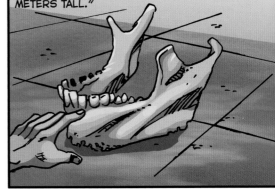

"IT WAS THE LOWER MANDIBLE OF A HUMAN-LIKE HOMINID! LARGER THAN ANYTHING LIKE IT EVER FOUND. I NAMED IT FOR THE GIANTS IN THE BOOK OF NUMBERS: 'WE SAW THE NEPHILIM THERE (THE DESCENDANTS OF ANAK COME FROM THE NEPHILIM). WE SEEMED LIKE GRASSHOPPERS IN OUR OWN EYES, AND WE LOOKED THE SAME TO THEM.' I ESTIMATED THE MAN TO BE ABOUT SEVEN METERS TALL."

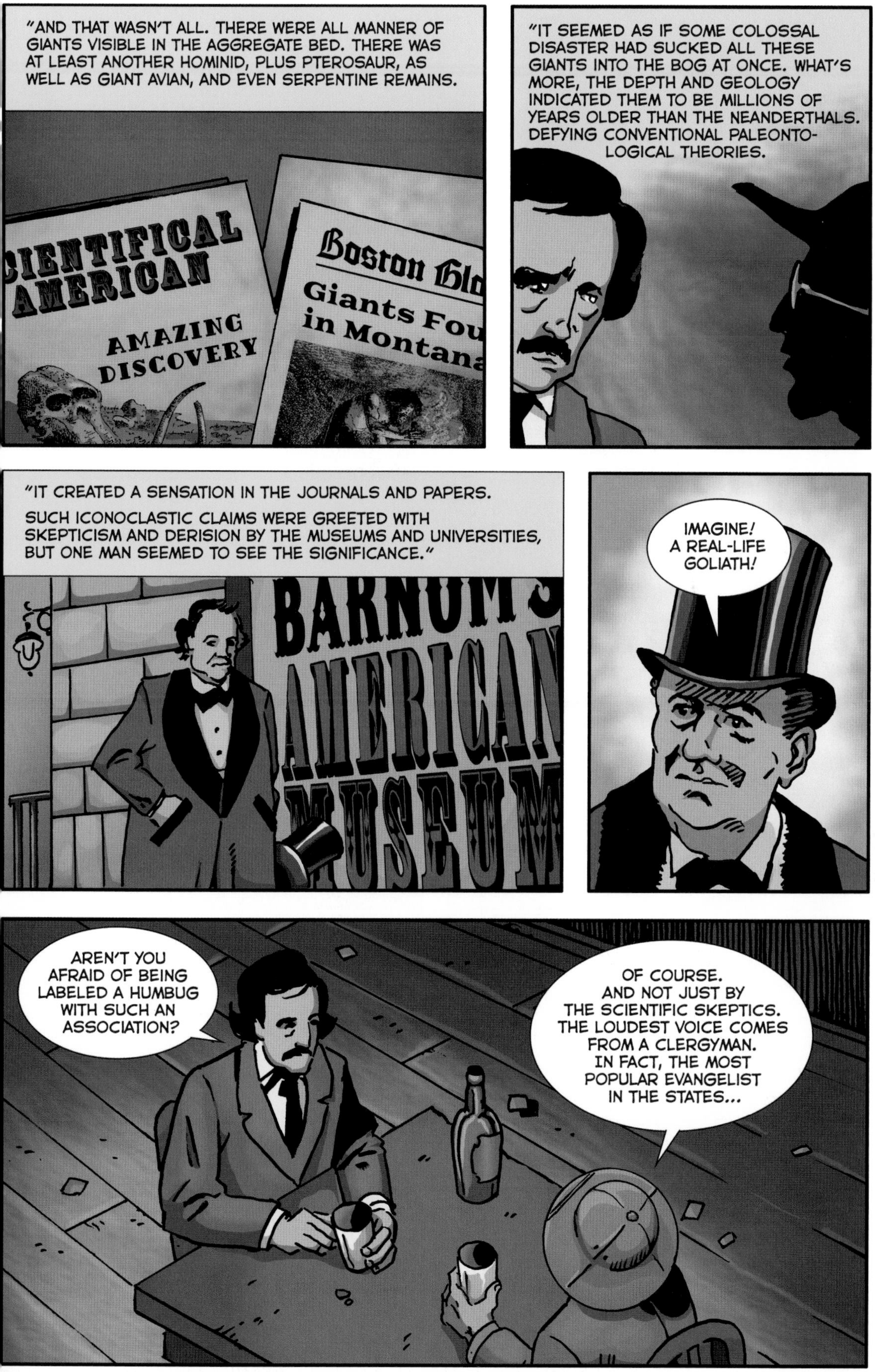
"AND THAT WASN'T ALL. THERE WERE ALL MANNER OF GIANTS VISIBLE IN THE AGGREGATE BED. THERE WAS AT LEAST ANOTHER HOMINID, PLUS PTEROSAUR, AS WELL AS GIANT AVIAN, AND EVEN SERPENTINE REMAINS.
CIENTIFICAL
AMERICAN
AMAZING DISCOVERY
Boston Glo
Giants Fou
in Montana
"IT SEEMED AS IF SOME COLOSSAL DISASTER HAD SUCKED ALL THESE GIANTS INTO THE BOG AT ONCE. WHAT'S MORE, THE DEPTH AND GEOLOGY INDICATED THEM TO BE MILLIONS OF YEARS OLDER THAN THE NEANDERTHALS. DEFYING CONVENTIONAL PALEONTOLOGICAL THEORIES.
"IT CREATED A SENSATION IN THE JOURNALS AND PAPERS.
SUCH ICONOCLASTIC CLAIMS WERE GREETED WITH SKEPTICISM AND DERISION BY THE MUSEUMS AND UNIVERSITIES, BUT ONE MAN SEEMED TO SEE THE SIGNIFICANCE."
BARNUM
AMERICAN
MUSEUM
IMAGINE! A REAL-LIFE GOLIATH!
AREN'T YOU AFRAID OF BEING LABELED A HUMBUG WITH SUCH AN ASSOCIATION?
OF COURSE. AND NOT JUST BY THE SCIENTIFIC SKEPTICS. THE LOUDEST VOICE COMES FROM A CLERGYMAN. IN FACT, THE MOST POPULAR EVANGELIST IN THE STATES...

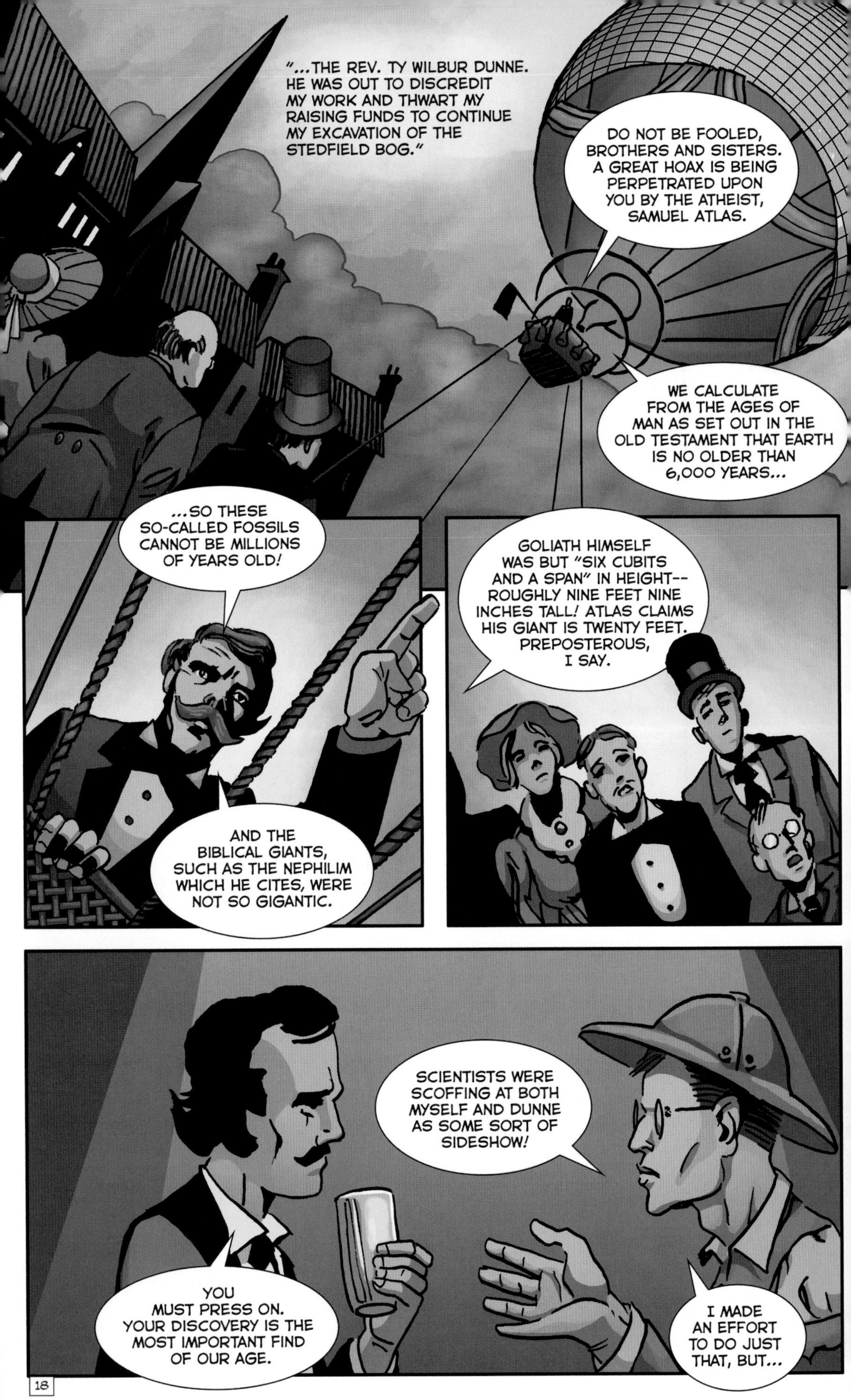
"...THE REV. TY WILBUR DUNNE. HE WAS OUT TO DISCREDIT MY WORK AND THWART MY RAISING FUNDS TO CONTINUE MY EXCAVATION OF THE STEDFIELD BOG."
DO NOT BE FOOLED, BROTHERS AND SISTERS. A GREAT HOAX IS BEING PERPETRATED UPON YOU BY THE ATHEIST, SAMUEL ATLAS.
WE CALCULATE FROM THE AGES OF MAN AS SET OUT IN THE OLD TESTAMENT THAT EARTH IS NO OLDER THAN 6,000 YEARS...
...SO THESE SO-CALLED FOSSILS CANNOT BE MILLIONS OF YEARS OLD!
AND THE BIBLICAL GIANTS, SUCH AS THE NEPHILIM WHICH HE CITES, WERE NOT SO GIGANTIC.
GOLIATH HIMSELF WAS BUT "SIX CUBITS AND A SPAN" IN HEIGHT-- ROUGHLY NINE FEET NINE INCHES TALL! ATLAS CLAIMS HIS GIANT IS TWENTY FEET. PREPOSTEROUS, I SAY.
SCIENTISTS WERE SCOFFING AT BOTH MYSELF AND DUNNE AS SOME SORT OF SIDESHOW!
YOU MUST PRESS ON. YOUR DISCOVERY IS THE MOST IMPORTANT FIND OF OUR AGE.
I MADE AN EFFORT TO DO JUST THAT, BUT...

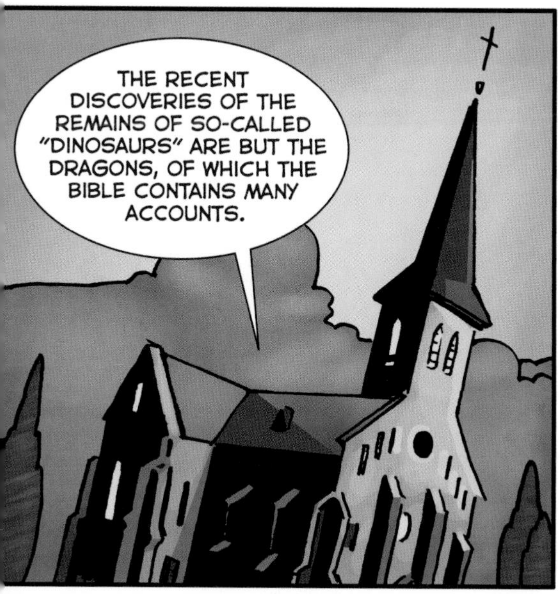
THE RECENT DISCOVERIES OF THE REMAINS OF SO-CALLED "DINOSAURS" ARE BUT THE DRAGONS, OF WHICH THE BIBLE CONTAINS MANY ACCOUNTS.

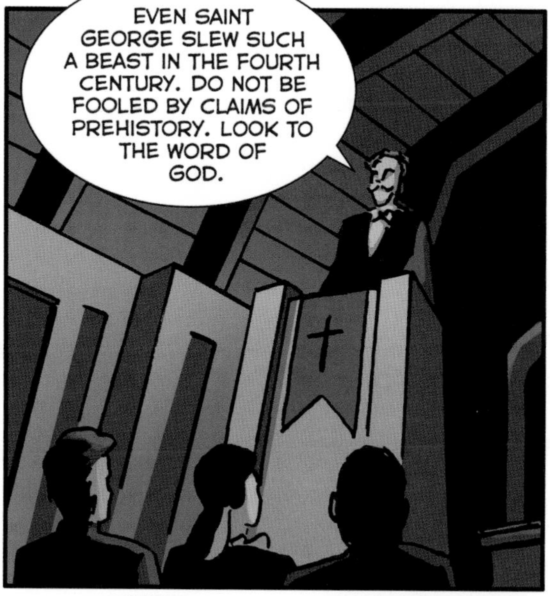
EVEN SAINT GEORGE SLEW SUCH A BEAST IN THE FOURTH CENTURY. DO NOT BE FOOLED BY CLAIMS OF PREHISTORY. LOOK TO THE WORD OF GOD.

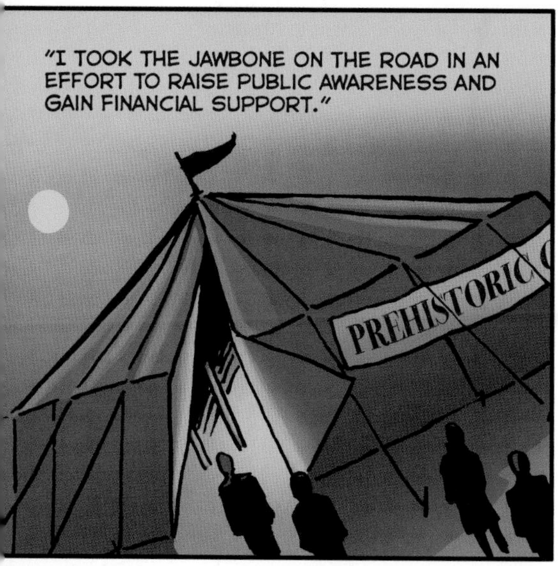
"I TOOK THE JAWBONE ON THE ROAD IN AN EFFORT TO RAISE PUBLIC AWARENESS AND GAIN FINANCIAL SUPPORT."
PREHISTORIC

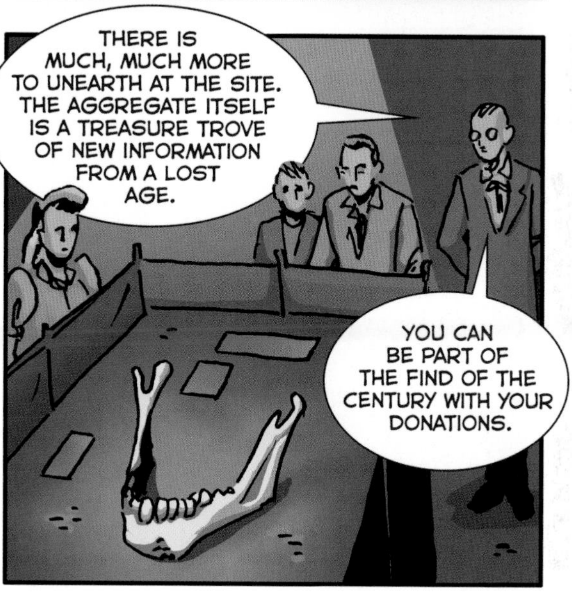
THERE IS MUCH, MUCH MORE TO UNEARTH AT THE SITE. THE AGGREGATE ITSELF IS A TREASURE TROVE OF NEW INFORMATION FROM A LOST AGE.
YOU CAN BE PART OF THE FIND OF THE CENTURY WITH YOUR DONATIONS.

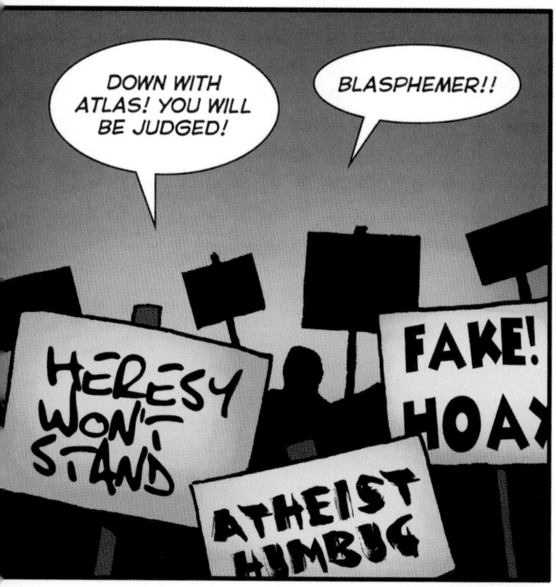
DOWN WITH ATLAS! YOU WILL BE JUDGED!
BLASPHEMER!!
HERESY WON'T STAND
FAKE!
ATHEIST HUMBUG

"DUNNE'S CAMPAIGN AND THE CONTINUED DISBELIEF FROM PALEONTOLOGISTS TOOK THEIR TOLL. ATTENDANCE FOR MY EXHIBITION FELL OFF VERY QUICKLY. DONATIONS BECAME ALMOST NON-EXISTENT. I WAS FACING HUMILIATION AND RUINATION."

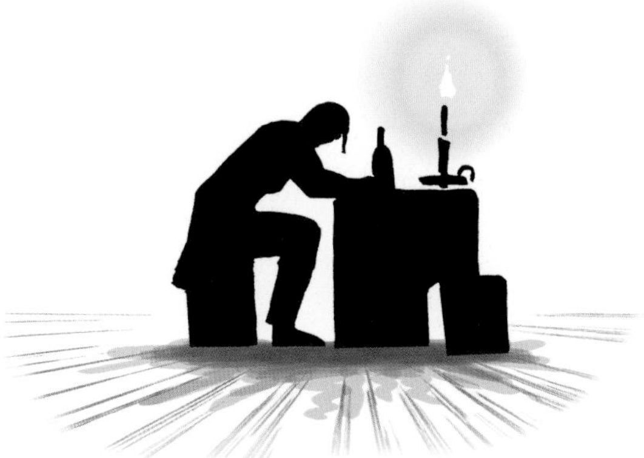

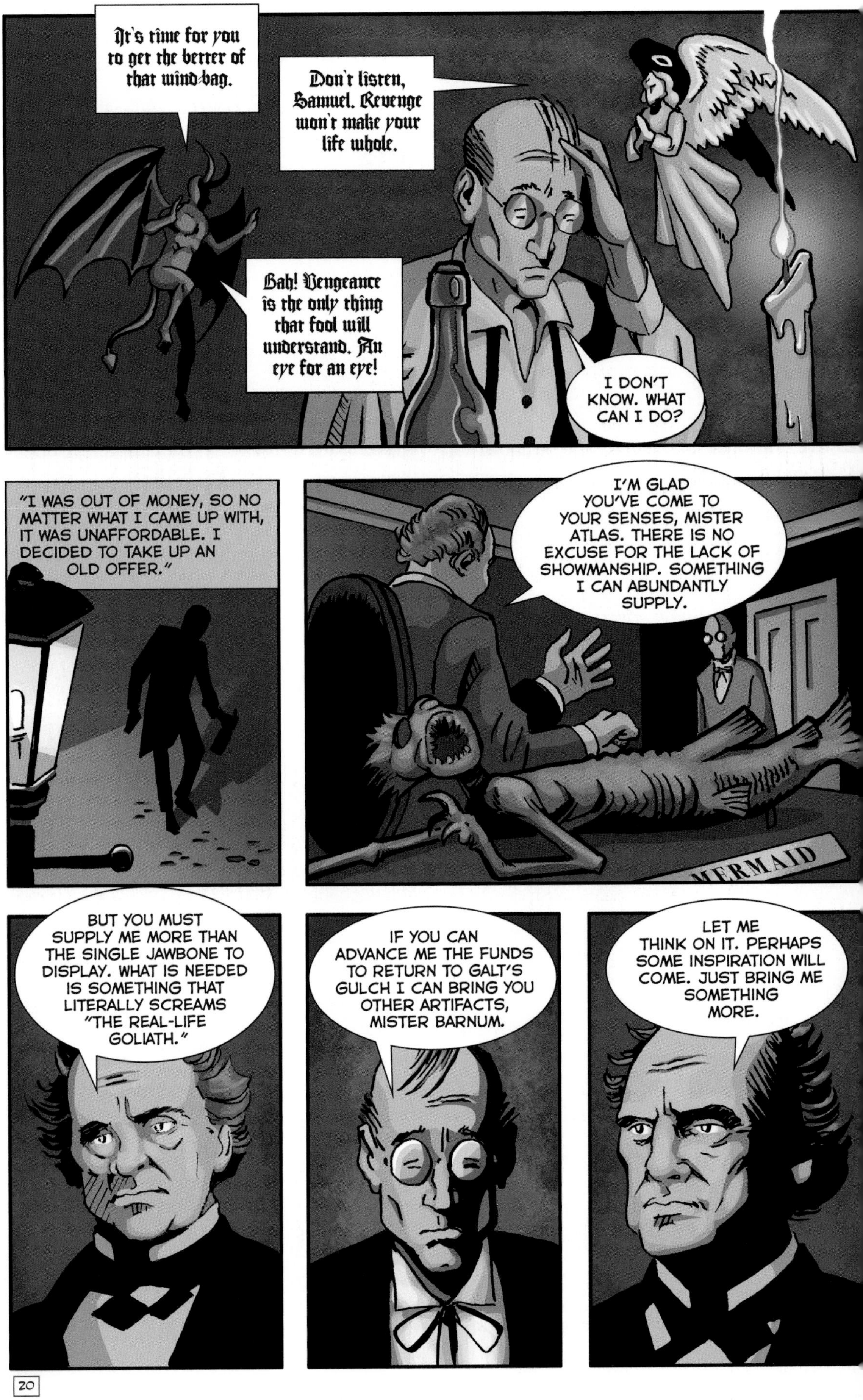
It's time for you to get the better of that wind-bag.
Don't listen, Samuel. Revenge won't make your life whole.
Bah! Vengeance is the only thing that fool will understand. An eye for an eye!
I DON'T KNOW. WHAT CAN I DO?
"I WAS OUT OF MONEY, SO NO MATTER WHAT I CAME UP WITH, IT WAS UNAFFORDABLE. I DECIDED TO TAKE UP AN OLD OFFER."
I'M GLAD YOU'VE COME TO YOUR SENSES, MISTER ATLAS. THERE IS NO EXCUSE FOR THE LACK OF SHOWMANSHIP. SOMETHING I CAN ABUNDANTLY SUPPLY.
MERMAID
BUT YOU MUST SUPPLY ME MORE THAN THE SINGLE JAWBONE TO DISPLAY. WHAT IS NEEDED IS SOMETHING THAT LITERALLY SCREAMS "THE REAL-LIFE GOLIATH."
IF YOU CAN ADVANCE ME THE FUNDS TO RETURN TO GALT'S GULCH I CAN BRING YOU OTHER ARTIFACTS, MISTER BARNUM.
LET ME THINK ON IT. PERHAPS SOME INSPIRATION WILL COME. JUST BRING ME SOMETHING MORE.

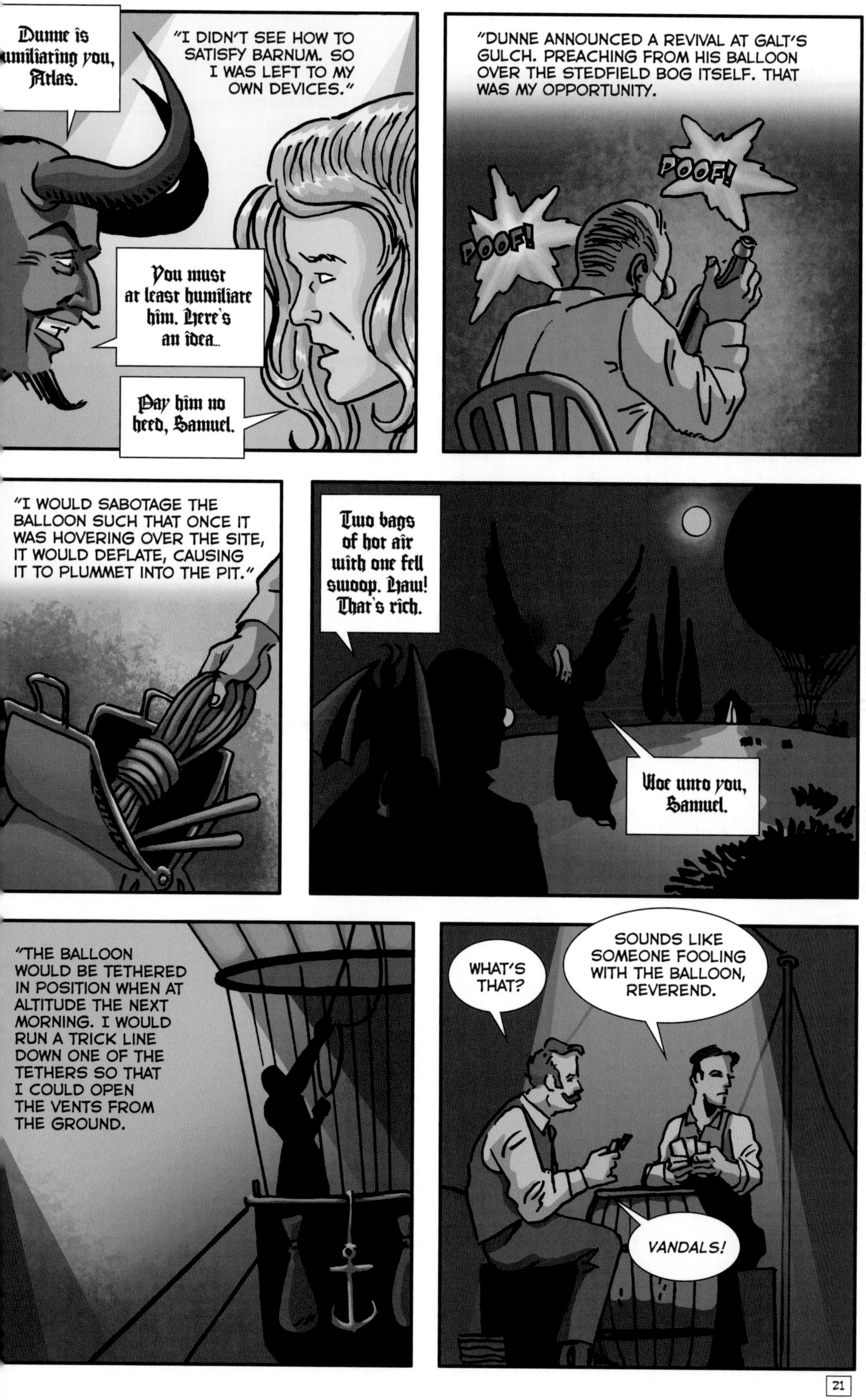
Dunne is umiliating you, Atlas.
"I DIDN'T SEE HOW TO SATISFY BARNUM. SO I WAS LEFT TO MY OWN DEVICES."
You must at least humiliate him. Here's an idea...
Pay him no heed, Samuel.
"DUNNE ANNOUNCED A REVIVAL AT GALT'S GULCH. PREACHING FROM HIS BALLOON OVER THE STEDFIELD BOG ITSELF. THAT WAS MY OPPORTUNITY.
POOF!
POOF!
"I WOULD SABOTAGE THE BALLOON SUCH THAT ONCE IT WAS HOVERING OVER THE SITE, IT WOULD DEFLATE, CAUSING IT TO PLUMMET INTO THE PIT."
Two bags of hot air with one fell swoop. Haw! That's rich.
Woe unto you, Samuel.
"THE BALLOON WOULD BE TETHERED IN POSITION WHEN AT ALTITUDE THE NEXT MORNING. I WOULD RUN A TRICK LINE DOWN ONE OF THE TETHERS SO THAT I COULD OPEN THE VENTS FROM THE GROUND.
WHAT'S THAT?
SOUNDS LIKE SOMEONE FOOLING WITH THE BALLOON, REVEREND.
VANDALS!

SCOUNDREL! OUT OF MY BALLOON!

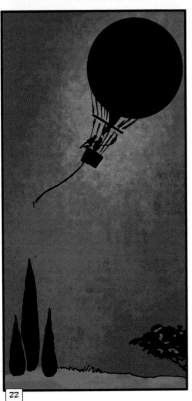

BOSS! THE MOORING!

UNGH! LET GO!

:ACK!:

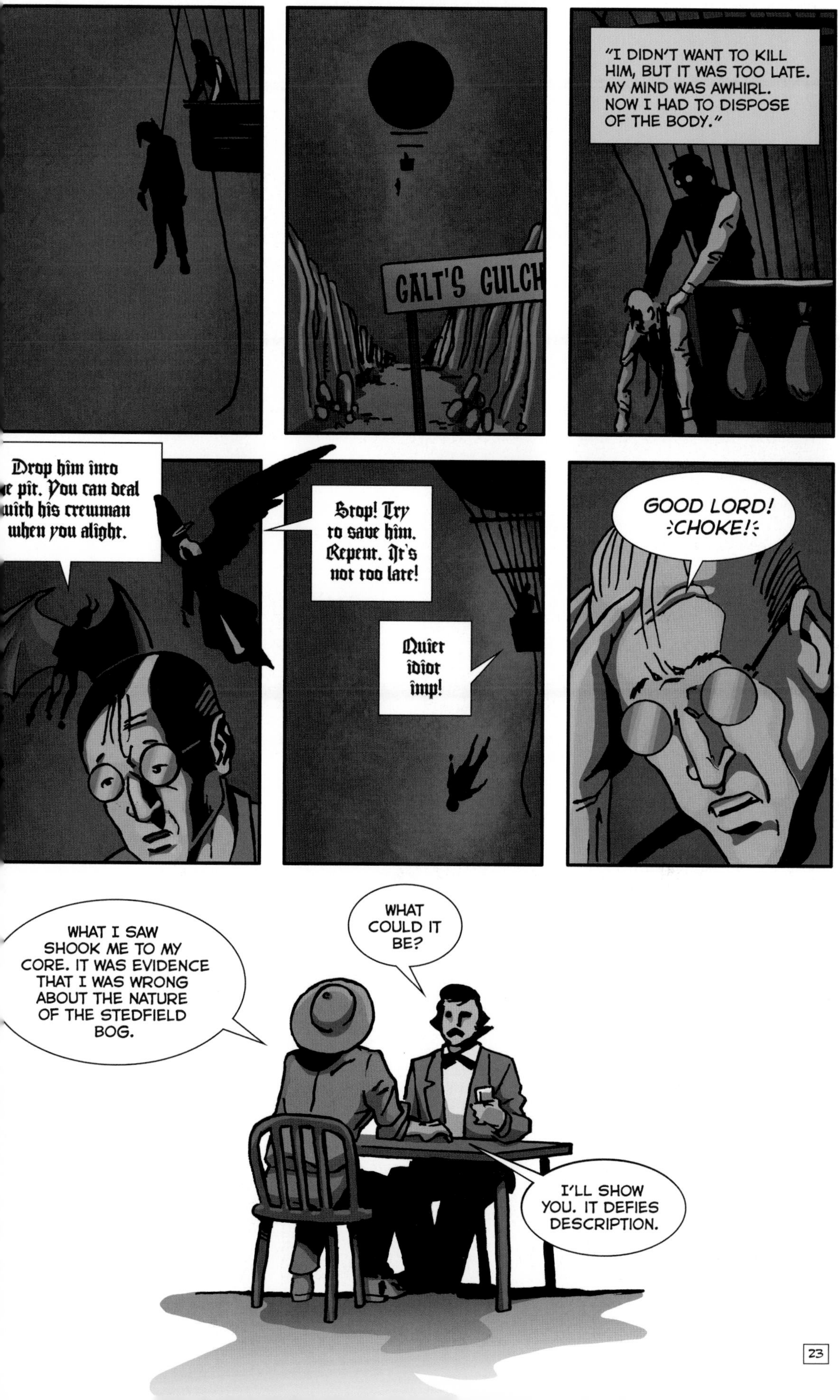
GALT'S GULCH
"I DIDN'T WANT TO KILL HIM, BUT IT WAS TOO LATE. MY MIND WAS AWHIRL. NOW I HAD TO DISPOSE OF THE BODY."
Drop him into e pit. You can deal ith his crewman when you alight.
Stop! Try to save him. Repent. It's not too late!
Quiet idiot imp!
GOOD LORD! CHOKE!
WHAT I SAW SHOOK ME TO MY CORE. IT WAS EVIDENCE THAT I WAS WRONG ABOUT THE NATURE OF THE STEDFIELD BOG.
WHAT COULD IT BE?
I'LL SHOW YOU. IT DEFIES DESCRIPTION.

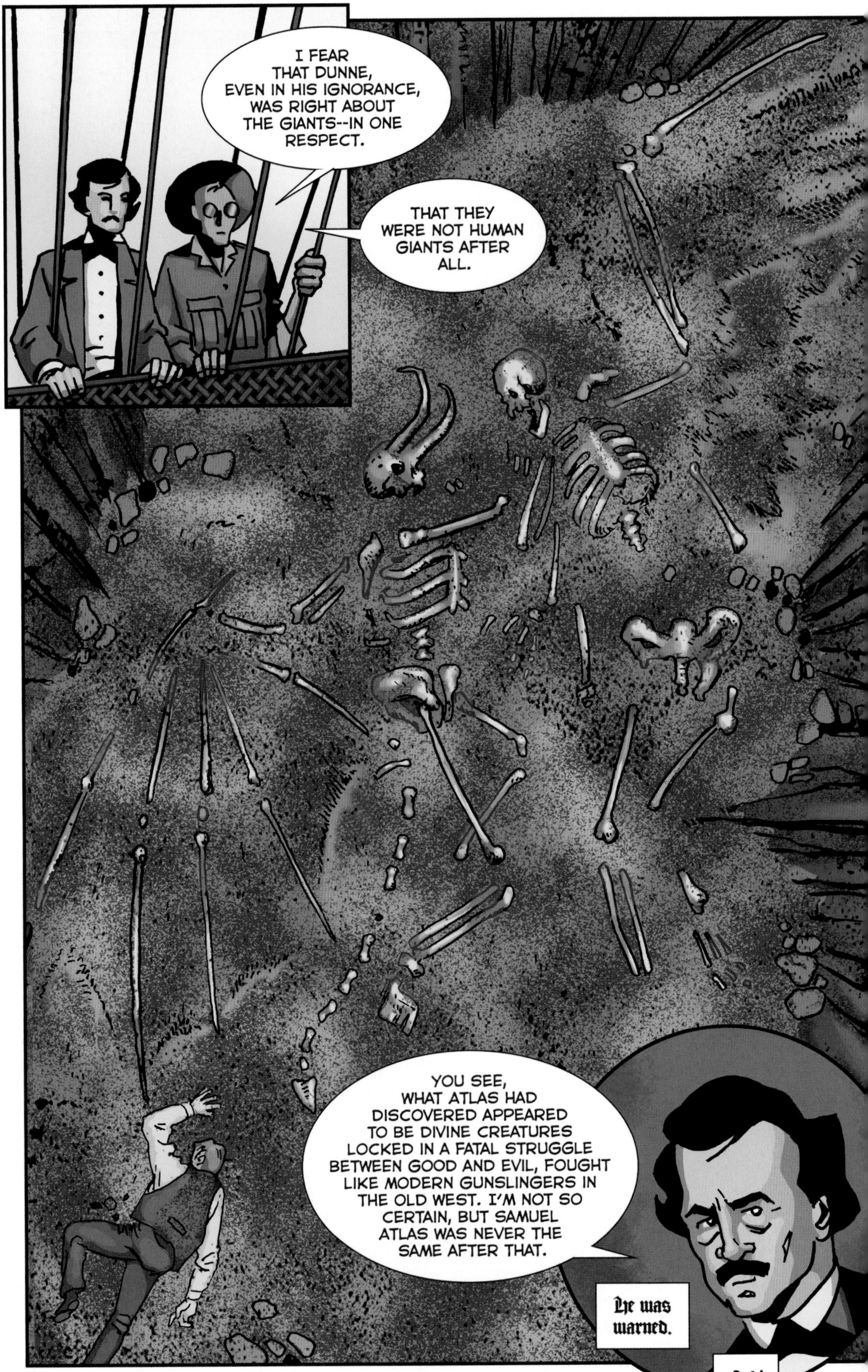
I FEAR THAT DUNNE, EVEN IN HIS IGNORANCE, WAS RIGHT ABOUT THE GIANTS--IN ONE RESPECT.
THAT THEY WERE NOT HUMAN GIANTS AFTER ALL.
YOU SEE, WHAT ATLAS HAD DISCOVERED APPEARED TO BE DIVINE CREATURES LOCKED IN A FATAL STRUGGLE BETWEEN GOOD AND EVIL, FOUGHT LIKE MODERN GUNSLINGERS IN THE OLD WEST. I'M NOT SO CERTAIN, BUT SAMUEL ATLAS WAS NEVER THE SAME AFTER THAT.
He was warned.
Bah!

Fin

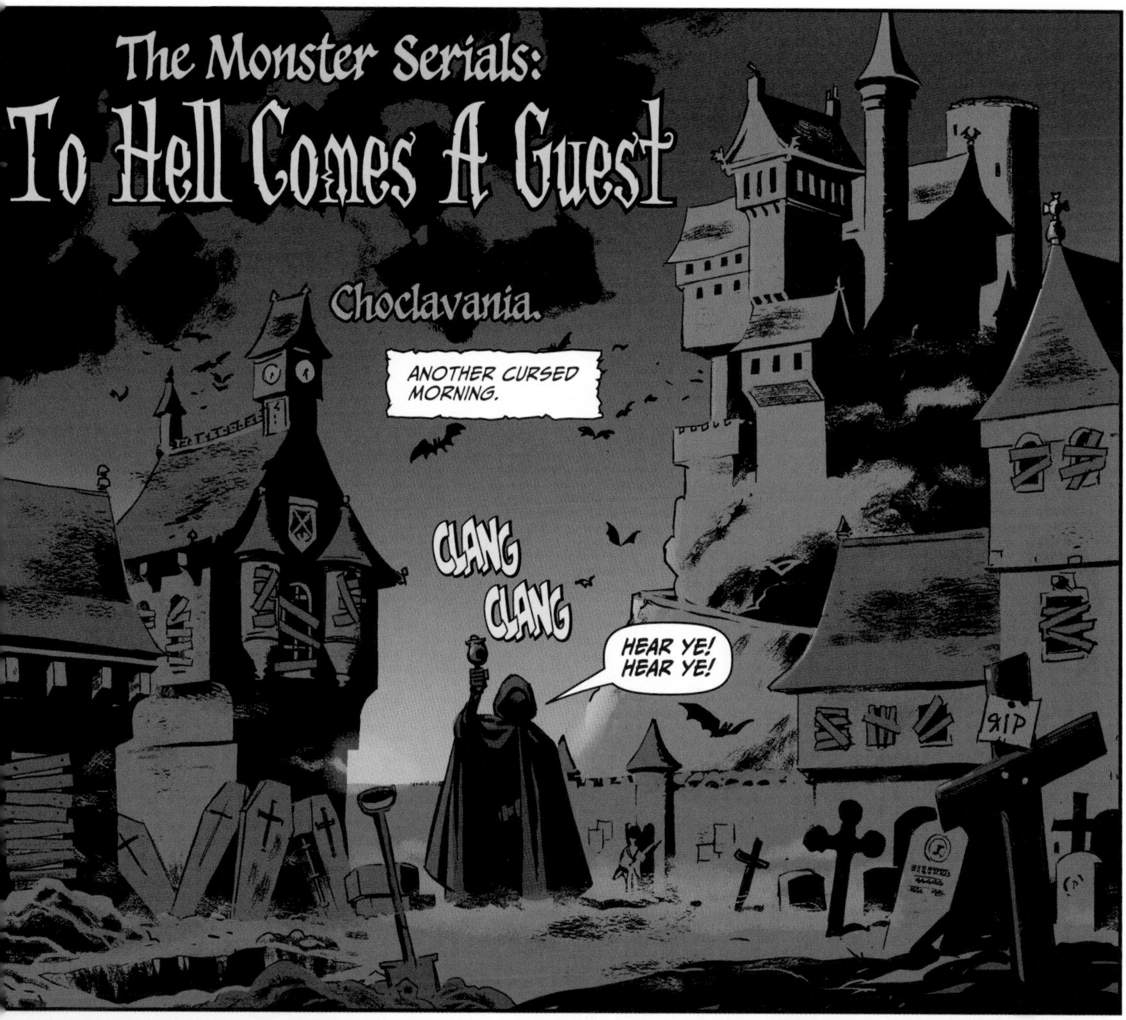
The Monster Serials:
To Hell Comes A Guest
Choclavania.
ANOTHER CURSED MORNING.
CLANG
CLANG
HEAR YE! HEAR YE!
RIP

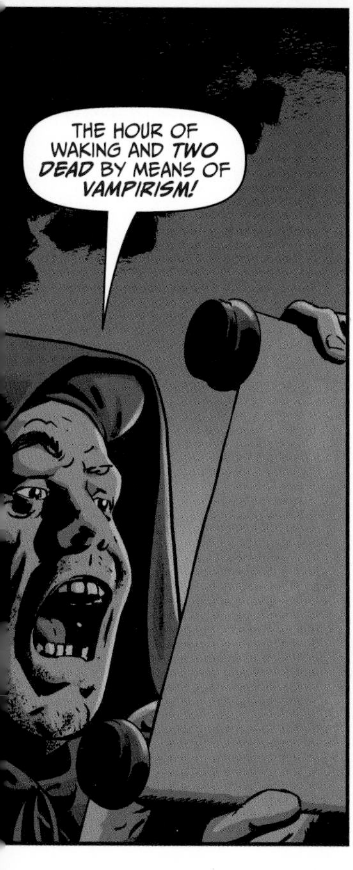
THE HOUR OF WAKING AND *TWO DEAD* BY MEANS OF *VAMPIRISM!*

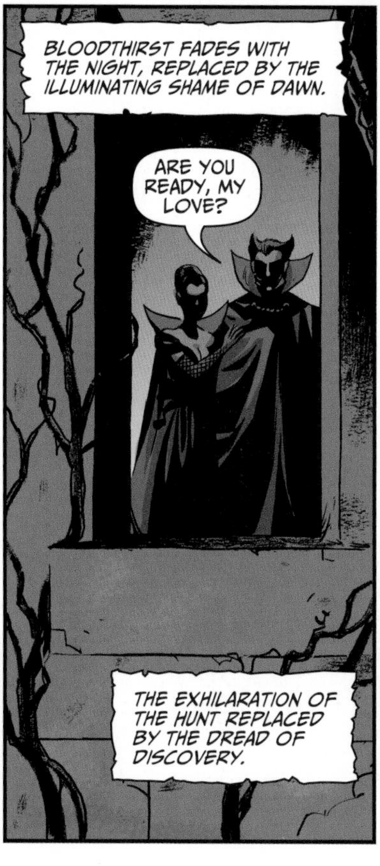
BLOODTHIRST FADES WITH THE NIGHT, REPLACED BY THE ILLUMINATING SHAME OF DAWN.
ARE YOU READY, MY LOVE?
THE EXHILARATION OF THE HUNT REPLACED BY THE DREAD OF DISCOVERY.

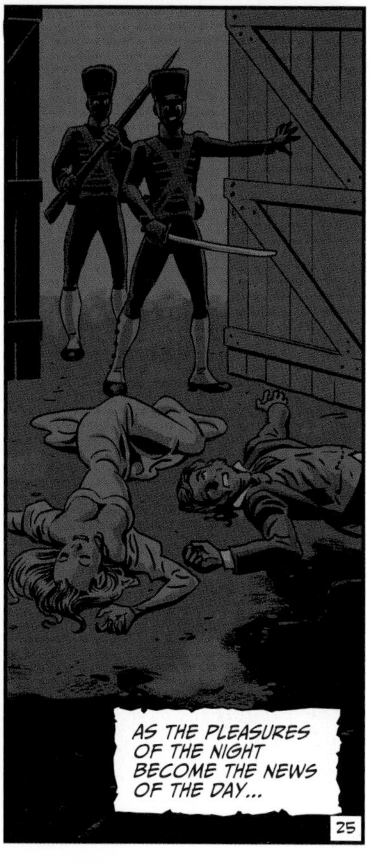
AS THE PLEASURES OF THE NIGHT BECOME THE NEWS OF THE DAY...

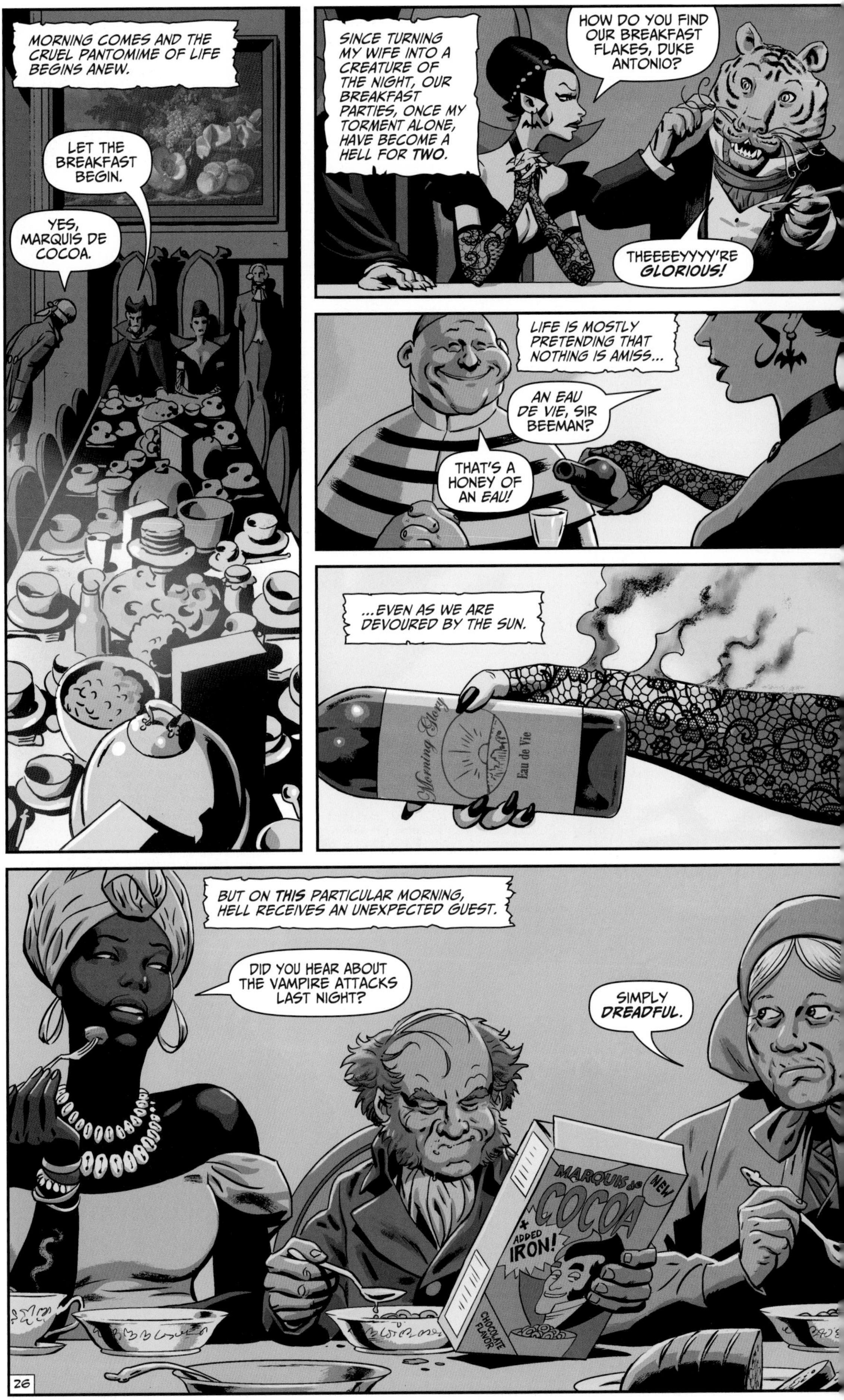
MORNING COMES AND THE CRUEL PANTOMIME OF LIFE BEGINS ANEW.
LET THE BREAKFAST BEGIN.
YES, MARQUIS DE COCOA.
SINCE TURNING MY WIFE INTO A CREATURE OF THE NIGHT, OUR BREAKFAST PARTIES, ONCE MY TORMENT ALONE, HAVE BECOME A HELL FOR TWO.
HOW DO YOU FIND OUR BREAKFAST FLAKES, DUKE ANTONIO?
THEEEEYYYY'RE GLORIOUS!
LIFE IS MOSTLY PRETENDING THAT NOTHING IS AMISS...
AN EAU DE VIE, SIR BEEMAN?
THAT'S A HONEY OF AN EAU!
...EVEN AS WE ARE DEVOURED BY THE SUN.
Morning Glory
Eau de Vie
BUT ON THIS PARTICULAR MORNING, HELL RECEIVES AN UNEXPECTED GUEST.
DID YOU HEAR ABOUT THE VAMPIRE ATTACKS LAST NIGHT?
SIMPLY DREADFUL.
MARQUIS de COCOA
NEW
+ ADDED IRON!
CHOCOLATE FLAVOR

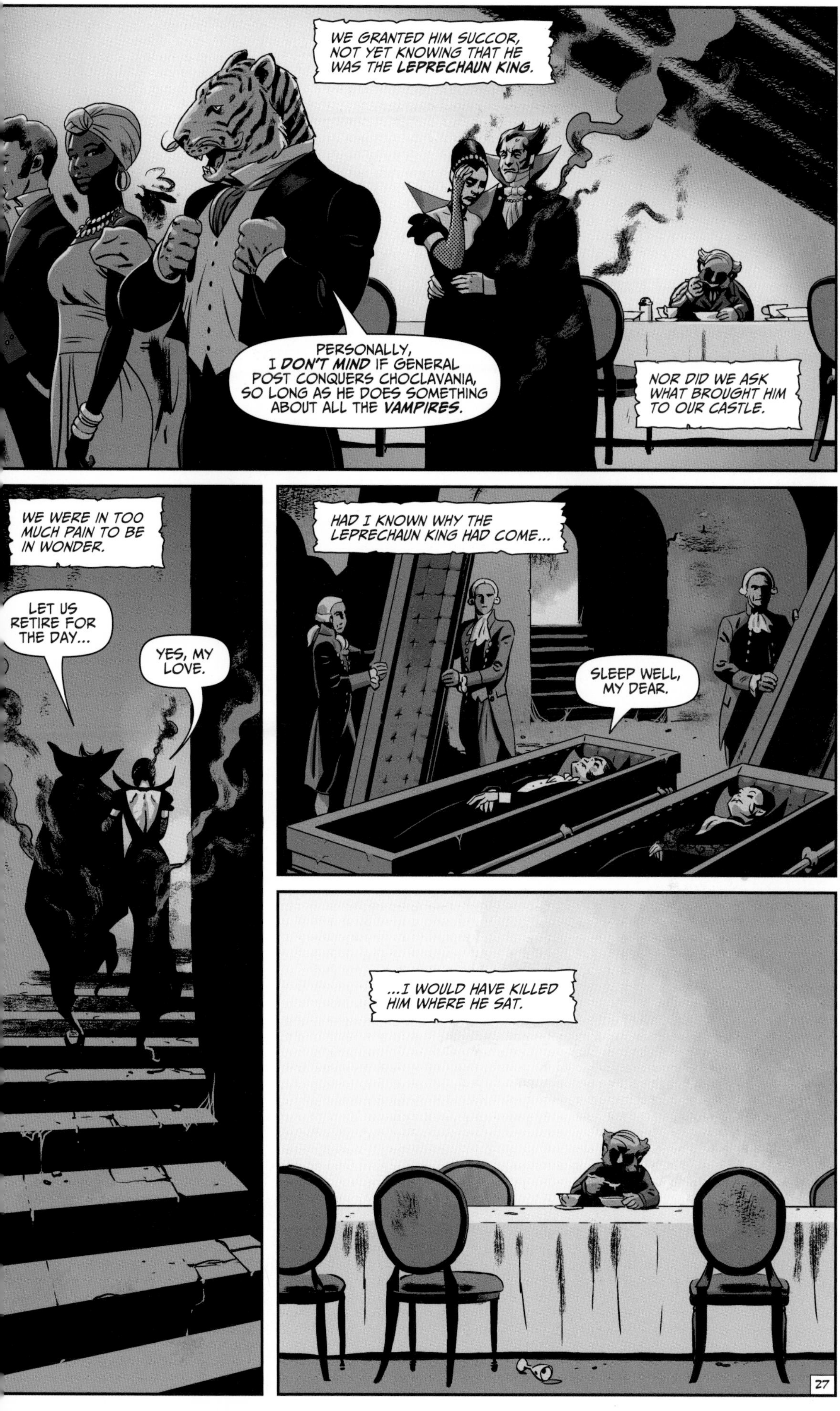
WE GRANTED HIM SUCCOR, NOT YET KNOWING THAT HE WAS THE **LEPRECHAUN KING.**
PERSONALLY, I ***DON'T MIND*** IF GENERAL POST CONQUERS CHOCLAVANIA, SO LONG AS HE DOES SOMETHING ABOUT ALL THE ***VAMPIRES.***
NOR DID WE ASK WHAT BROUGHT HIM TO OUR CASTLE.
WE WERE IN TOO MUCH PAIN TO BE IN WONDER.
LET US RETIRE FOR THE DAY...
YES, MY LOVE.
HAD I KNOWN WHY THE LEPRECHAUN KING HAD COME...
SLEEP WELL, MY DEAR.
...I WOULD HAVE KILLED HIM WHERE HE SAT.

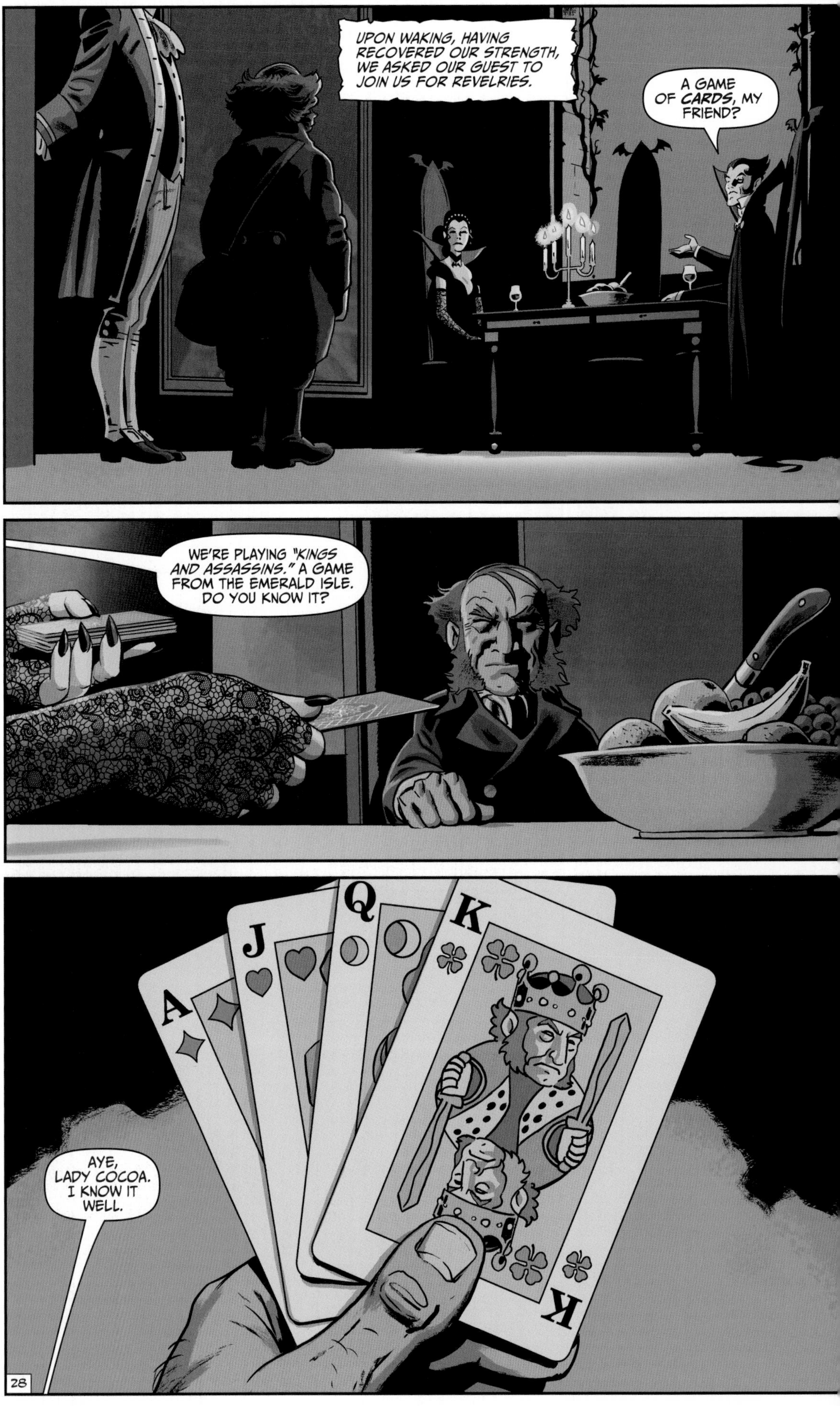
UPON WAKING, HAVING RECOVERED OUR STRENGTH, WE ASKED OUR GUEST TO JOIN US FOR REVELRIES.
A GAME OF CARDS, MY FRIEND?
WE'RE PLAYING "KINGS AND ASSASSINS." A GAME FROM THE EMERALD ISLE. DO YOU KNOW IT?
A
J
Q
K
K
AYE, LADY COCOA. I KNOW IT WELL.

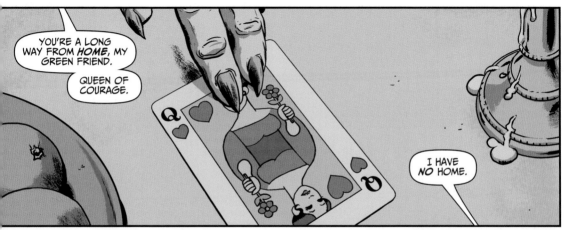

YOU'RE A LONG WAY FROM *HOME,* MY GREEN FRIEND.

QUEEN OF COURAGE.

I HAVE *NO* HOME.

NOT SINCE IT BE *CONQUERED* BY *GENERAL POST.*

KING OF WEALTH.

OUR *SYMPATHIES.* IN THIS CASTLE, WE KNOW WELL THE GENERAL'S CRIMES.

IN MY EXPERIENCE, CASTLE WALLS NOT ONLY PROTECT, BUT *INSULATE.*

HOW CAN YOU *POSSIBLY* KNOW OF THE SUFFERING OUTSIDE THEM?

GENERAL POST IS...HE'S *MY FATHER.*

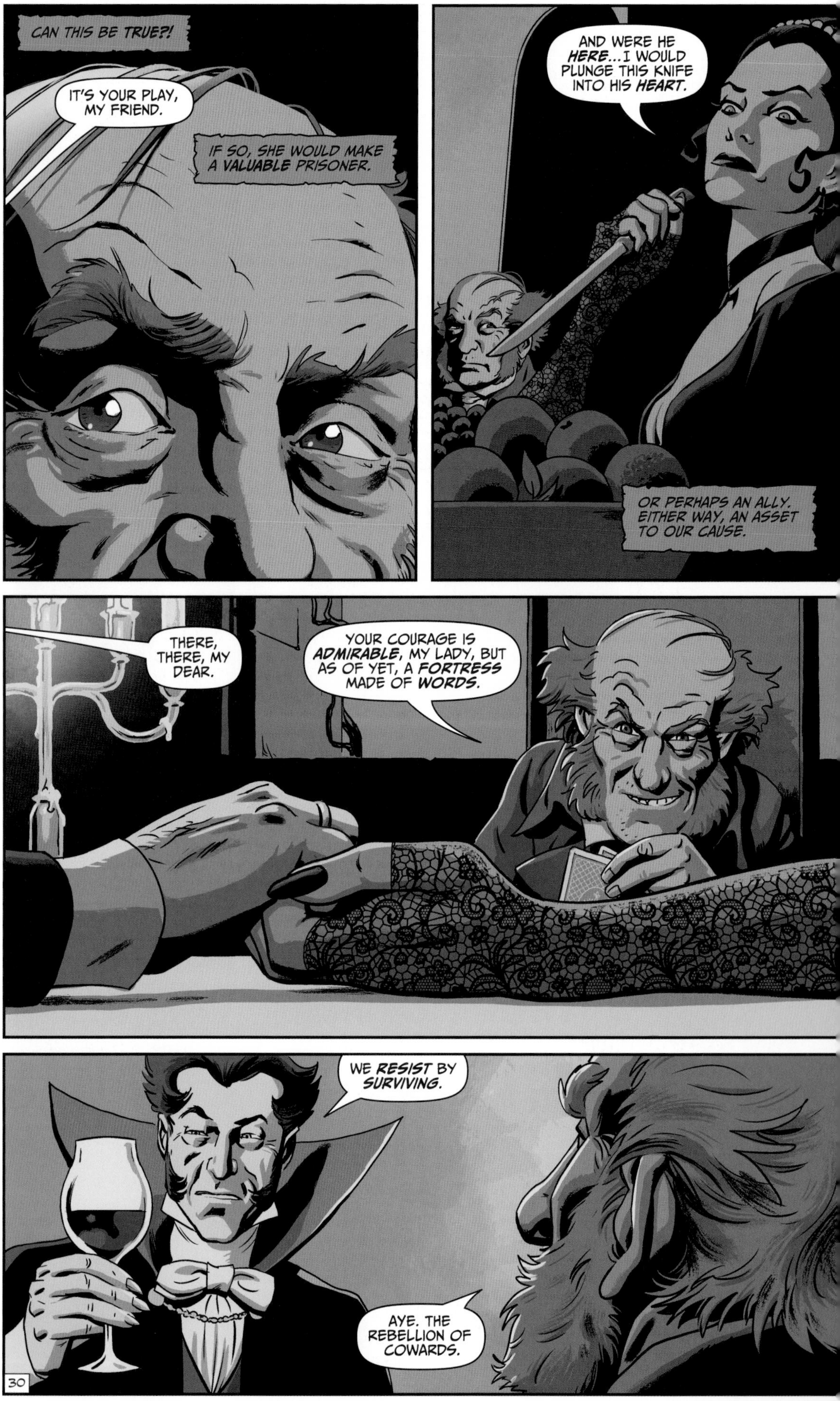
CAN THIS BE TRUE?!
IT'S YOUR PLAY, MY FRIEND.
IF SO, SHE WOULD MAKE A VALUABLE PRISONER.
AND WERE HE HERE...I WOULD PLUNGE THIS KNIFE INTO HIS HEART.
OR PERHAPS AN ALLY. EITHER WAY, AN ASSET TO OUR CAUSE.
THERE, THERE, MY DEAR.
YOUR COURAGE IS ADMIRABLE, MY LADY, BUT AS OF YET, A FORTRESS MADE OF WORDS.
WE RESIST BY SURVIVING.
AYE. THE REBELLION OF COWARDS.
30

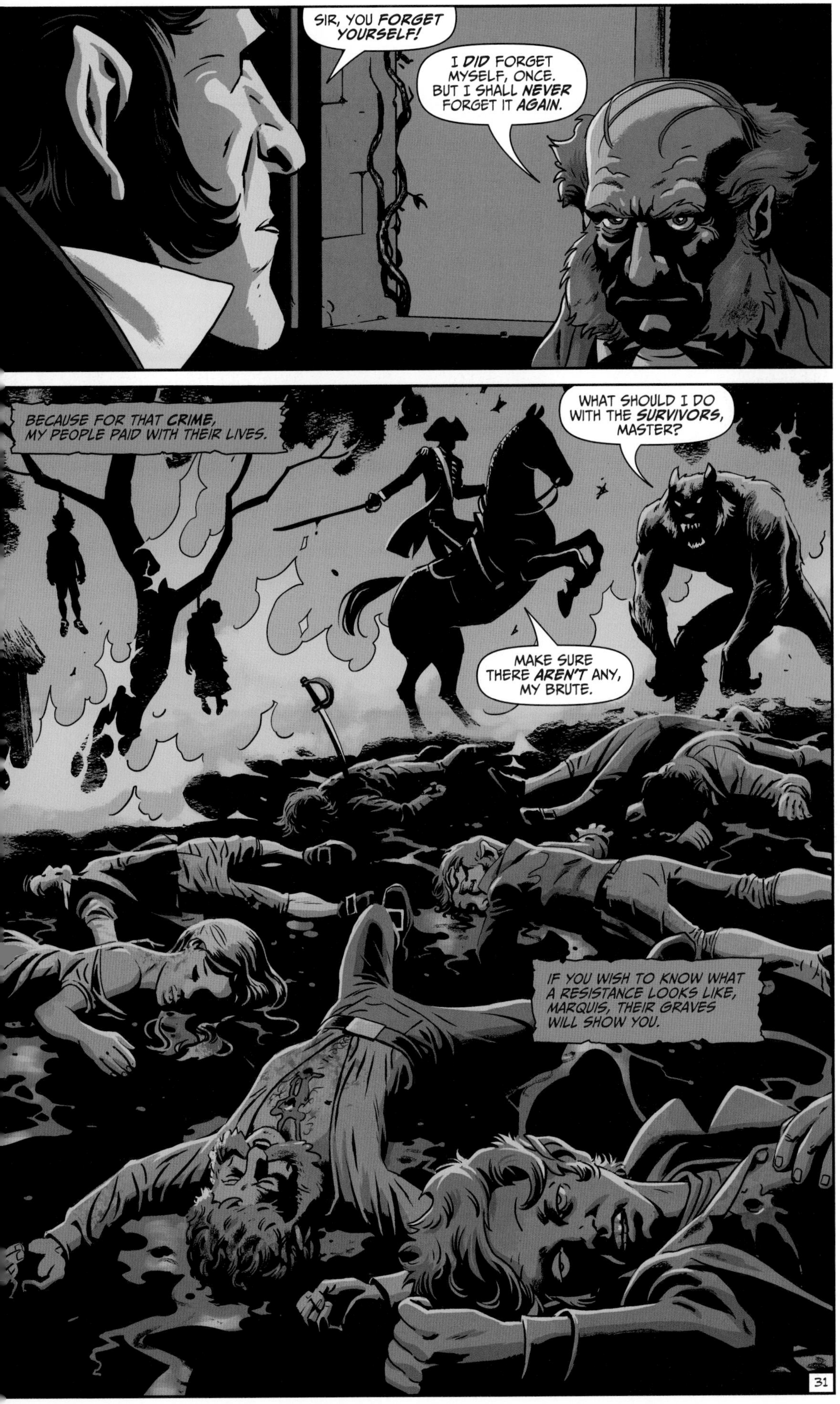
SIR, YOU FORGET YOURSELF!
I DID FORGET MYSELF, ONCE. BUT I SHALL NEVER FORGET IT AGAIN.
BECAUSE FOR THAT CRIME, MY PEOPLE PAID WITH THEIR LIVES.
WHAT SHOULD I DO WITH THE SURVIVORS, MASTER?
MAKE SURE THERE AREN'T ANY, MY BRUTE.
IF YOU WISH TO KNOW WHAT A RESISTANCE LOOKS LIKE, MARQUIS, THEIR GRAVES WILL SHOW YOU.

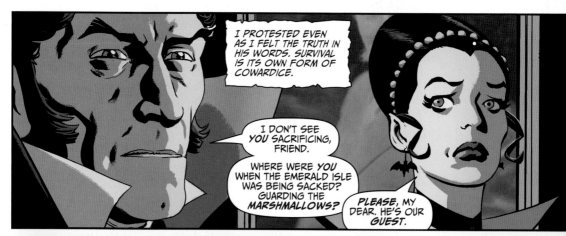

I PROTESTED EVEN AS I FELT THE TRUTH IN HIS WORDS. SURVIVAL IS ITS OWN FORM OF COWARDICE.

I DON'T SEE *YOU* SACRIFICING, FRIEND.

WHERE WERE *YOU* WHEN THE EMERALD ISLE WAS BEING SACKED? GUARDING THE *MARSHMALLOWS*?

PLEASE, MY DEAR. HE'S OUR *GUEST*.

NO, MY LADY. HE'S *RIGHT* TO SHAME ME.

YOU HAVE LAIN YOUR CARDS UPON THE TABLE. ALLOW ME TO LAY MINE...

I AM THE *LEPRECHAUN KING* DETHRONED.

AND I AM HEADED TO FORTRESS HONEYCOMB TO CONFRONT GENERAL POST. TO DIE AT *HIS* HAND OR WATCH HIM DIE AT *MINE*.

AND WHAT DOES *DYING* ACCOMPLISH? OTHER THAN REDUCING THE BELIEVERS IN YOUR CAUSE BY *ONE*.

A HORROR UNCHALLENGED IS PERFORMED WITH PERMISSION.

EVEN IN FAILURE, EVEN IN *DEATH*, A SINGLE *ACT* IS WORTH A MILLION CONDEMNATIONS.

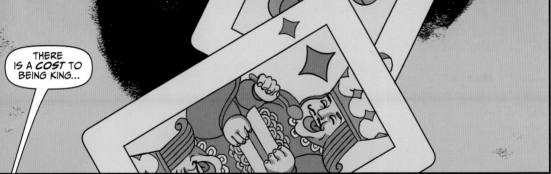

THERE IS A *COST* TO BEING KING...

I GO TO FORTRESS HONEYCOMB TO SHOW THE GENERAL THE COST OF MISRULE...

...AND TO PAY THE DEBT FOR *MY OWN*.

33

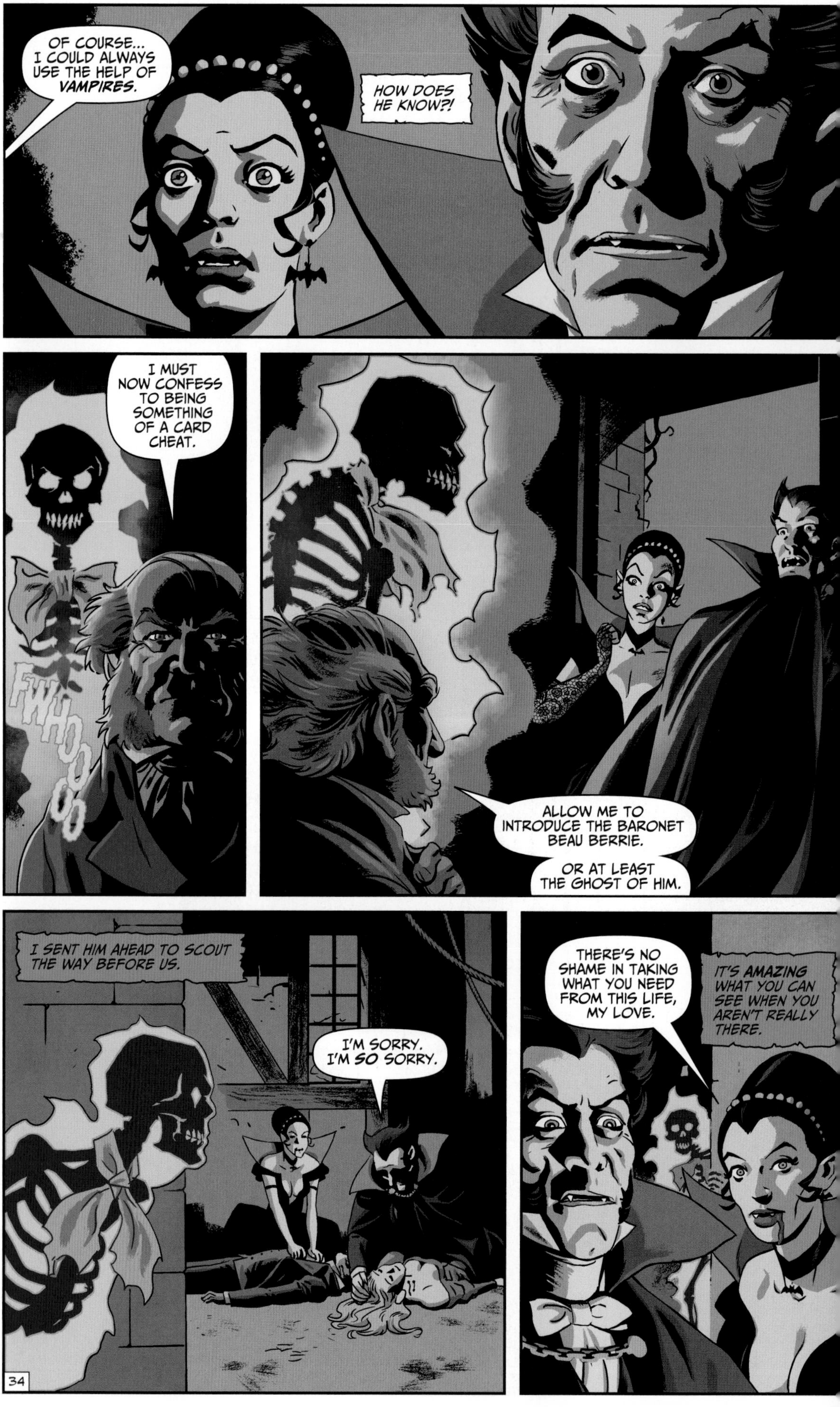
OF COURSE... I COULD ALWAYS USE THE HELP OF *VAMPIRES*.
HOW DOES HE KNOW?!
I MUST NOW CONFESS TO BEING SOMETHING OF A CARD CHEAT.
FWHOOOO
ALLOW ME TO INTRODUCE THE BARONET BEAU BERRIE.
OR AT LEAST THE GHOST OF HIM.
I SENT HIM AHEAD TO SCOUT THE WAY BEFORE US.
I'M SORRY. I'M *SO* SORRY.
THERE'S NO SHAME IN TAKING WHAT YOU NEED FROM THIS LIFE, MY LOVE.
IT'S *AMAZING* WHAT YOU CAN SEE WHEN YOU AREN'T REALLY THERE.

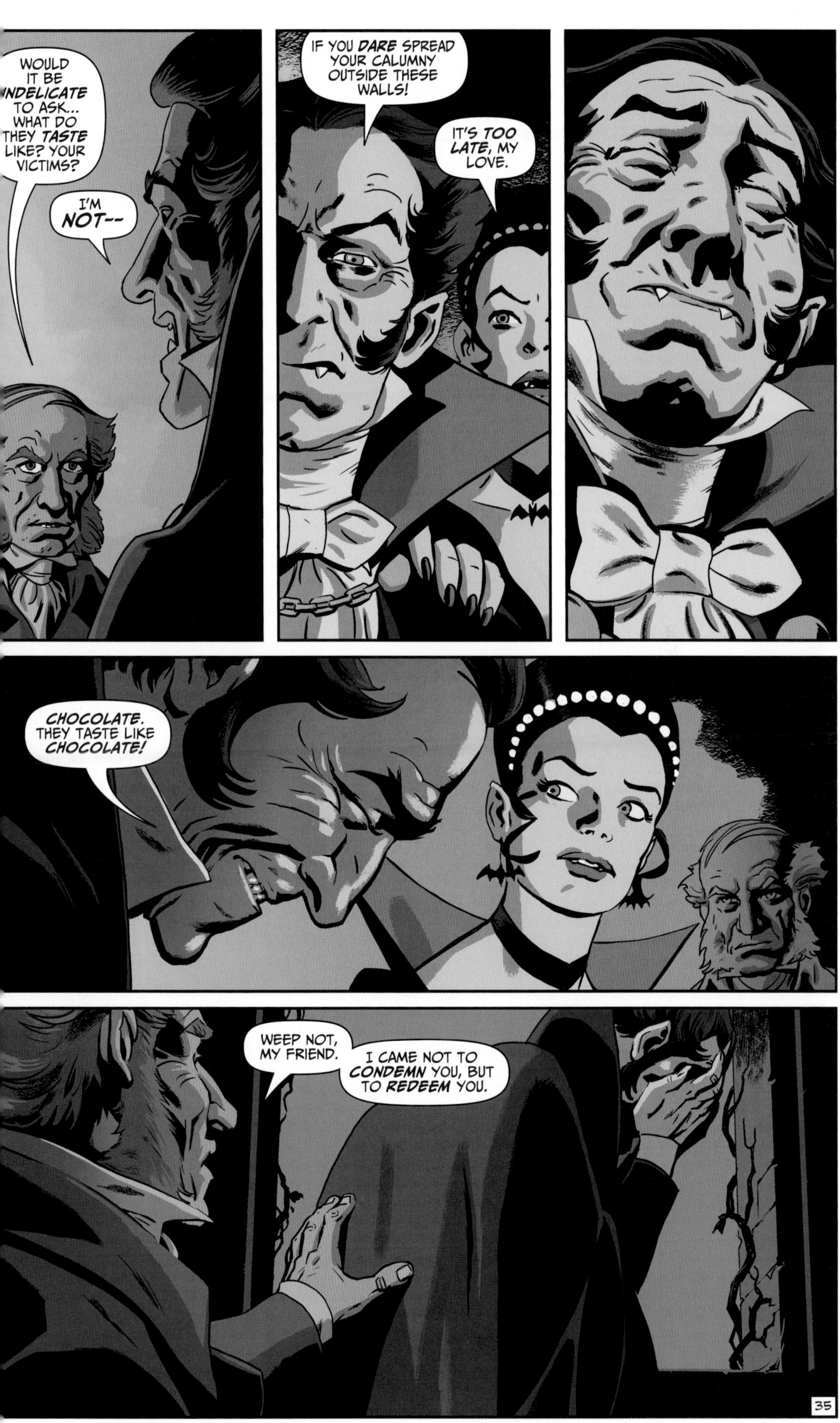

WOULD IT BE INDELICATE TO ASK... WHAT DO THEY TASTE LIKE? YOUR VICTIMS?
I'M NOT--
IF YOU DARE SPREAD YOUR CALUMNY OUTSIDE THESE WALLS!
IT'S TOO LATE, MY LOVE.
CHOCOLATE. THEY TASTE LIKE CHOCOLATE!
WEEP NOT, MY FRIEND.
I CAME NOT TO CONDEMN YOU, BUT TO REDEEM YOU.

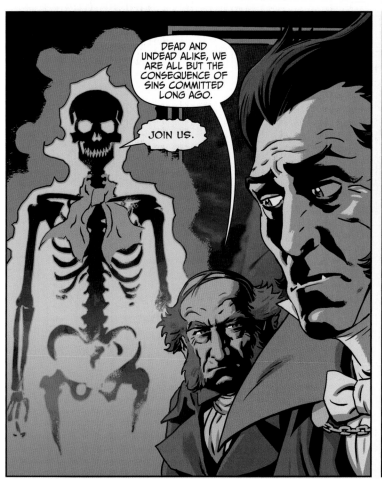

DEAD AND UNDEAD ALIKE, WE ARE ALL BUT THE CONSEQUENCE OF SINS COMMITTED LONG AGO.

JOIN US.

YOU DON'T UNDERSTAND WHAT IT IS TO LIVE IN HIDING. TO BE HUNTED BY THE *WORLD*.

WHAT IT TOOK TO BUILD EVEN WHAT *LITTLE* LIFE WE HAVE HERE!

YOU ARE NOT ONLY HUNTED, BUT HUNTER AS WELL.

YOU WILL *KILL AGAIN*, MARQUIS. THAT WE KNOW. THE ONLY QUESTION IS WHETHER IT SHALL BE IN THE *LIBERATION* OF THY LAND, OR IN THE PRESERVATION OF A *COWARD*.

I MAY INDEED BE A *COWARD*, BUT THAT COWARDICE IS THE THIN WALL THAT PROTECTS US. YOU MAY STAY THE NIGHT, BUT TOMORROW YOU AND YOUR FRIEND MUST *LEAVE*.

PLEASE, MY LOVE--

MY DECISION IS *FINAL*. WHAT YOU DO, YOU DO *ALONE*.

VERY WELL.

ANOTHER DAY, ANOTHER WASTED OPPORTUNITY AT LIFE.

I HAD SHAMED MYSELF DEEPLY. I ONLY WISH MY DEAR WIFE HAD NOT BEEN THERE TO WITNESS IT.

I KNEW SHE WAS GONE THE MOMENT I SAW THE NOTE. ONE DOES NOT NEED TO READ AN EPITAPH TO KNOW IT MARKS A DEATH.

THOUGH THE DEATH BE MY OWN.

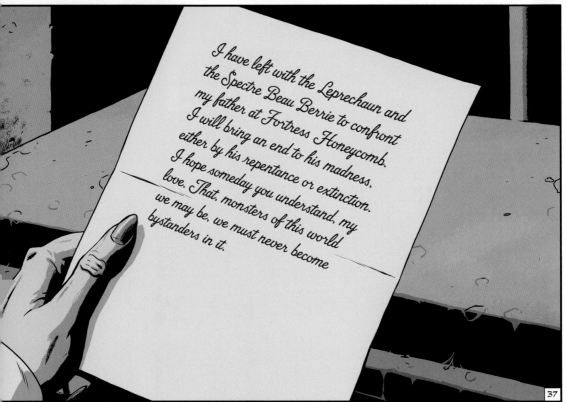

I have left with the Leprechaun and the Spectre Beau Berrie to confront my father at Fortress Honeycomb. I will bring an end to his madness, either by his repentance or extinction. I hope someday you understand, my love. That, monsters of this world we may be, we must never become bystanders in it.

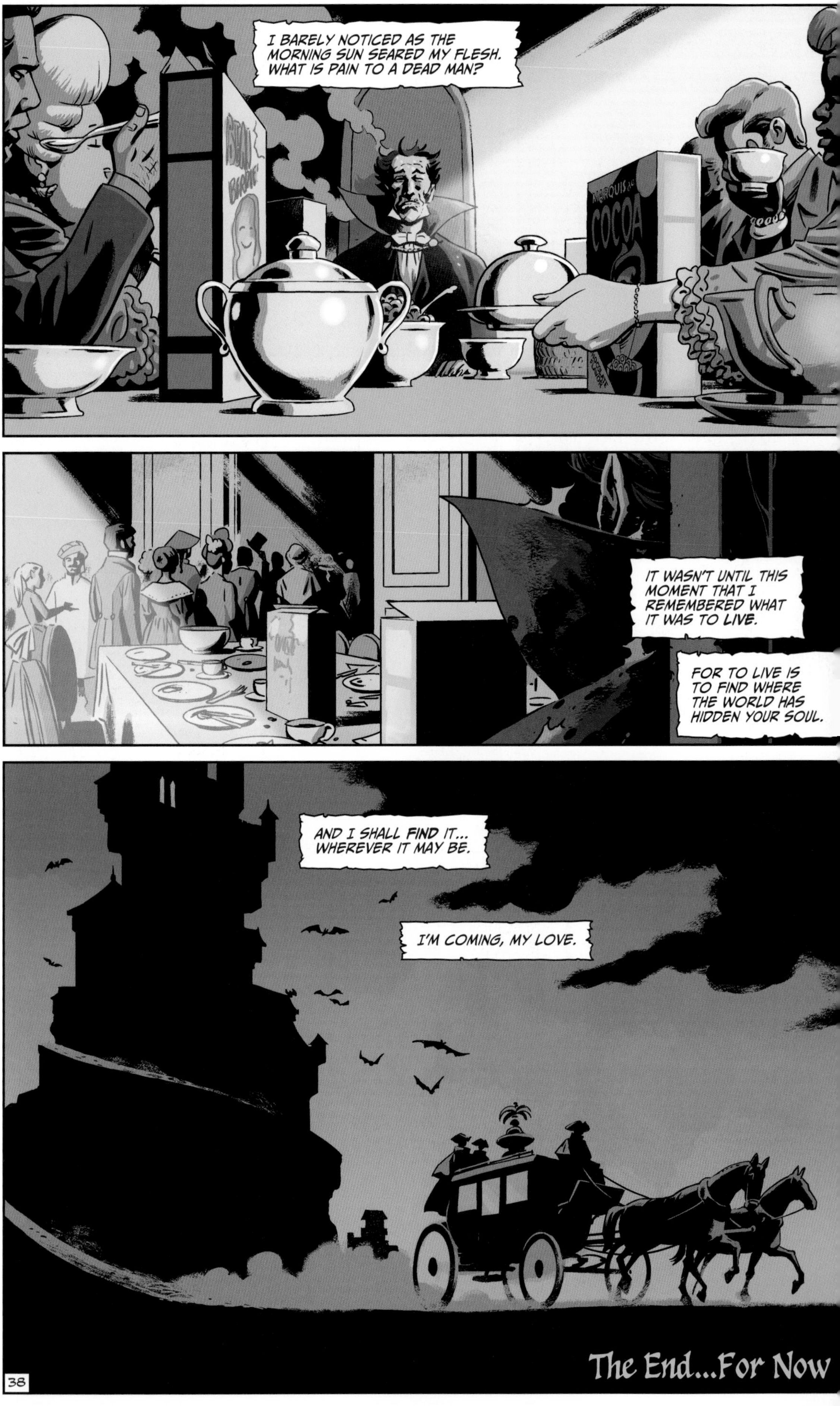
I BARELY NOTICED AS THE MORNING SUN SEARED MY FLESH. WHAT IS PAIN TO A DEAD MAN?
IT WASN'T UNTIL THIS MOMENT THAT I REMEMBERED WHAT IT WAS TO **LIVE**.
FOR TO LIVE IS TO FIND WHERE THE WORLD HAS HIDDEN YOUR SOUL.
AND I SHALL **FIND** IT... WHEREVER IT MAY BE.
I'M COMING, MY LOVE.
The End...For Now

A Tipple of Amontillado

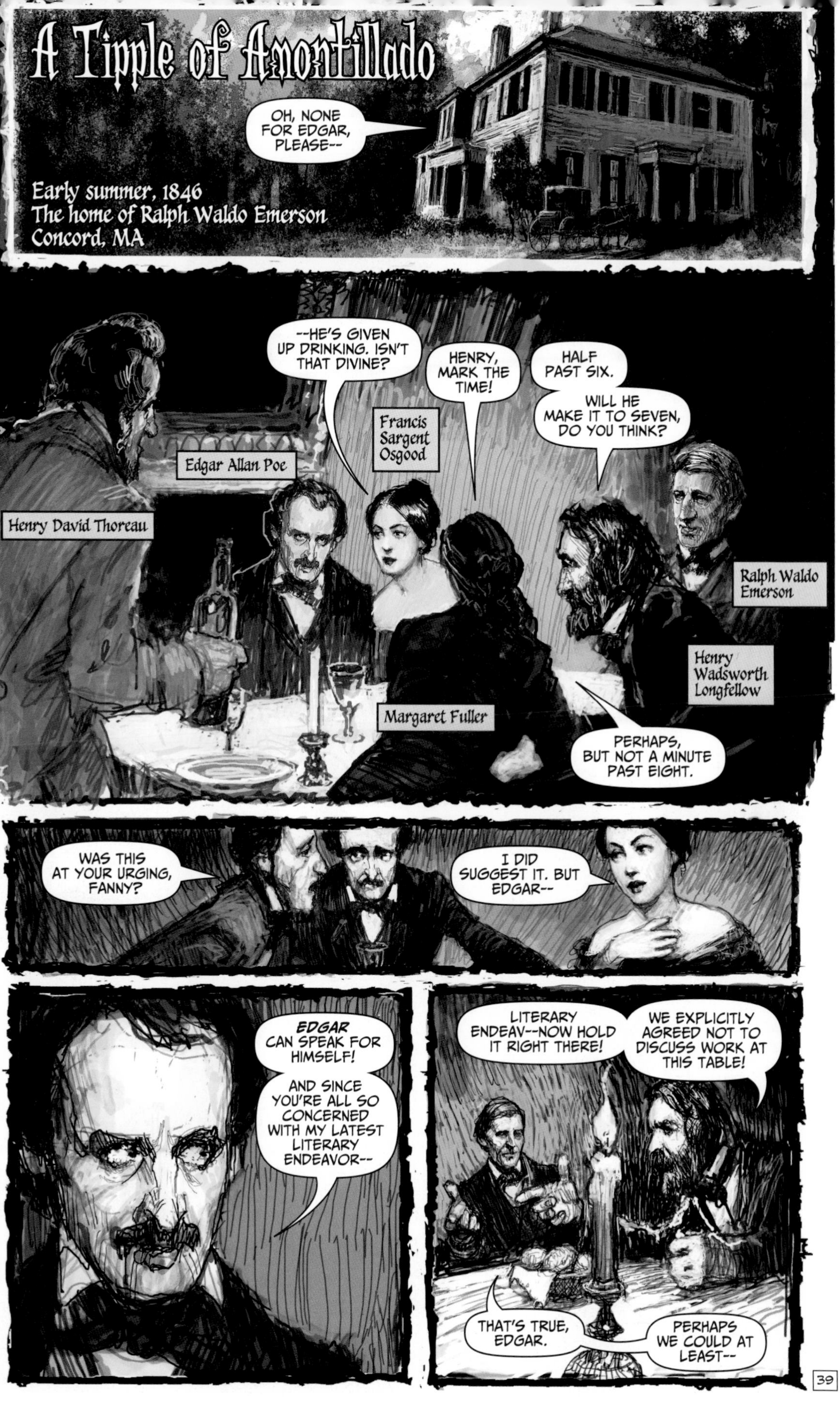

OH, NONE FOR EDGAR, PLEASE--
Early summer, 1846
The home of Ralph Waldo Emerson
Concord, MA
--HE'S GIVEN UP DRINKING. ISN'T THAT DIVINE?
HENRY, MARK THE TIME!
HALF PAST SIX.
WILL HE MAKE IT TO SEVEN, DO YOU THINK?
Francis Sargent Osgood
Edgar Allan Poe
Henry David Thoreau
Ralph Waldo Emerson
Henry Wadsworth Longfellow
Margaret Fuller
PERHAPS, BUT NOT A MINUTE PAST EIGHT.
WAS THIS AT YOUR URGING, FANNY?
I DID SUGGEST IT. BUT EDGAR--
EDGAR CAN SPEAK FOR HIMSELF!
AND SINCE YOU'RE ALL SO CONCERNED WITH MY LATEST LITERARY ENDEAVOR--
LITERARY ENDEAV--NOW HOLD IT RIGHT THERE!
WE EXPLICITLY AGREED NOT TO DISCUSS WORK AT THIS TABLE!
THAT'S TRUE, EDGAR.
PERHAPS WE COULD AT LEAST--

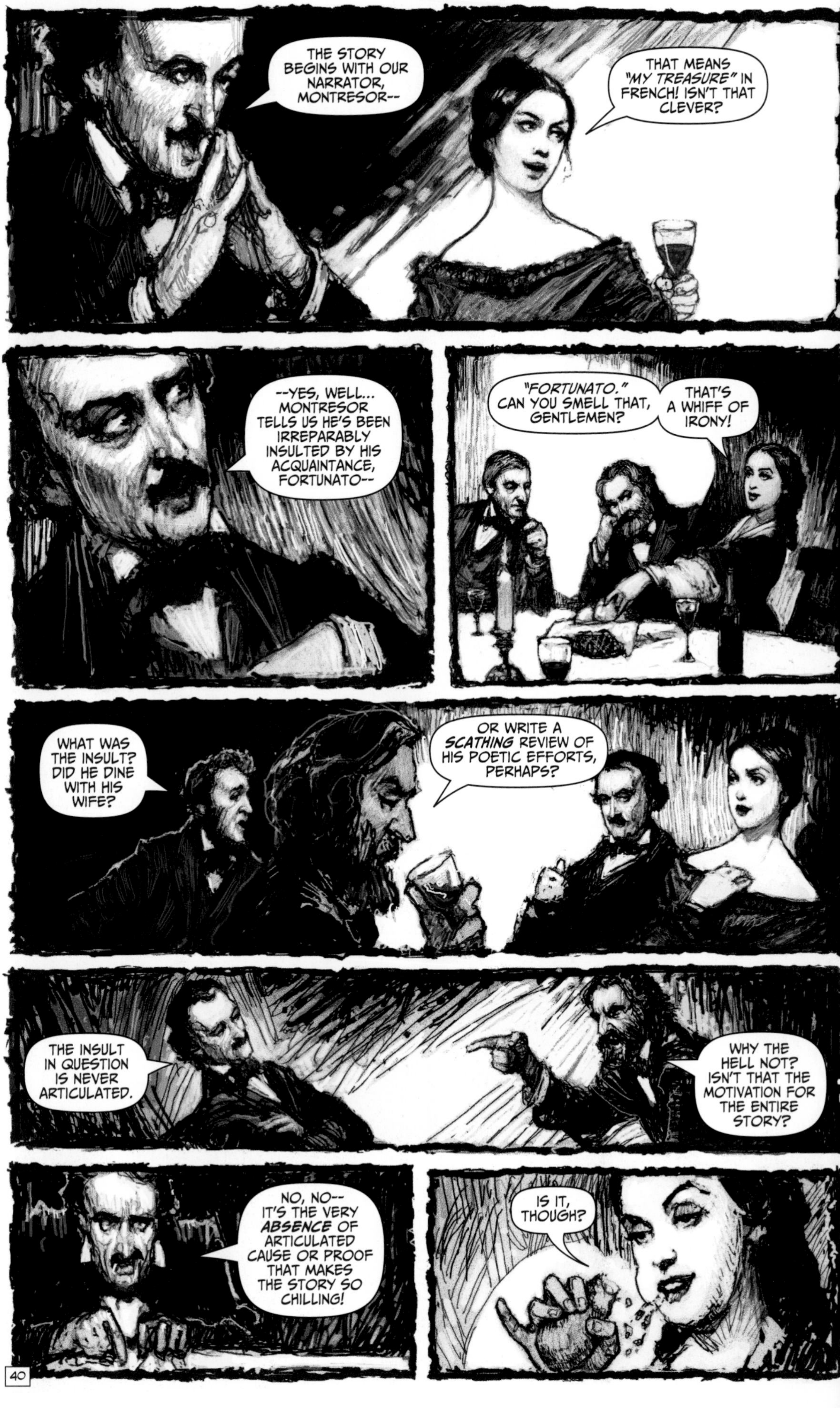
THE STORY BEGINS WITH OUR NARRATOR, MONTRESOR--
THAT MEANS *"MY TREASURE"* IN FRENCH! ISN'T THAT CLEVER?
--YES, WELL... MONTRESOR TELLS US HE'S BEEN IRREPARABLY INSULTED BY HIS ACQUAINTANCE, FORTUNATO--
"FORTUNATO." CAN YOU SMELL THAT, GENTLEMEN?
THAT'S A WHIFF OF IRONY!
WHAT WAS THE INSULT? DID HE DINE WITH HIS WIFE?
OR WRITE A ***SCATHING*** REVIEW OF HIS POETIC EFFORTS, PERHAPS?
THE INSULT IN QUESTION IS NEVER ARTICULATED.
WHY THE HELL NOT? ISN'T THAT THE MOTIVATION FOR THE ENTIRE STORY?
NO, NO-- IT'S THE VERY ***ABSENCE*** OF ARTICULATED CAUSE OR PROOF THAT MAKES THE STORY SO CHILLING!
IS IT, THOUGH?

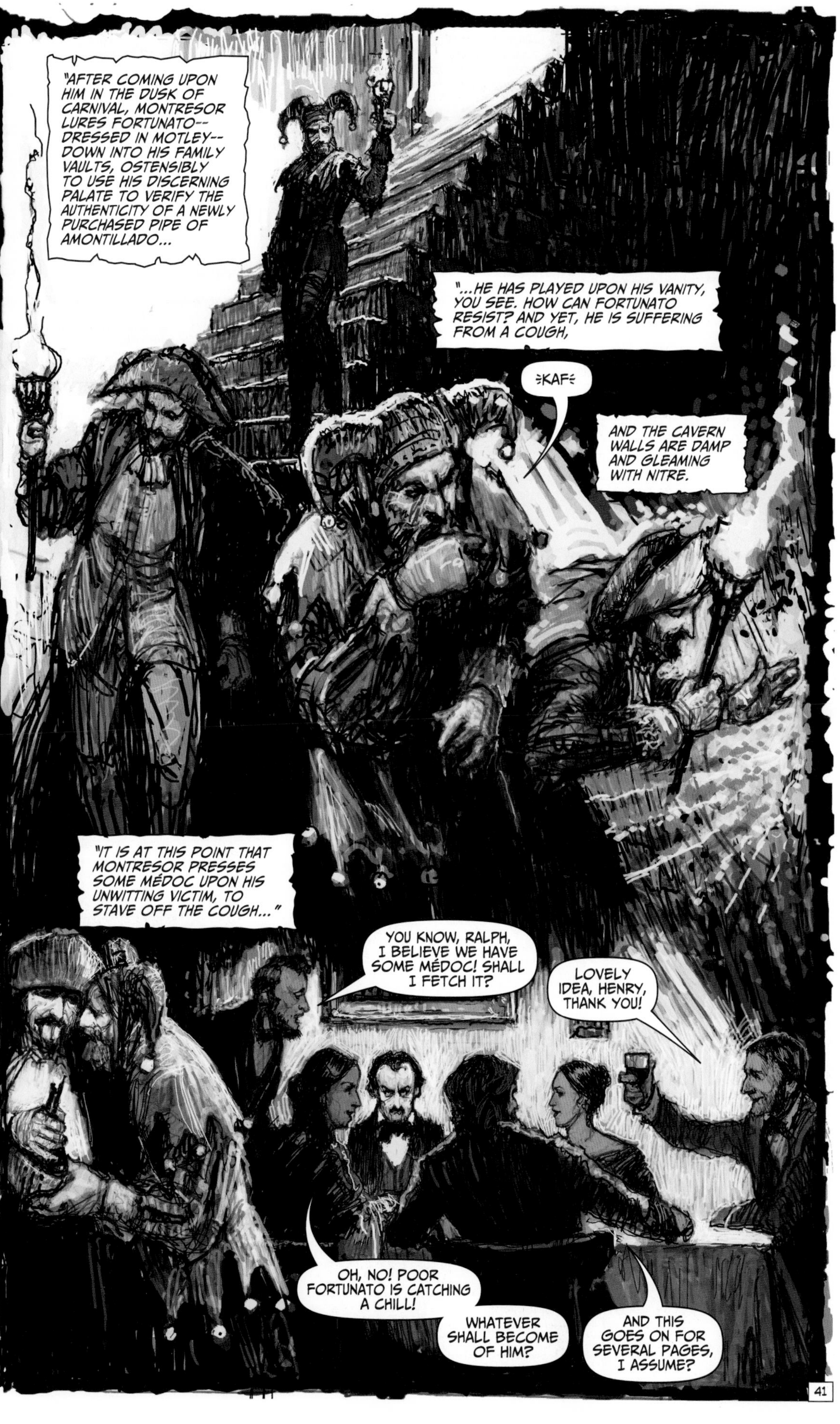
"AFTER COMING UPON HIM IN THE DUSK OF CARNIVAL, MONTRESOR LURES FORTUNATO--DRESSED IN MOTLEY--DOWN INTO HIS FAMILY VAULTS, OSTENSIBLY TO USE HIS DISCERNING PALATE TO VERIFY THE AUTHENTICITY OF A NEWLY PURCHASED PIPE OF AMONTILLADO...
"...HE HAS PLAYED UPON HIS VANITY, YOU SEE. HOW CAN FORTUNATO RESIST? AND YET, HE IS SUFFERING FROM A COUGH,
KAF
AND THE CAVERN WALLS ARE DAMP AND GLEAMING WITH NITRE.
"IT IS AT THIS POINT THAT MONTRESOR PRESSES SOME MÉDOC UPON HIS UNWITTING VICTIM, TO STAVE OFF THE COUGH..."
YOU KNOW, RALPH, I BELIEVE WE HAVE SOME MÉDOC! SHALL I FETCH IT?
LOVELY IDEA, HENRY, THANK YOU!
OH, NO! POOR FORTUNATO IS CATCHING A CHILL!
WHATEVER SHALL BECOME OF HIM?
AND THIS GOES ON FOR SEVERAL PAGES, I ASSUME?

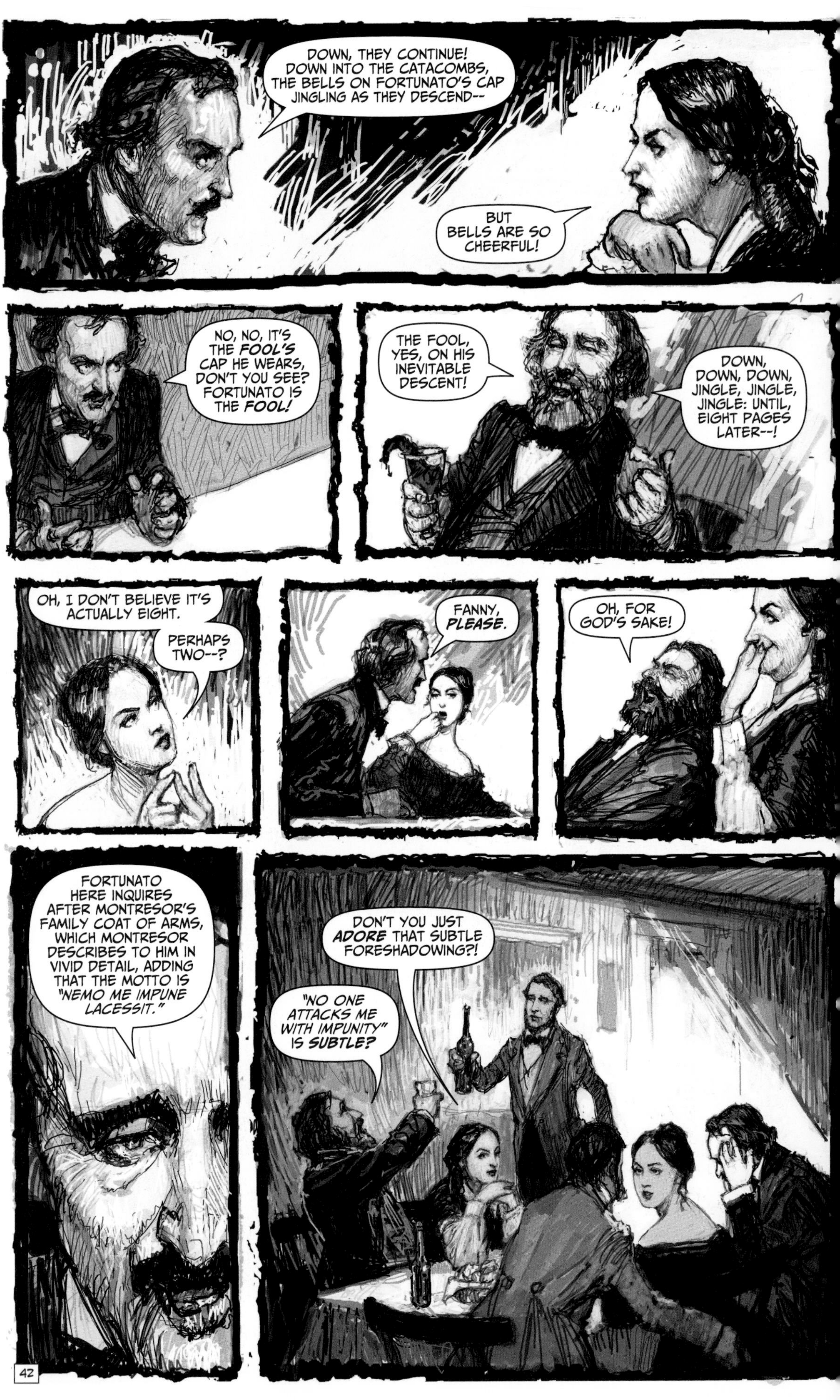
DOWN, THEY CONTINUE! DOWN INTO THE CATACOMBS, THE BELLS ON FORTUNATO'S CAP JINGLING AS THEY DESCEND--
BUT BELLS ARE SO CHEERFUL!
NO, NO, IT'S THE ***FOOL'S*** CAP HE WEARS, DON'T YOU SEE? FORTUNATO IS THE ***FOOL!***
THE FOOL, YES, ON HIS INEVITABLE DESCENT!
DOWN, DOWN, DOWN, JINGLE, JINGLE, JINGLE: UNTIL, EIGHT PAGES LATER--!
OH, I DON'T BELIEVE IT'S ACTUALLY EIGHT.
PERHAPS TWO--?
FANNY, ***PLEASE.***
OH, FOR GOD'S SAKE!
FORTUNATO HERE INQUIRES AFTER MONTRESOR'S FAMILY COAT OF ARMS, WHICH MONTRESOR DESCRIBES TO HIM IN VIVID DETAIL, ADDING THAT THE MOTTO IS *"NEMO ME IMPUNE LACESSIT."*
DON'T YOU JUST ***ADORE*** THAT SUBTLE FORESHADOWING?!
"NO ONE ATTACKS ME WITH IMPUNITY" IS ***SUBTLE?***

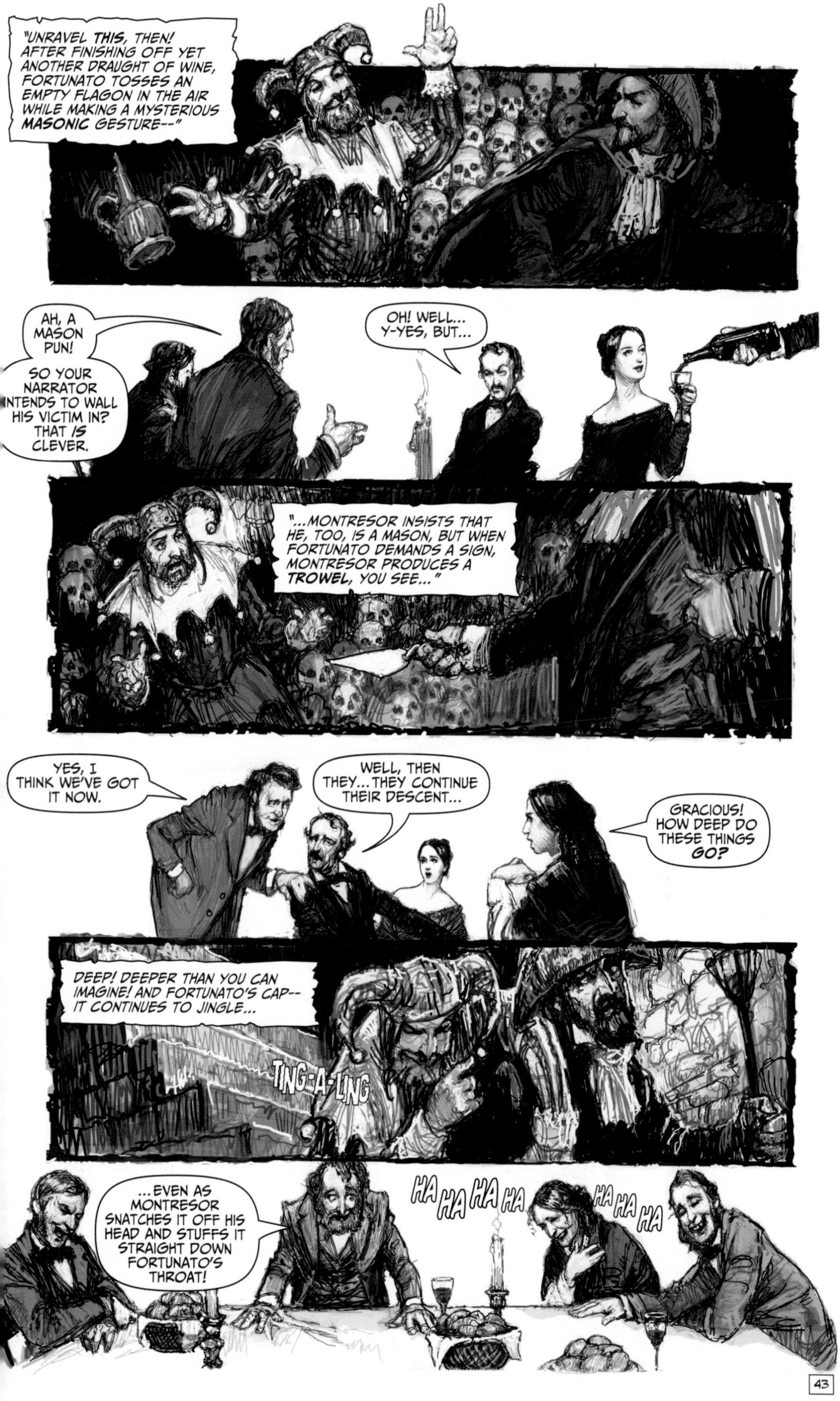
"UNRAVEL THIS, THEN! AFTER FINISHING OFF YET ANOTHER DRAUGHT OF WINE, FORTUNATO TOSSES AN EMPTY FLAGON IN THE AIR WHILE MAKING A MYSTERIOUS MASONIC GESTURE--"
AH, A MASON PUN!
SO YOUR NARRATOR INTENDS TO WALL HIS VICTIM IN? THAT IS CLEVER.
OH! WELL... Y-YES, BUT...
"...MONTRESOR INSISTS THAT HE, TOO, IS A MASON, BUT WHEN FORTUNATO DEMANDS A SIGN, MONTRESOR PRODUCES A TROWEL, YOU SEE..."
YES, I THINK WE'VE GOT IT NOW.
WELL, THEN THEY... THEY CONTINUE THEIR DESCENT...
GRACIOUS! HOW DEEP DO THESE THINGS GO?
DEEP! DEEPER THAN YOU CAN IMAGINE! AND FORTUNATO'S CAP-- IT CONTINUES TO JINGLE...
TING-A-LING
...EVEN AS MONTRESOR SNATCHES IT OFF HIS HEAD AND STUFFS IT STRAIGHT DOWN FORTUNATO'S THROAT!
HA HA HA HA
HA HA HA HA

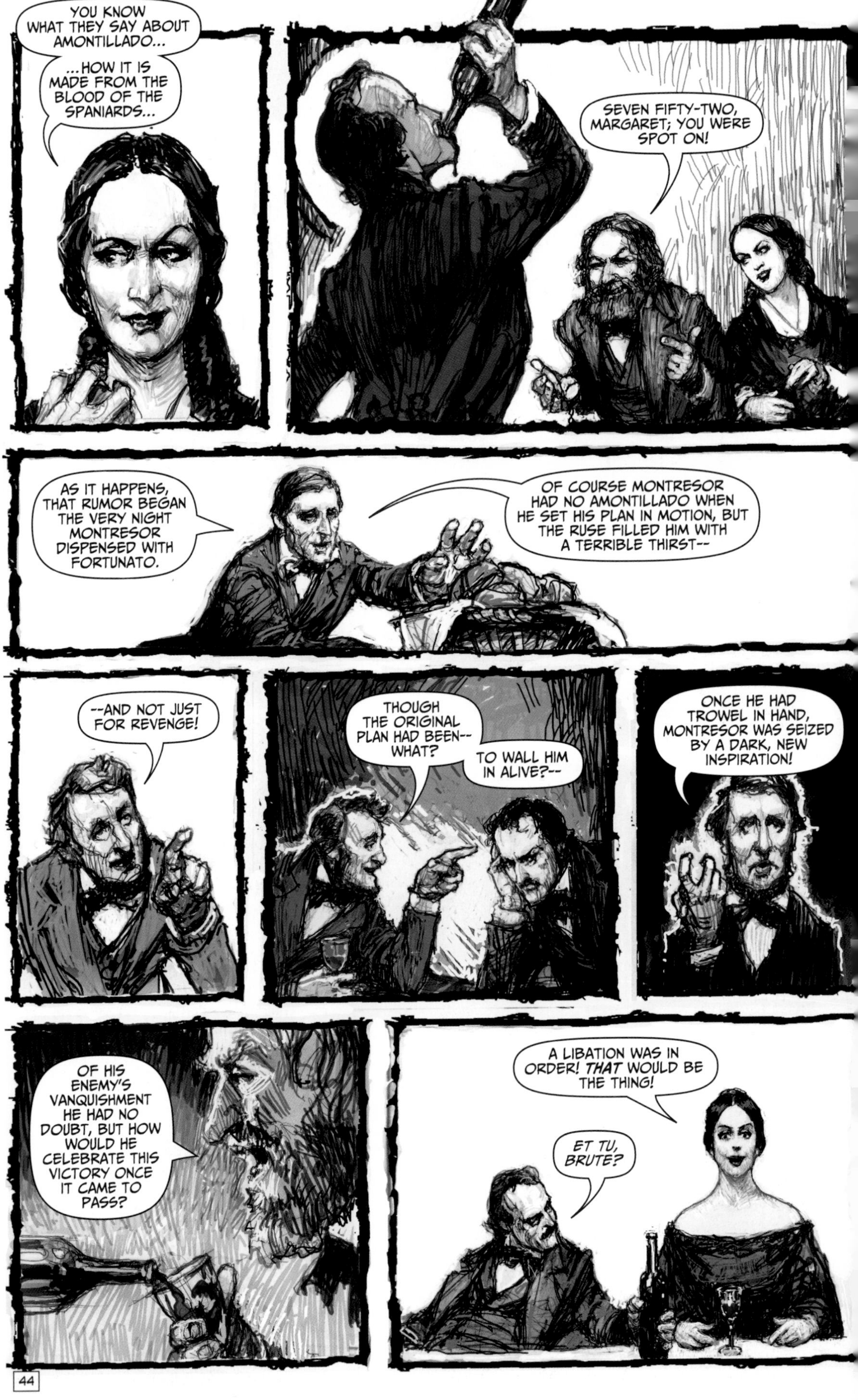
YOU KNOW WHAT THEY SAY ABOUT AMONTILLADO...
...HOW IT IS MADE FROM THE BLOOD OF THE SPANIARDS...
SEVEN FIFTY-TWO, MARGARET; YOU WERE SPOT ON!
AS IT HAPPENS, THAT RUMOR BEGAN THE VERY NIGHT MONTRESOR DISPENSED WITH FORTUNATO.
OF COURSE MONTRESOR HAD NO AMONTILLADO WHEN HE SET HIS PLAN IN MOTION, BUT THE RUSE FILLED HIM WITH A TERRIBLE THIRST--
--AND NOT JUST FOR REVENGE!
THOUGH THE ORIGINAL PLAN HAD BEEN-- WHAT?
TO WALL HIM IN ALIVE?--
ONCE HE HAD TROWEL IN HAND, MONTRESOR WAS SEIZED BY A DARK, NEW INSPIRATION!
OF HIS ENEMY'S VANQUISHMENT HE HAD NO DOUBT, BUT HOW WOULD HE CELEBRATE THIS VICTORY ONCE IT CAME TO PASS?
A LIBATION WAS IN ORDER! *THAT* WOULD BE THE THING!
ET TU, BRUTE?

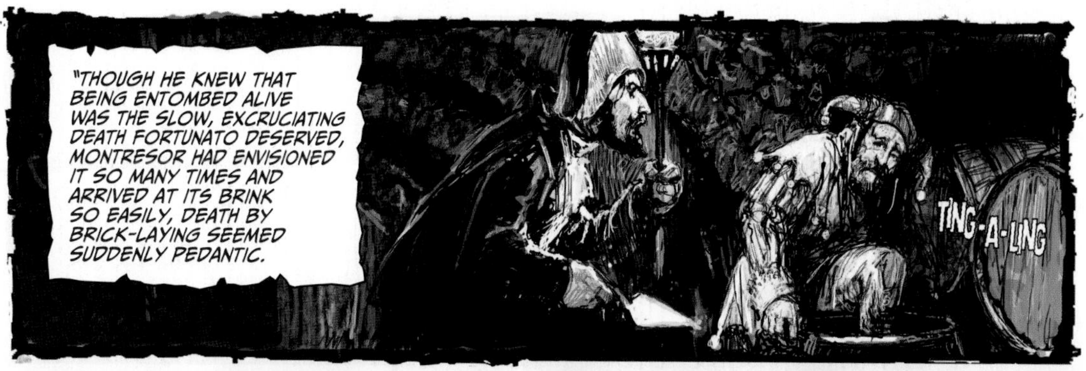
"THOUGH HE KNEW THAT BEING ENTOMBED ALIVE WAS THE SLOW, EXCRUCIATING DEATH FORTUNATO DESERVED, MONTRESOR HAD ENVISIONED IT SO MANY TIMES AND ARRIVED AT ITS BRINK SO EASILY, DEATH BY BRICK-LAYING SEEMED SUDDENLY PEDANTIC.
TING-A-LING
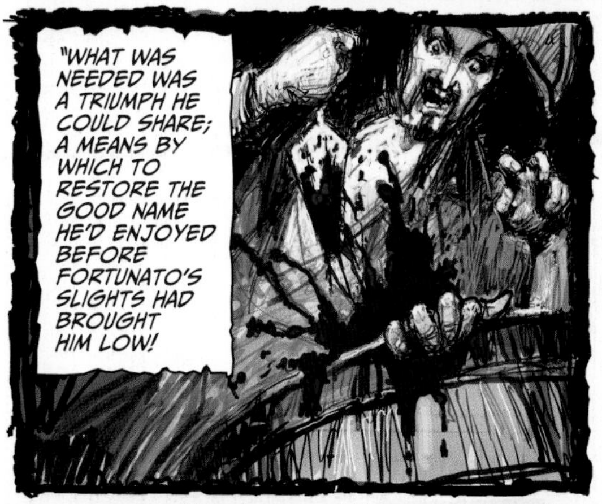
"WHAT WAS NEEDED WAS A TRIUMPH HE COULD SHARE; A MEANS BY WHICH TO RESTORE THE GOOD NAME HE'D ENJOYED BEFORE FORTUNATO'S SLIGHTS HAD BROUGHT HIM LOW!
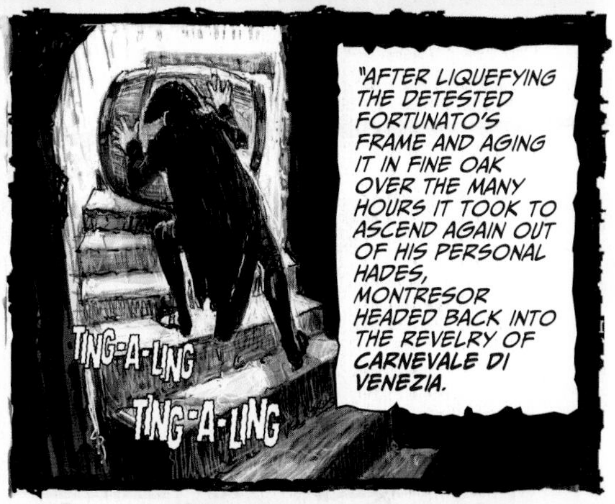
TING-A-LING
TING-A-LING
"AFTER LIQUEFYING THE DETESTED FORTUNATO'S FRAME AND AGING IT IN FINE OAK OVER THE MANY HOURS IT TOOK TO ASCEND AGAIN OUT OF HIS PERSONAL HADES, MONTRESOR HEADED BACK INTO THE REVELRY OF **CARNEVALE DI VENEZIA.**
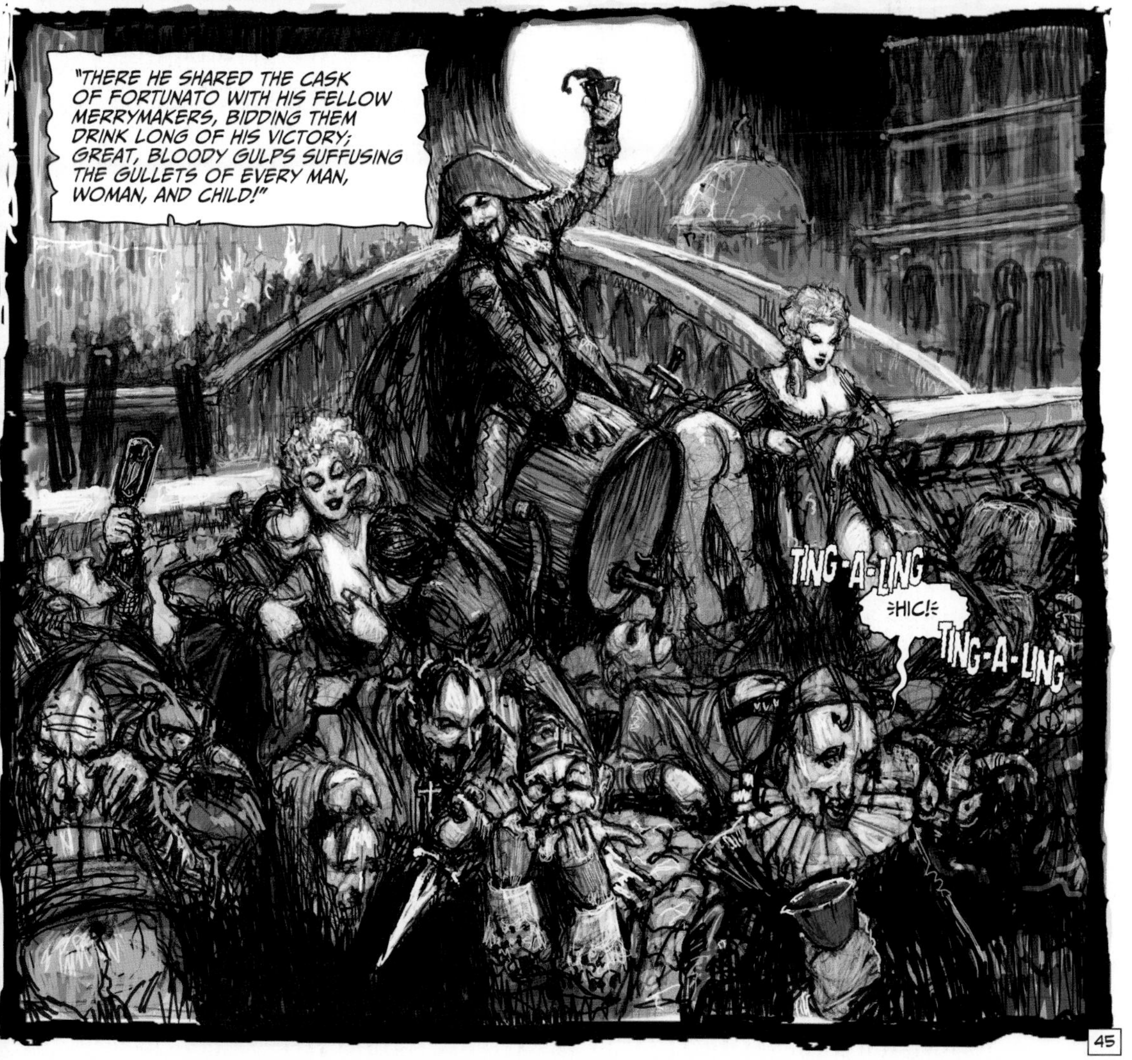
"THERE HE SHARED THE CASK OF FORTUNATO WITH HIS FELLOW MERRYMAKERS, BIDDING THEM DRINK LONG OF HIS VICTORY; GREAT, BLOODY GULPS SUFFUSING THE GULLETS OF EVERY MAN, WOMAN, AND CHILD!"
TING-A-LING
HIC!
TING-A-LING

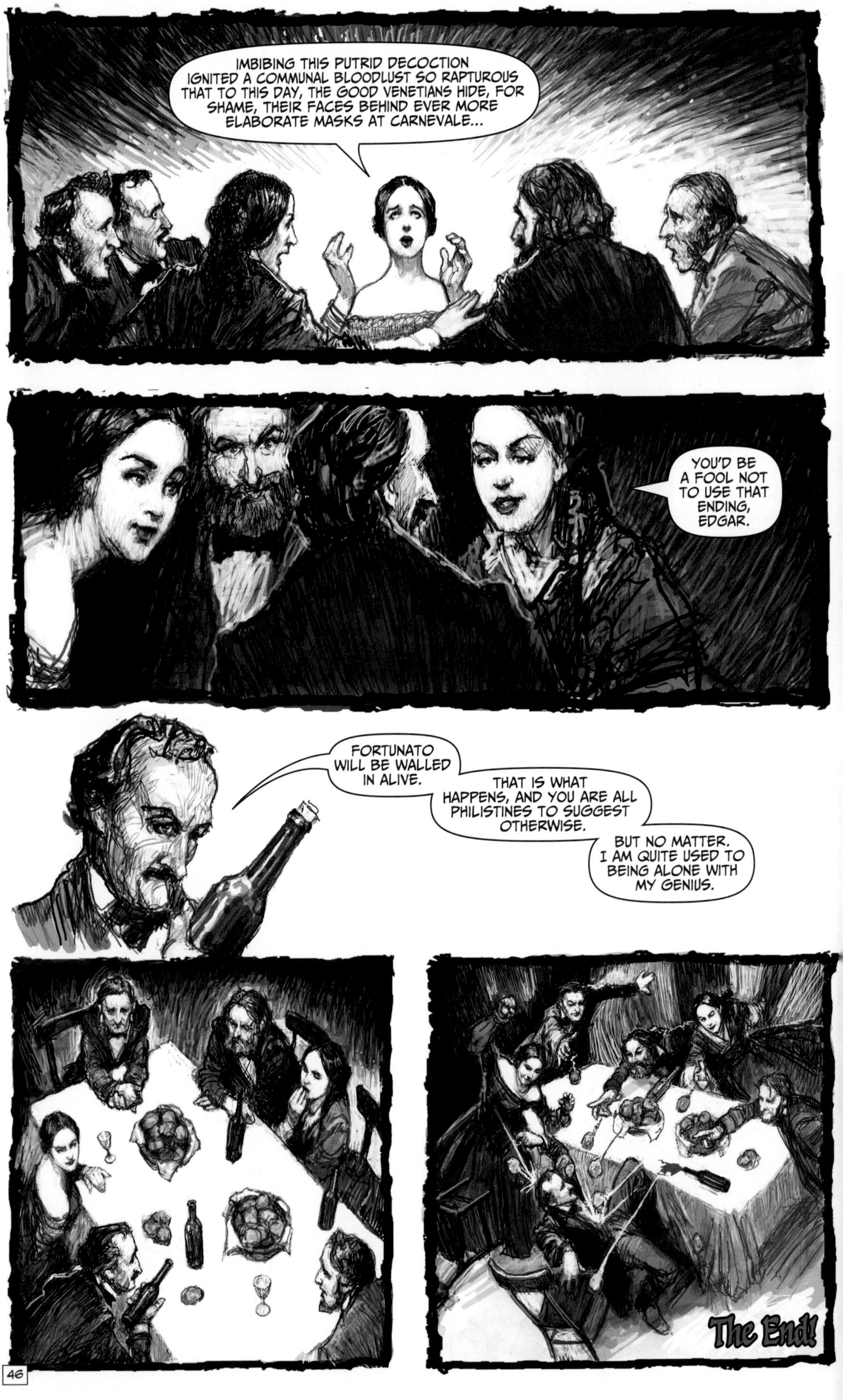
IMBIBING THIS PUTRID DECOCTION IGNITED A COMMUNAL BLOODLUST SO RAPTUROUS THAT TO THIS DAY, THE GOOD VENETIANS HIDE, FOR SHAME, THEIR FACES BEHIND EVER MORE ELABORATE MASKS AT CARNEVALE...
YOU'D BE A FOOL NOT TO USE THAT ENDING, EDGAR.
FORTUNATO WILL BE WALLED IN ALIVE.
THAT IS WHAT HAPPENS, AND YOU ARE ALL PHILISTINES TO SUGGEST OTHERWISE.
BUT NO MATTER. I AM QUITE USED TO BEING ALONE WITH MY GENIUS.
The End!

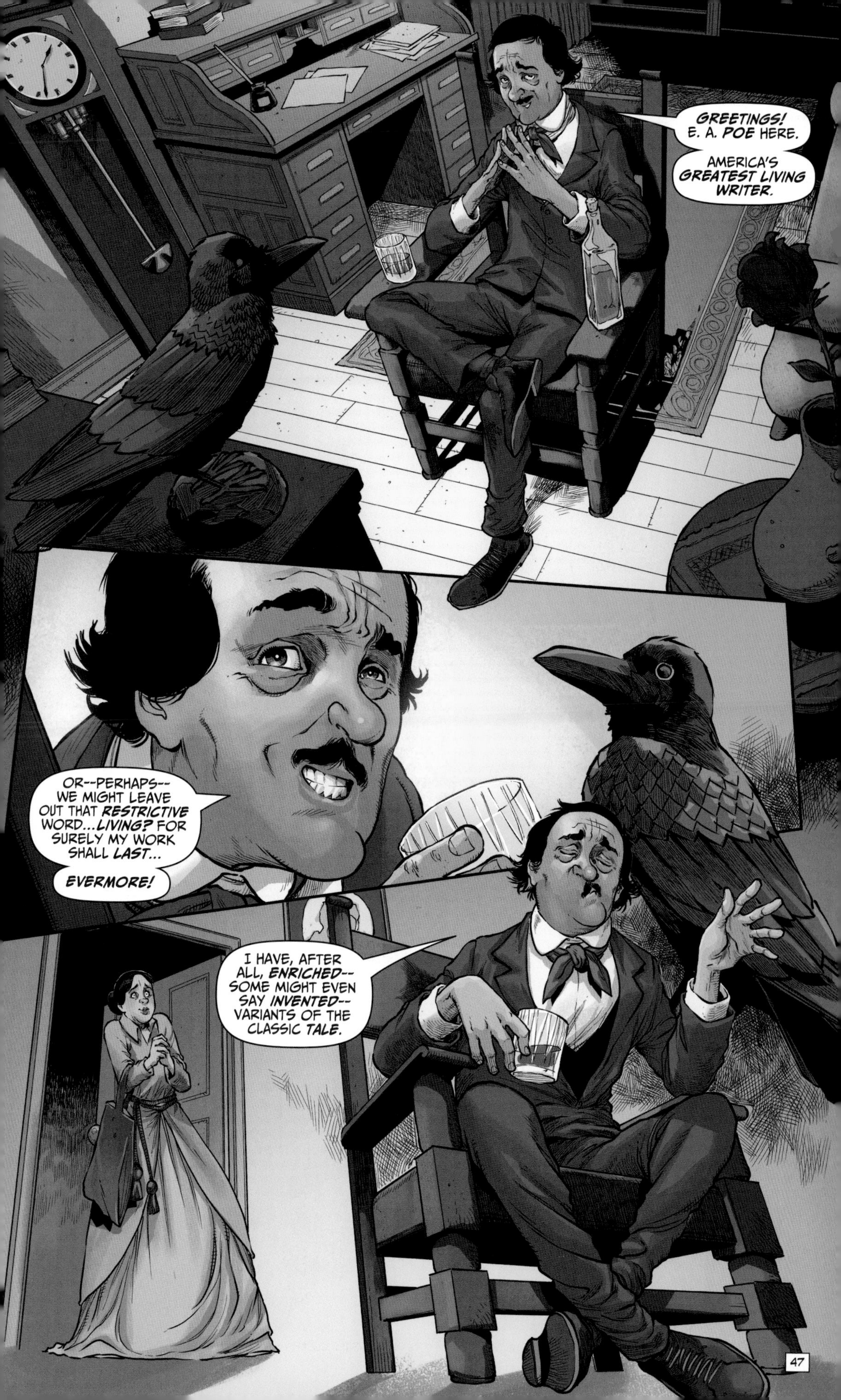
GREETINGS! E. A. POE HERE.
AMERICA'S GREATEST LIVING WRITER.
OR--PERHAPS-- WE MIGHT LEAVE OUT THAT RESTRICTIVE WORD...LIVING? FOR SURELY MY WORK SHALL LAST...
EVERMORE!
I HAVE, AFTER ALL, ENRICHED-- SOME MIGHT EVEN SAY INVENTED-- VARIANTS OF THE CLASSIC TALE.

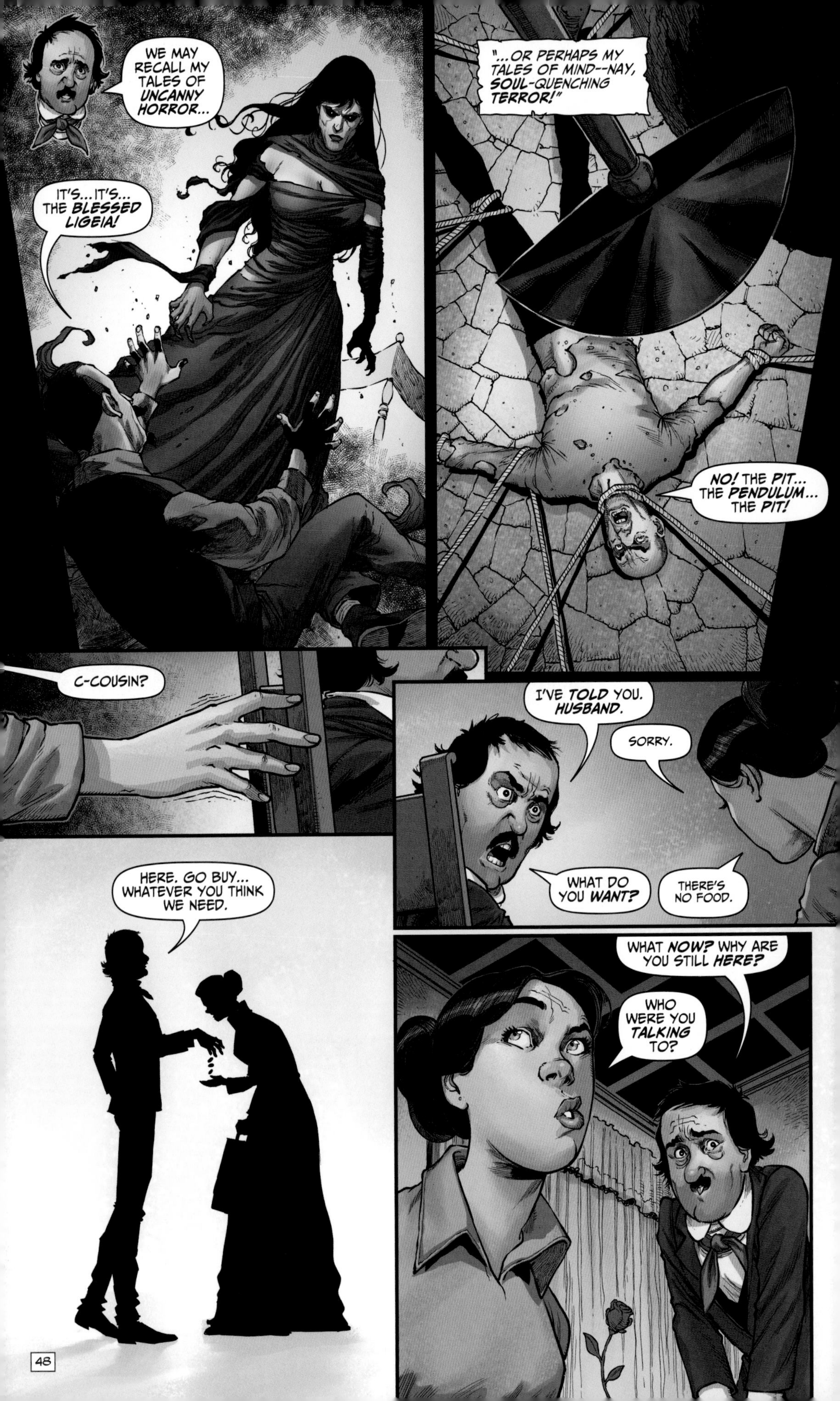
WE MAY RECALL MY TALES OF UNCANNY HORROR...
IT'S...IT'S... THE BLESSED LIGEIA!
"...OR PERHAPS MY TALES OF MIND--NAY, SOUL-QUENCHING TERROR!"
NO! THE PIT... THE PENDULUM... THE PIT!
C-COUSIN?
I'VE TOLD YOU. HUSBAND.
SORRY.
WHAT DO YOU WANT?
THERE'S NO FOOD.
HERE. GO BUY... WHATEVER YOU THINK WE NEED.
WHAT NOW? WHY ARE YOU STILL HERE?
WHO WERE YOU TALKING TO?

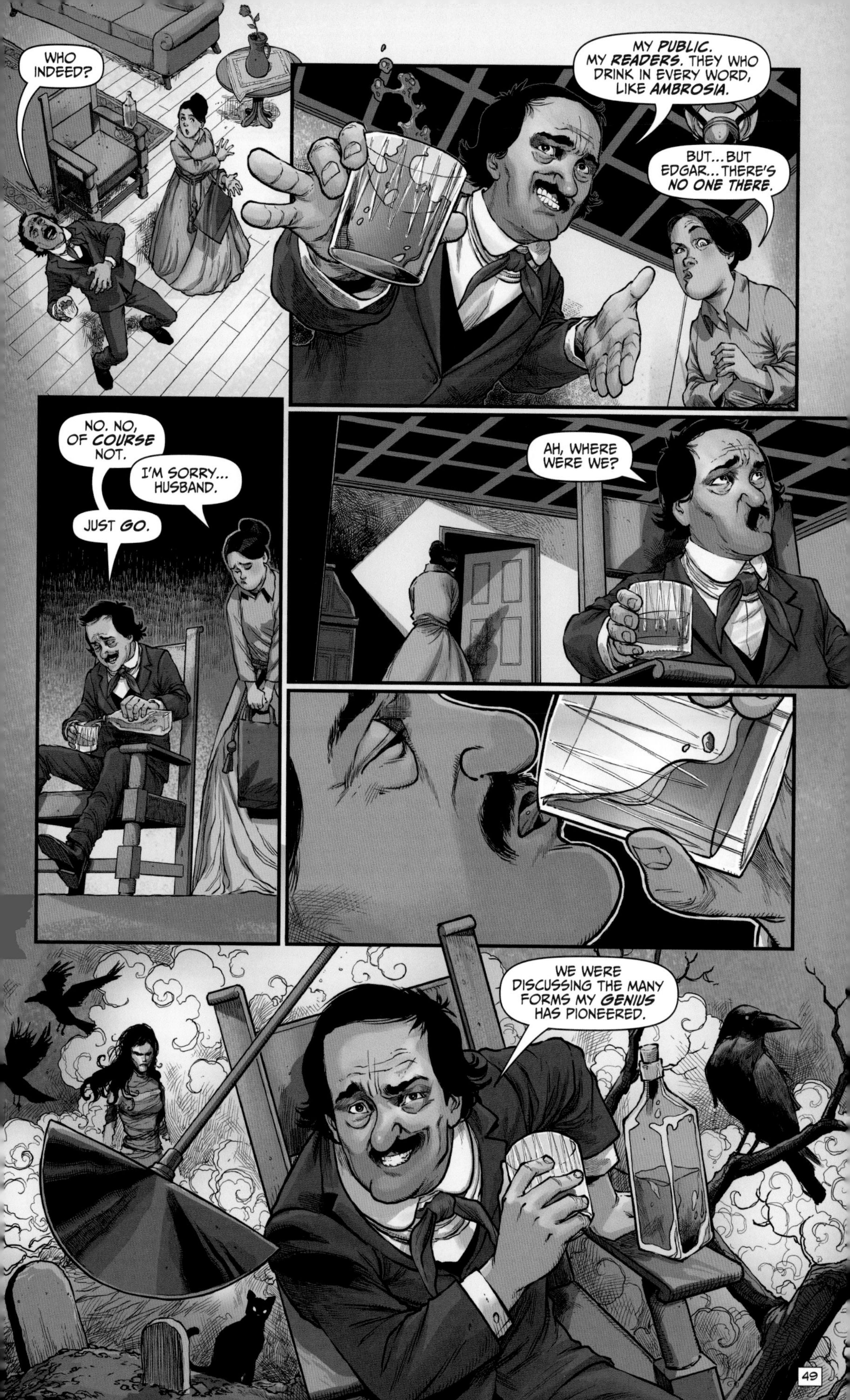
WHO INDEED?
MY PUBLIC. MY READERS. THEY WHO DRINK IN EVERY WORD, LIKE AMBROSIA.
BUT...BUT EDGAR...THERE'S NO ONE THERE.
NO. NO, OF COURSE NOT.
I'M SORRY... HUSBAND.
JUST GO.
AH, WHERE WERE WE?
WE WERE DISCUSSING THE MANY FORMS MY GENIUS HAS PIONEERED.

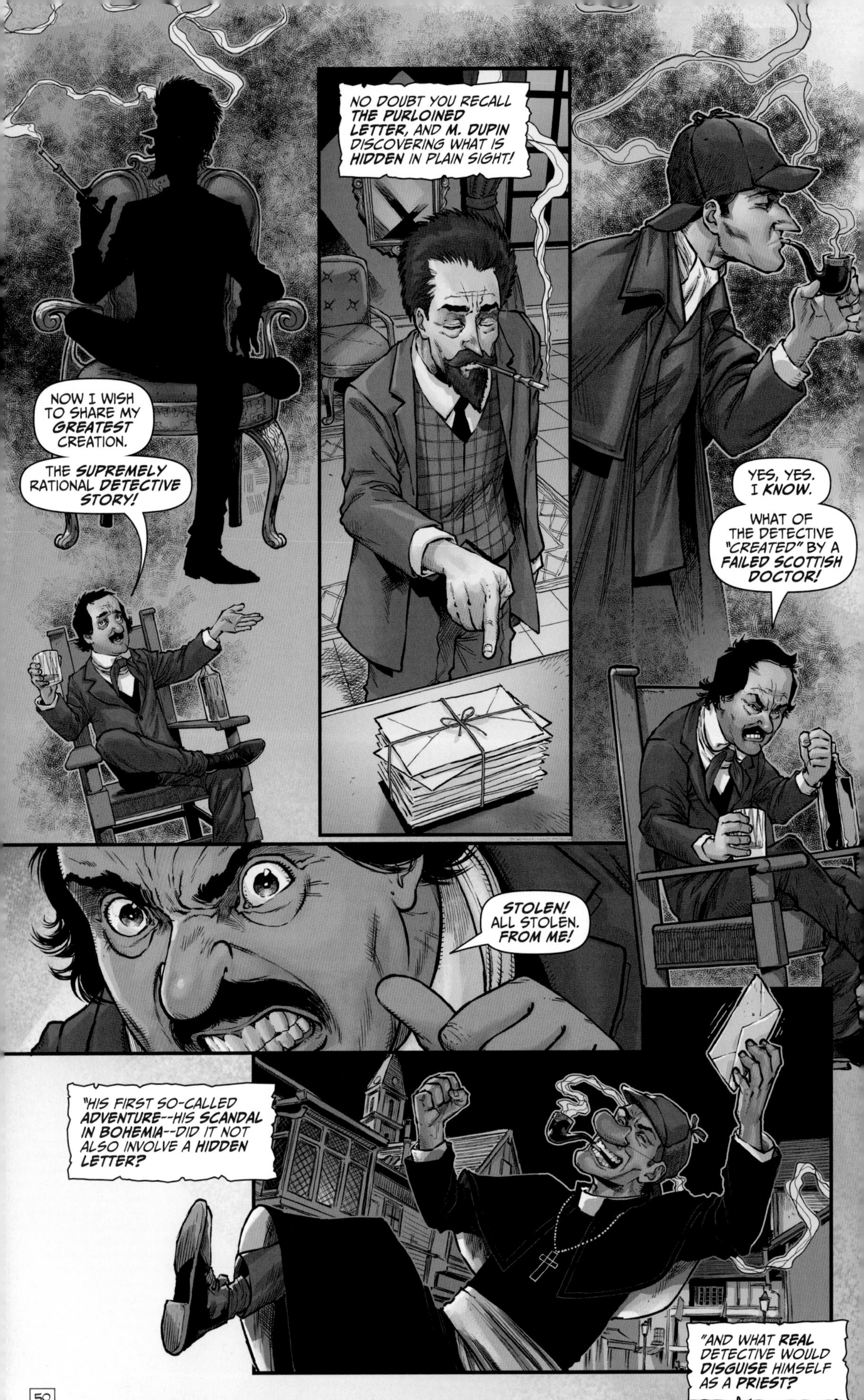
NOW I WISH TO SHARE MY **GREATEST** CREATION.
THE **SUPREMELY** RATIONAL **DETECTIVE STORY!**
NO DOUBT YOU RECALL **THE PURLOINED LETTER**, AND **M. DUPIN** DISCOVERING WHAT IS **HIDDEN** IN PLAIN SIGHT!
YES, YES. I **KNOW.**
WHAT OF THE DETECTIVE "**CREATED**" BY A **FAILED SCOTTISH DOCTOR!**
STOLEN! ALL STOLEN. **FROM ME!**
"HIS FIRST SO-CALLED **ADVENTURE**--HIS **SCANDAL IN BOHEMIA**--DID IT NOT ALSO INVOLVE A **HIDDEN LETTER?**
"AND WHAT **REAL** DETECTIVE WOULD **DISGUISE** HIMSELF AS A **PRIEST?**

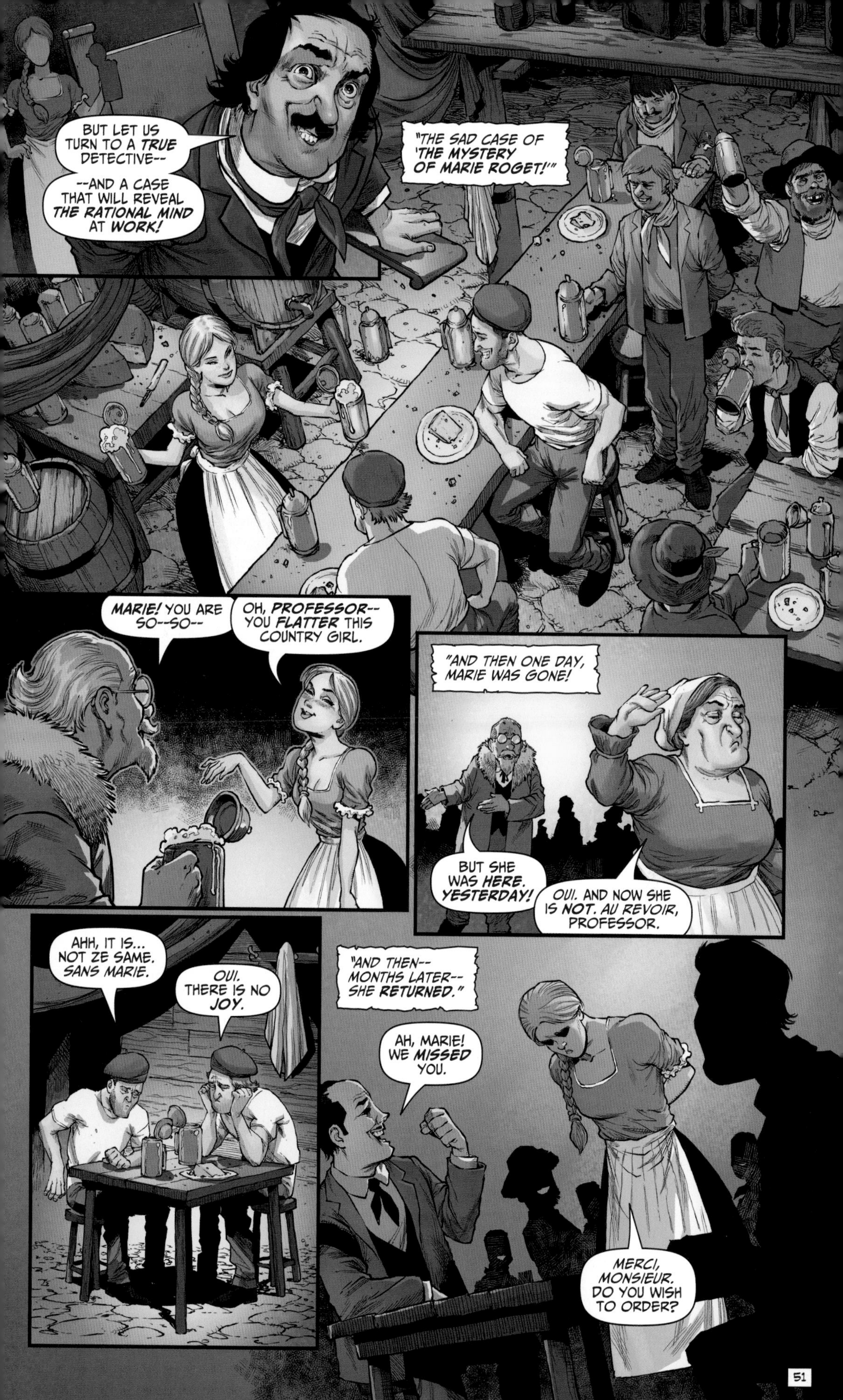

BUT LET US TURN TO A TRUE DETECTIVE--
--AND A CASE THAT WILL REVEAL THE RATIONAL MIND AT WORK!
"THE SAD CASE OF 'THE MYSTERY OF MARIE ROGET!'"
MARIE! YOU ARE SO--SO--
OH, PROFESSOR--YOU FLATTER THIS COUNTRY GIRL.
"AND THEN ONE DAY, MARIE WAS GONE!
BUT SHE WAS HERE. YESTERDAY!
OUI. AND NOW SHE IS NOT. AU REVOIR, PROFESSOR.
AHH, IT IS... NOT ZE SAME. SANS MARIE.
OUI. THERE IS NO JOY.
"AND THEN--MONTHS LATER--SHE RETURNED."
AH, MARIE! WE MISSED YOU.
MERCI, MONSIEUR. DO YOU WISH TO ORDER?

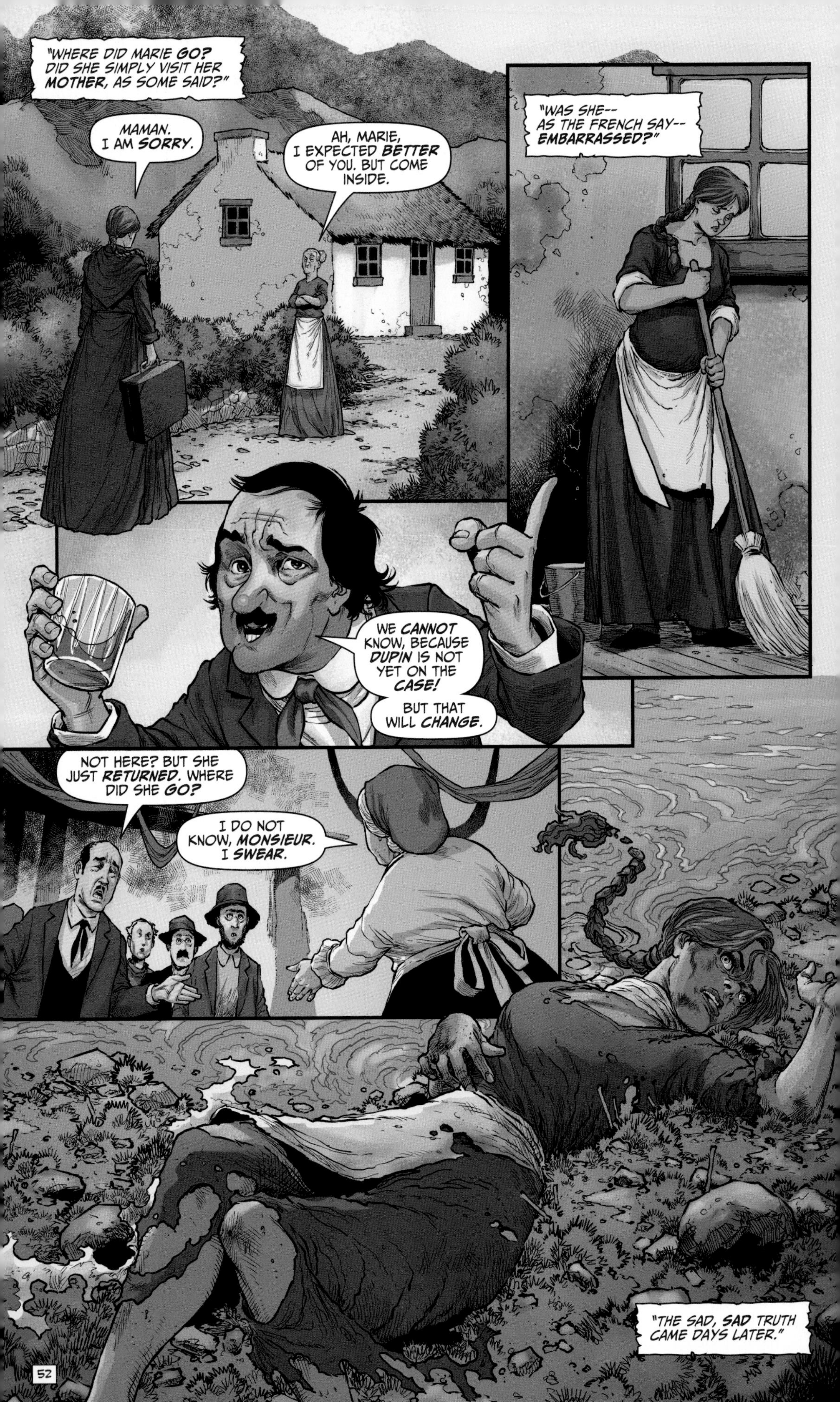

"WHERE DID MARIE GO? DID SHE SIMPLY VISIT HER MOTHER, AS SOME SAID?"
MAMAN. I AM SORRY.
AH, MARIE, I EXPECTED BETTER OF YOU. BUT COME INSIDE.
"WAS SHE-- AS THE FRENCH SAY-- EMBARRASSED?"
WE CANNOT KNOW, BECAUSE DUPIN IS NOT YET ON THE CASE!
BUT THAT WILL CHANGE.
NOT HERE? BUT SHE JUST RETURNED. WHERE DID SHE GO?
I DO NOT KNOW, MONSIEUR. I SWEAR.
"THE SAD, SAD TRUTH CAME DAYS LATER."

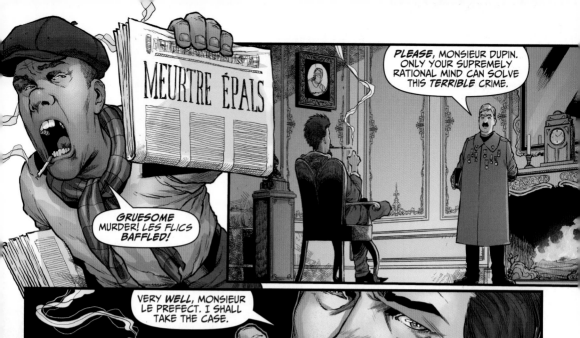

GRUESOME MURDER! LES FLICS BAFFLED!

MEURTRE ÉPAIS

PLEASE, MONSIEUR DUPIN. ONLY YOUR SUPREMELY RATIONAL MIND CAN SOLVE THIS *TERRIBLE* CRIME.

VERY *WELL*, MONSIEUR LE PREFECT. I SHALL TAKE THE CASE.

OH, *MERCI!* SHALL WE GO AND EXAMINE THE *CRIME* SCENE?

NON, MONSIEUR. THAT WILL NOT BE NÉCESSAIRE.

ONLY AN INFERIOR MIND MUST GO *IN PERSON.*

THE *TRUE,* THE *RATIONAL,* DETECTIVE, NEEDS ONLY HIS *CEREBRAL CORTEX* TO SOLVE ANY CRIME.

S'ILS VOUS PLAIT, MONSIEUR DUPIN. L'EVIDENCE.

THE MURDER WEAPON, MONSIEUR-- HER OWN *SCARF.*

MERCI. THE TABLE, PLEASE.

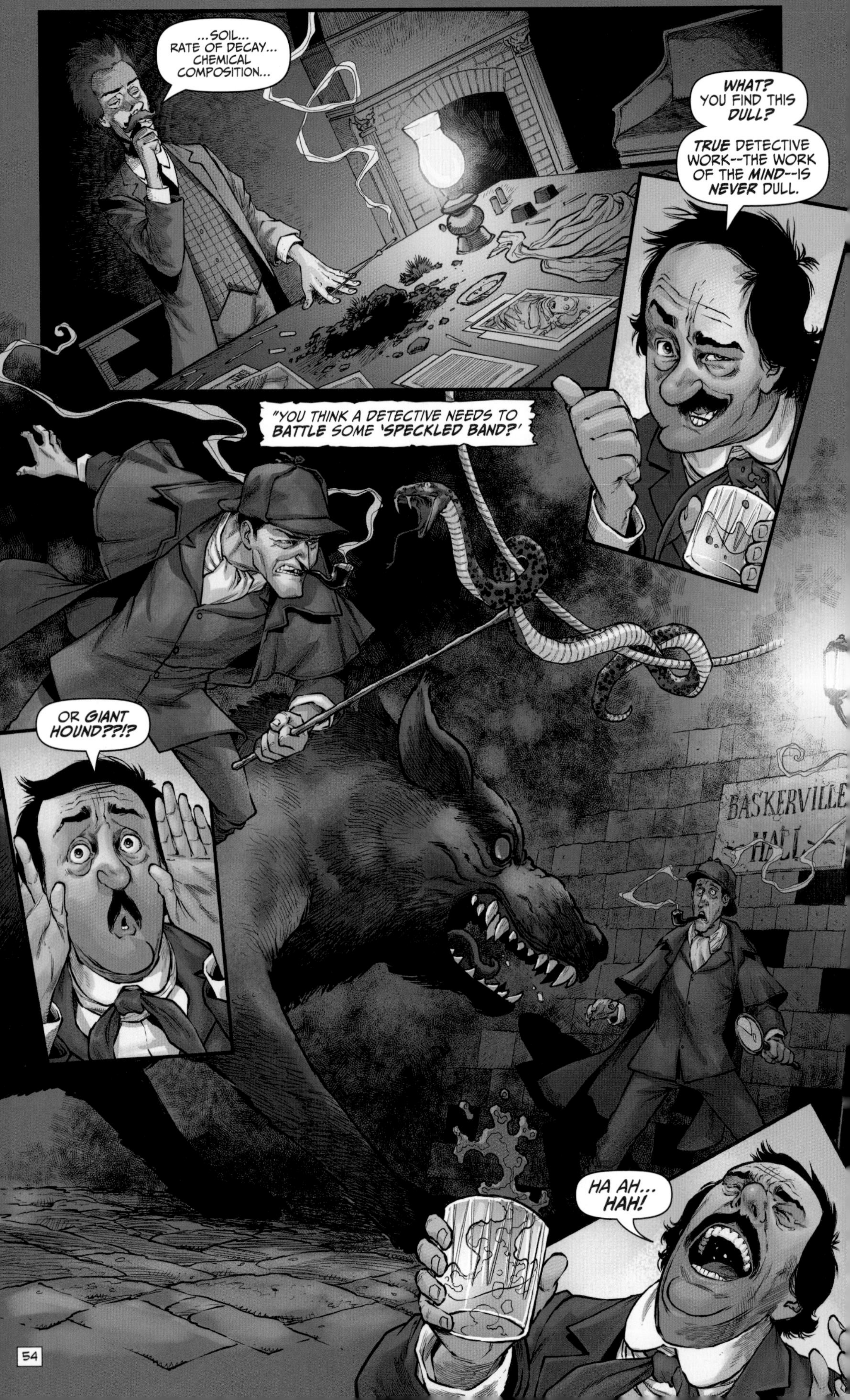

...SOIL... RATE OF DECAY... CHEMICAL COMPOSITION...
WHAT? YOU FIND THIS *DULL?*
TRUE DETECTIVE WORK--THE WORK OF THE *MIND*--IS *NEVER* DULL.
"YOU THINK A DETECTIVE NEEDS TO BATTLE SOME *'SPECKLED BAND?'*
OR *GIANT HOUND??!?*
BASKERVILLE HALL
HA AH... HAH!

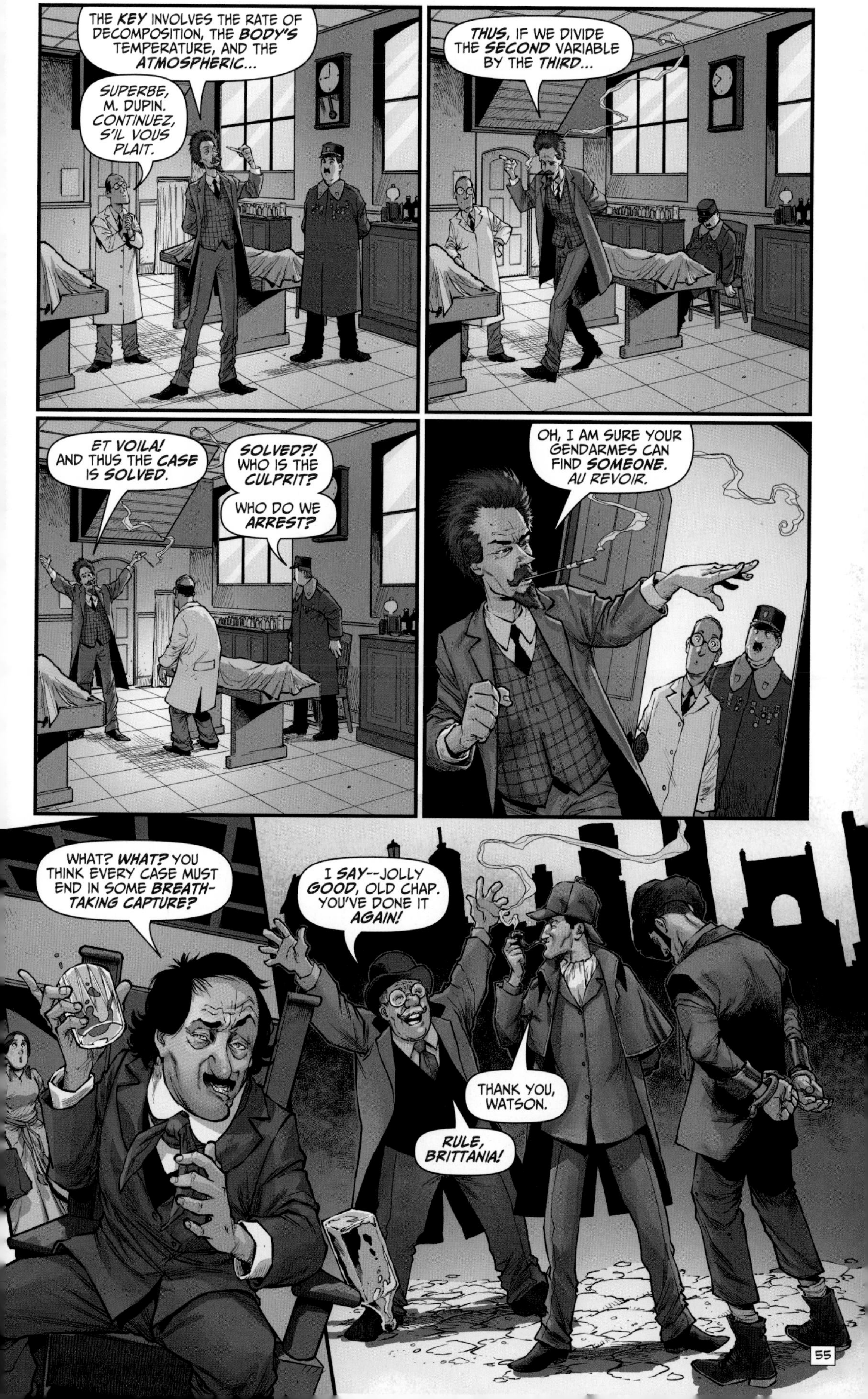
THE KEY INVOLVES THE RATE OF DECOMPOSITION, THE BODY'S TEMPERATURE, AND THE ATMOSPHERIC...
SUPERBE, M. DUPIN. CONTINUEZ, S'IL VOUS PLAIT.
THUS, IF WE DIVIDE THE SECOND VARIABLE BY THE THIRD...
ET VOILA! AND THUS THE CASE IS SOLVED.
SOLVED?! WHO IS THE CULPRIT?
WHO DO WE ARREST?
OH, I AM SURE YOUR GENDARMES CAN FIND SOMEONE. AU REVOIR.
WHAT? WHAT? YOU THINK EVERY CASE MUST END IN SOME BREATH-TAKING CAPTURE?
I SAY--JOLLY GOOD, OLD CHAP. YOU'VE DONE IT AGAIN!
THANK YOU, WATSON.
RULE, BRITTANIA!

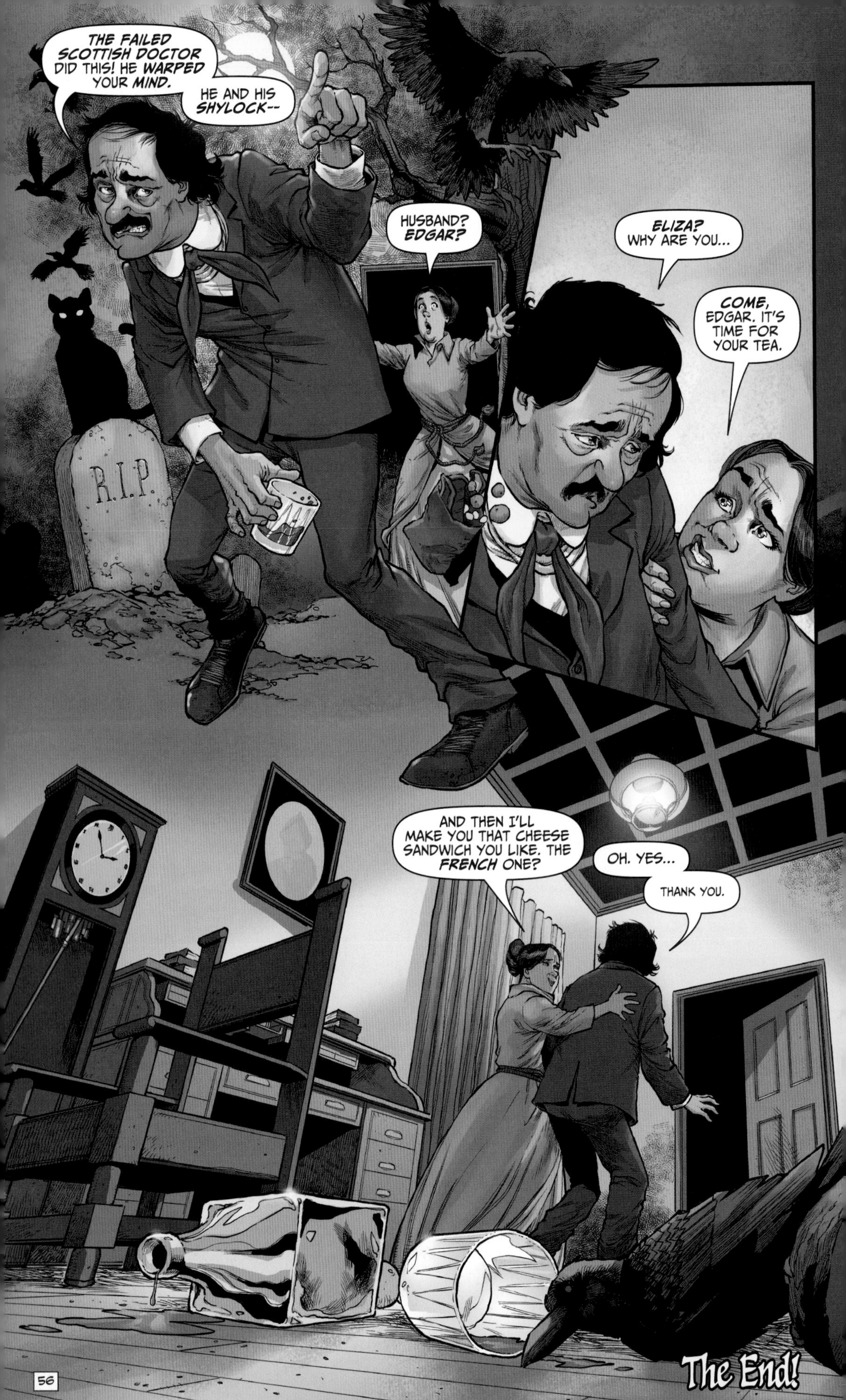
THE FAILED SCOTTISH DOCTOR DID THIS! HE WARPED YOUR MIND.
HE AND HIS SHYLOCK--
R.I.P.
HUSBAND? EDGAR?
ELIZA? WHY ARE YOU...
COME, EDGAR. IT'S TIME FOR YOUR TEA.
AND THEN I'LL MAKE YOU THAT CHEESE SANDWICH YOU LIKE. THE FRENCH ONE?
OH. YES...
THANK YOU.
The End!

The future!

I'VE NEARLY FOUND IT!

THE WORKS OF MY ANCESTOR *EDGAR ALLAN POE*, THE GREATEST POET WHO EVER LIVED, LOST FOR *CENTURIES*...

BAROOOOM!!

HUP!

...SOON WILL BE RESTORED TO THIS FALLEN WORLD.

ALL THANKS TO ME...

POENULUS EDGARALLAN, ARCHAEOLOGIST.

COULD IT BE...?

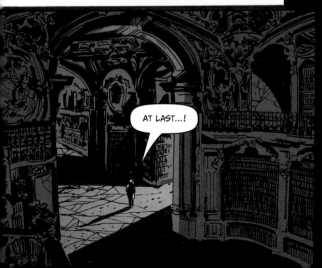

AT LAST...!

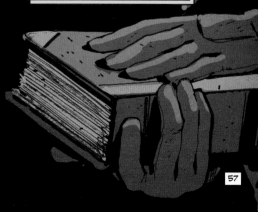

THE ONLY COPY OF THE COLLECTED WORKS OF EDGAR ALLAN POE IN EXISTENCE!

57

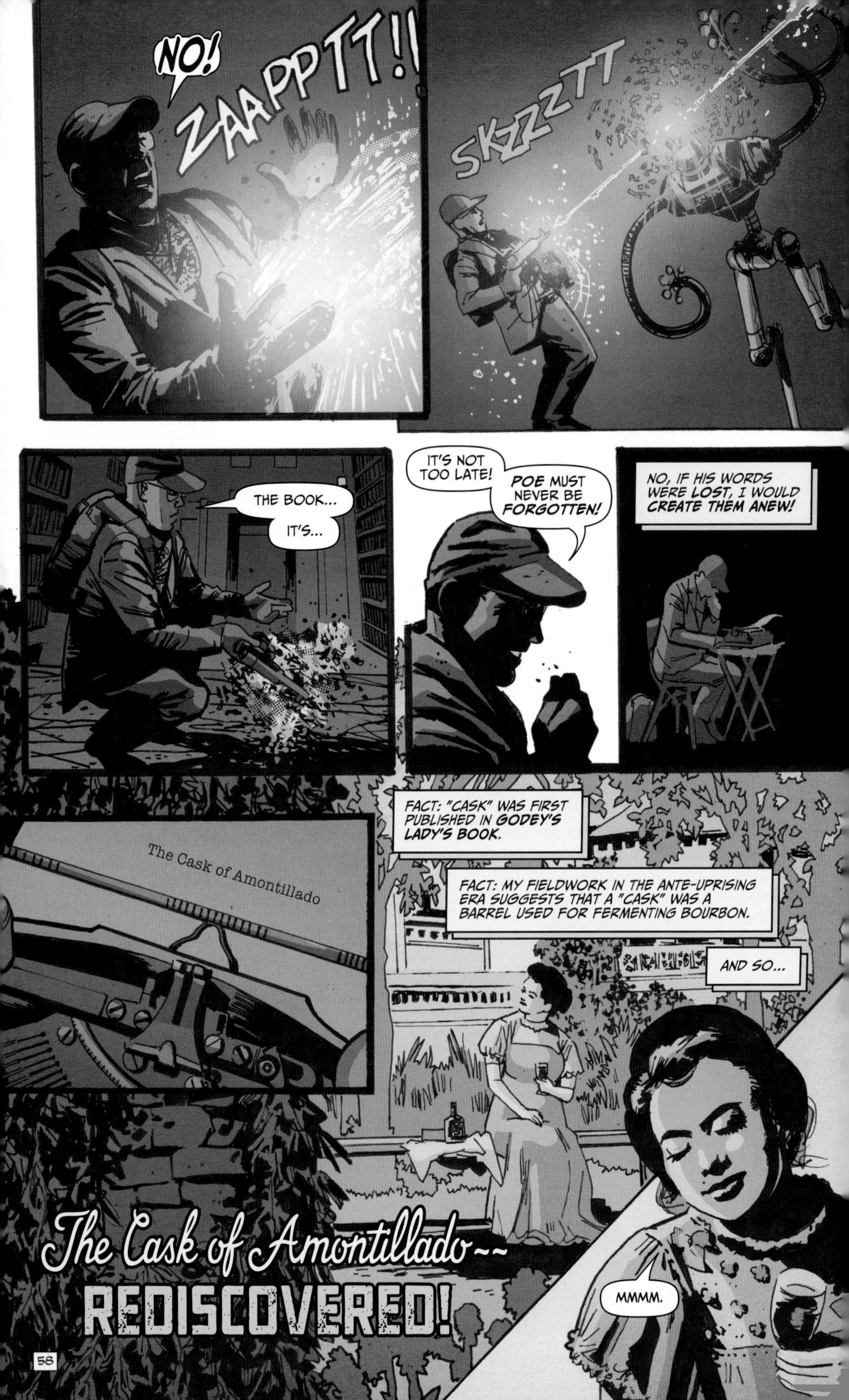
NO!
ZAAPPTT!!
SKZZZTT
THE BOOK...
IT'S...
IT'S NOT TOO LATE!
POE MUST NEVER BE FORGOTTEN!
NO, IF HIS WORDS WERE LOST, I WOULD CREATE THEM ANEW!
The Cask of Amontillado
FACT: "CASK" WAS FIRST PUBLISHED IN GODEY'S LADY'S BOOK.
FACT: MY FIELDWORK IN THE ANTE-UPRISING ERA SUGGESTS THAT A "CASK" WAS A BARREL USED FOR FERMENTING BOURBON.
AND SO...
The Cask of Amontillado~~
REDISCOVERED!
MMMM.

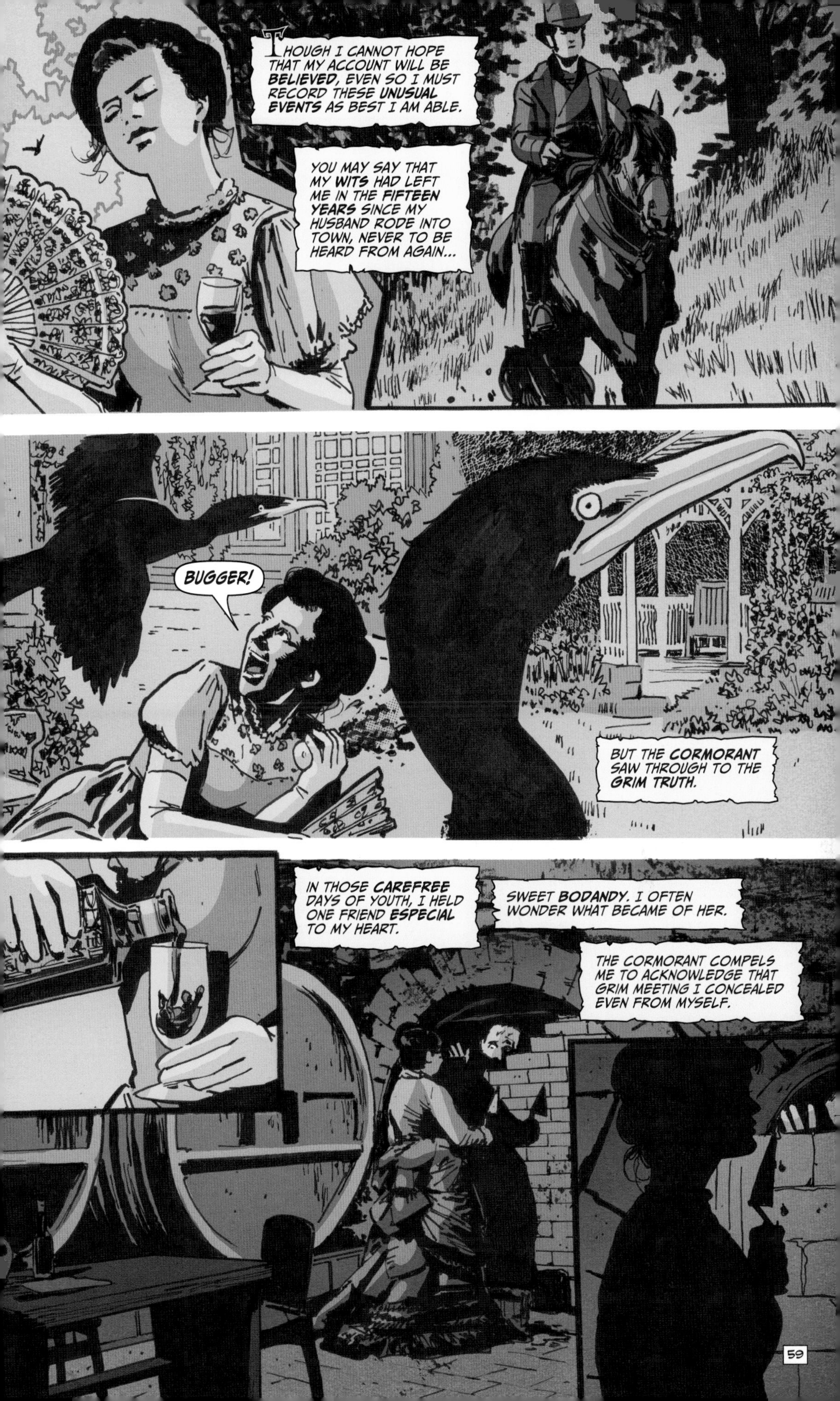
THOUGH I CANNOT HOPE THAT MY ACCOUNT WILL BE BELIEVED, EVEN SO I MUST RECORD THESE UNUSUAL EVENTS AS BEST I AM ABLE.
YOU MAY SAY THAT MY WITS HAD LEFT ME IN THE FIFTEEN YEARS SINCE MY HUSBAND RODE INTO TOWN, NEVER TO BE HEARD FROM AGAIN...
BUGGER!
BUT THE CORMORANT SAW THROUGH TO THE GRIM TRUTH.
IN THOSE CAREFREE DAYS OF YOUTH, I HELD ONE FRIEND ESPECIAL TO MY HEART.
SWEET BODANDY. I OFTEN WONDER WHAT BECAME OF HER.
THE CORMORANT COMPELS ME TO ACKNOWLEDGE THAT GRIM MEETING I CONCEALED EVEN FROM MYSELF.

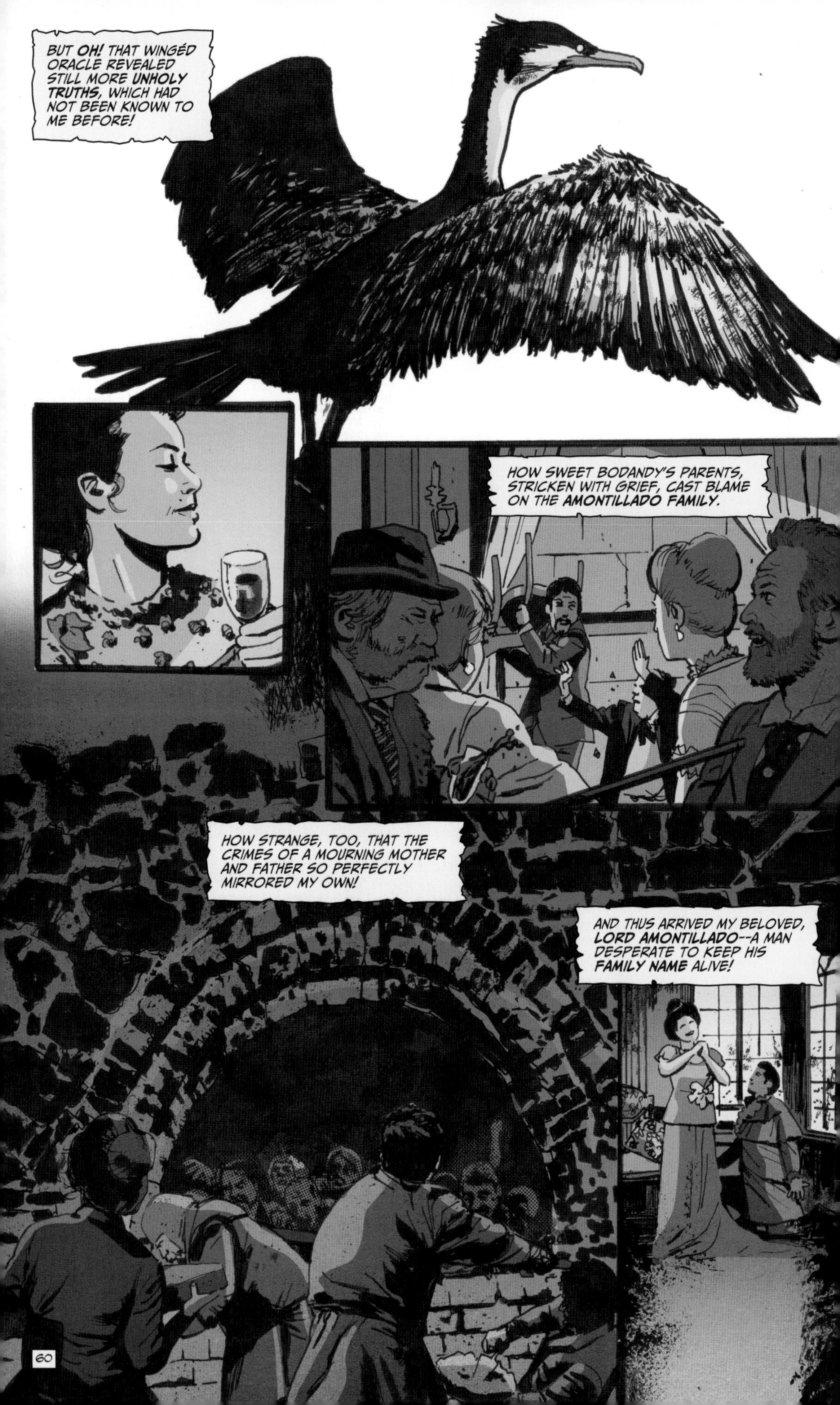
BUT OH! THAT WINGÉD ORACLE REVEALED STILL MORE UNHOLY TRUTHS, WHICH HAD NOT BEEN KNOWN TO ME BEFORE!
HOW SWEET BODANDY'S PARENTS, STRICKEN WITH GRIEF, CAST BLAME ON THE AMONTILLADO FAMILY.
HOW STRANGE, TOO, THAT THE CRIMES OF A MOURNING MOTHER AND FATHER SO PERFECTLY MIRRORED MY OWN!
AND THUS ARRIVED MY BELOVED, LORD AMONTILLADO--A MAN DESPERATE TO KEEP HIS FAMILY NAME ALIVE!

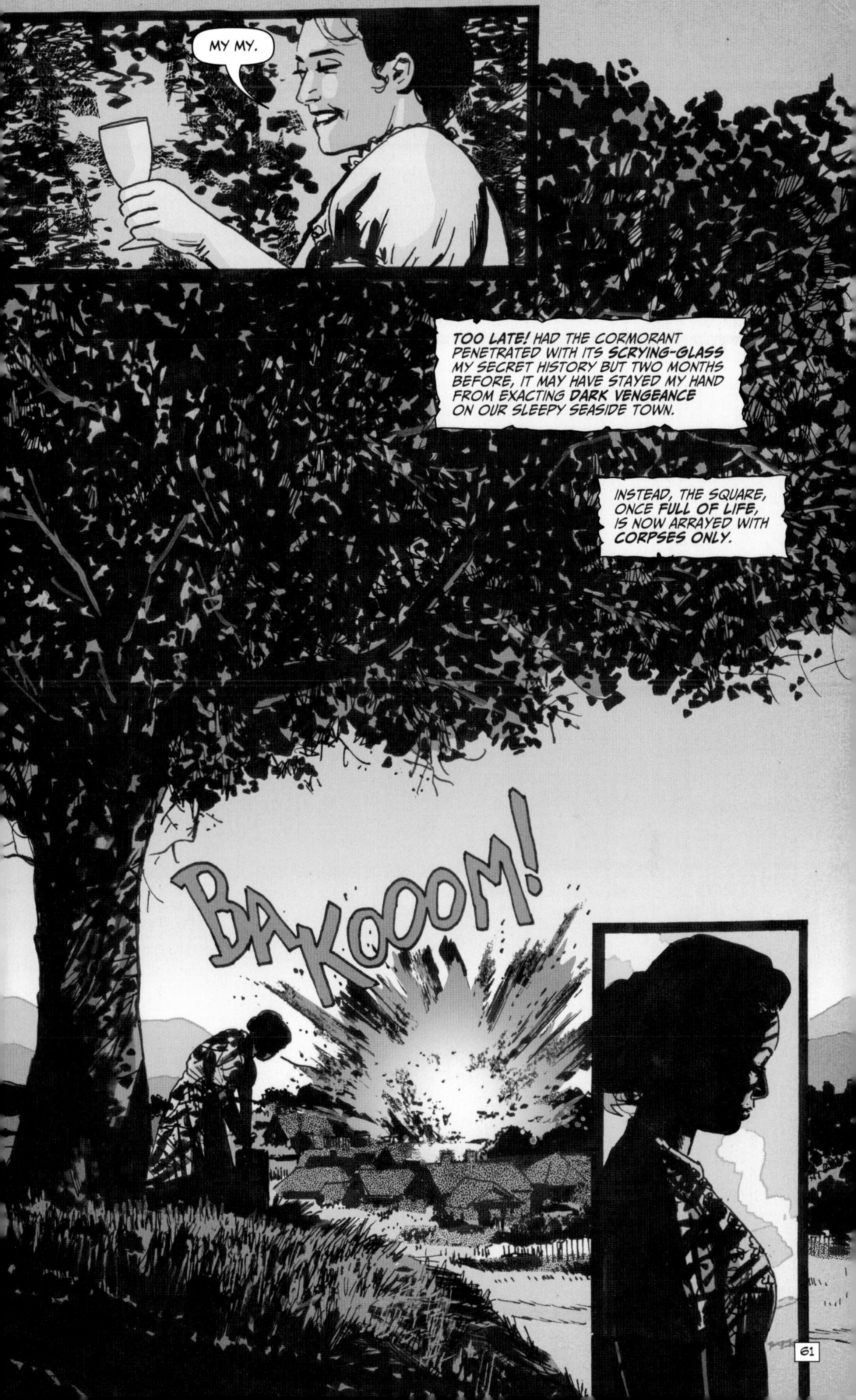
MY MY.
TOO LATE! HAD THE CORMORANT PENETRATED WITH ITS SCRYING-GLASS MY SECRET HISTORY BUT TWO MONTHS BEFORE, IT MAY HAVE STAYED MY HAND FROM EXACTING DARK VENGEANCE ON OUR SLEEPY SEASIDE TOWN.
INSTEAD, THE SQUARE, ONCE FULL OF LIFE, IS NOW ARRAYED WITH CORPSES ONLY.
BAKOOOM!

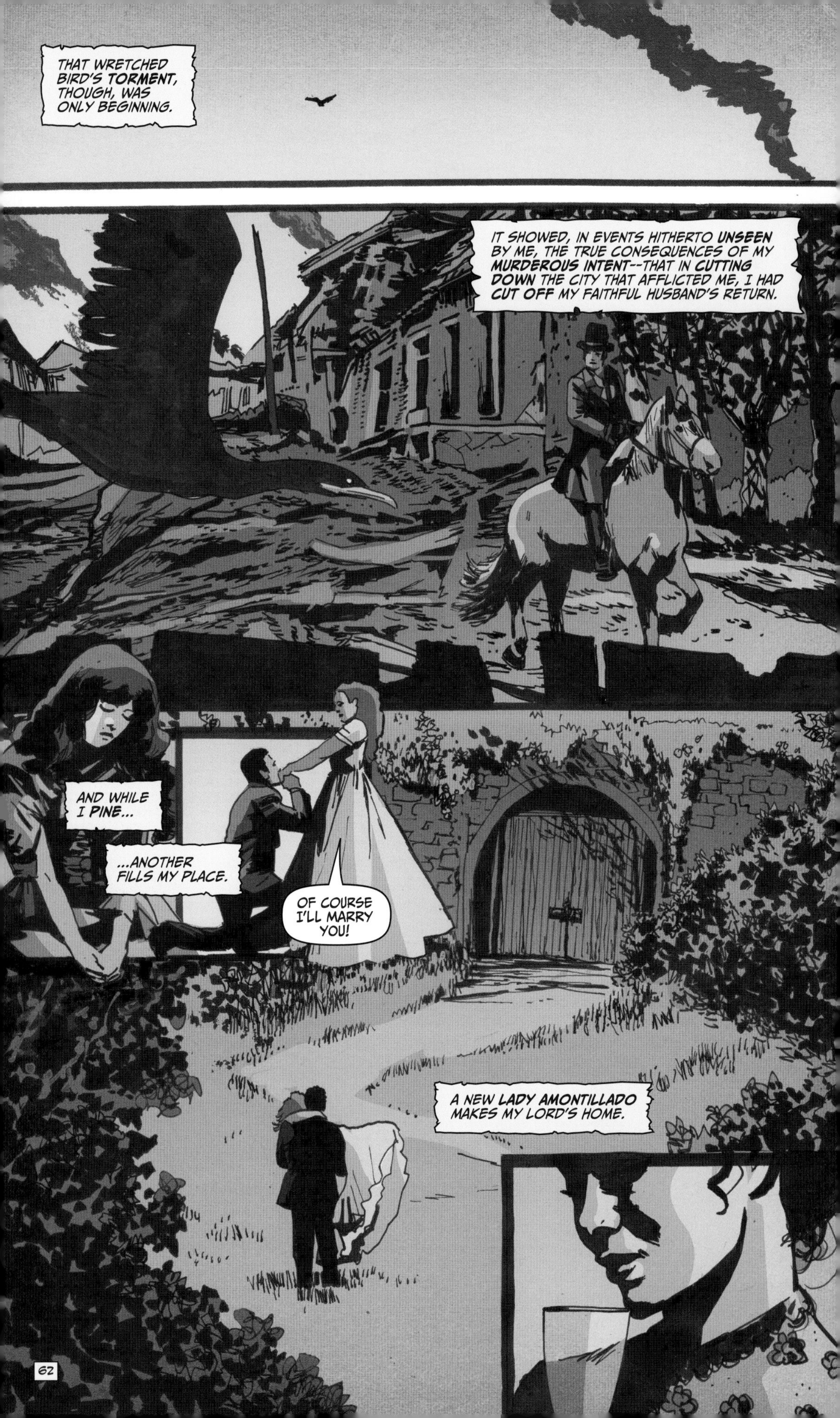
THAT WRETCHED BIRD'S **TORMENT**, THOUGH, WAS ONLY BEGINNING.
IT SHOWED, IN EVENTS HITHERTO **UNSEEN** BY ME, THE TRUE CONSEQUENCES OF MY **MURDEROUS INTENT**--THAT IN **CUTTING DOWN** THE CITY THAT AFFLICTED ME, I HAD **CUT OFF** MY FAITHFUL HUSBAND'S RETURN.
AND WHILE I **PINE**...
...ANOTHER FILLS MY PLACE.
OF COURSE I'LL MARRY YOU!
A NEW **LADY AMONTILLADO** MAKES MY LORD'S HOME.

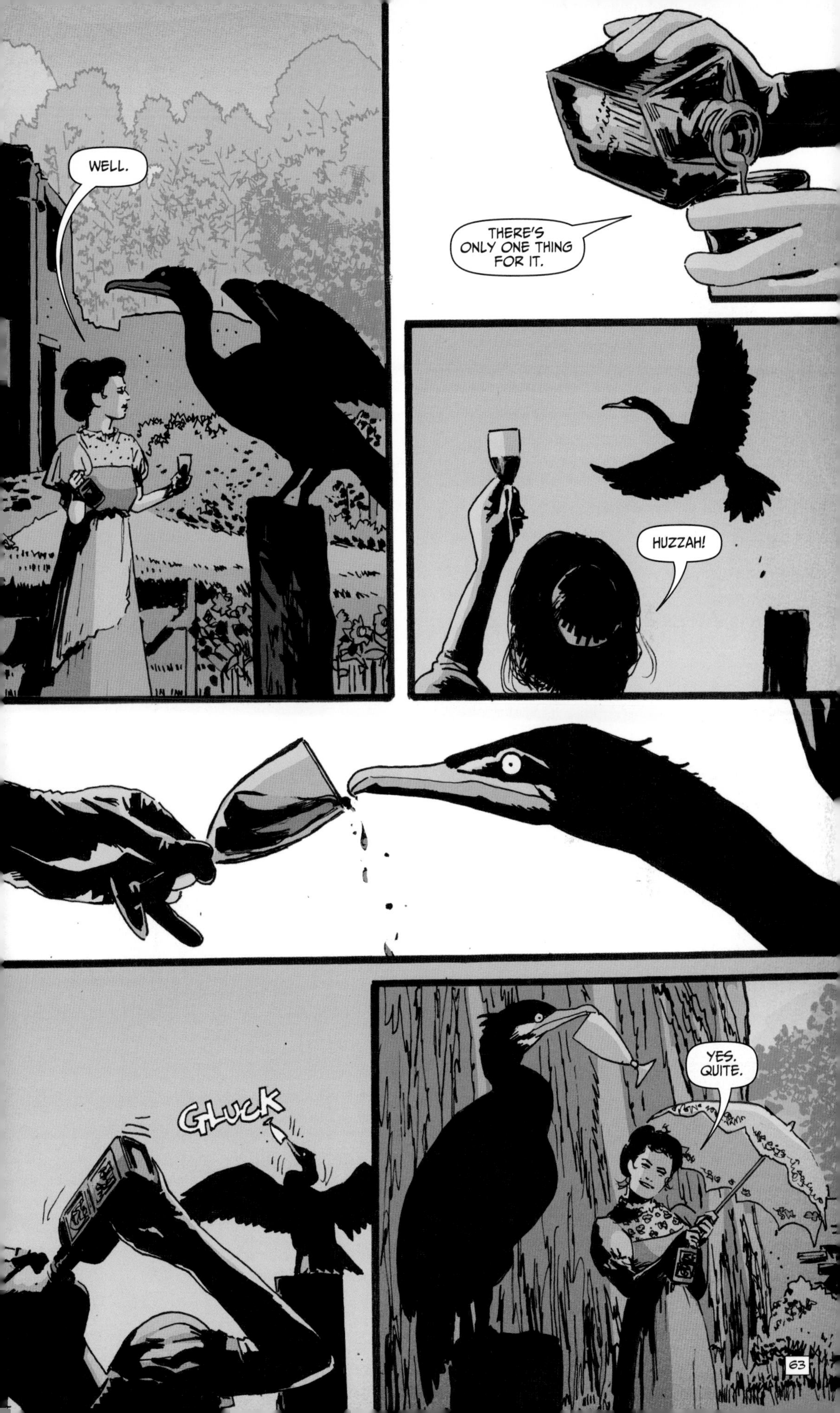

WELL.
THERE'S ONLY ONE THING FOR IT.
HUZZAH!
GLUCK
YES. QUITE.

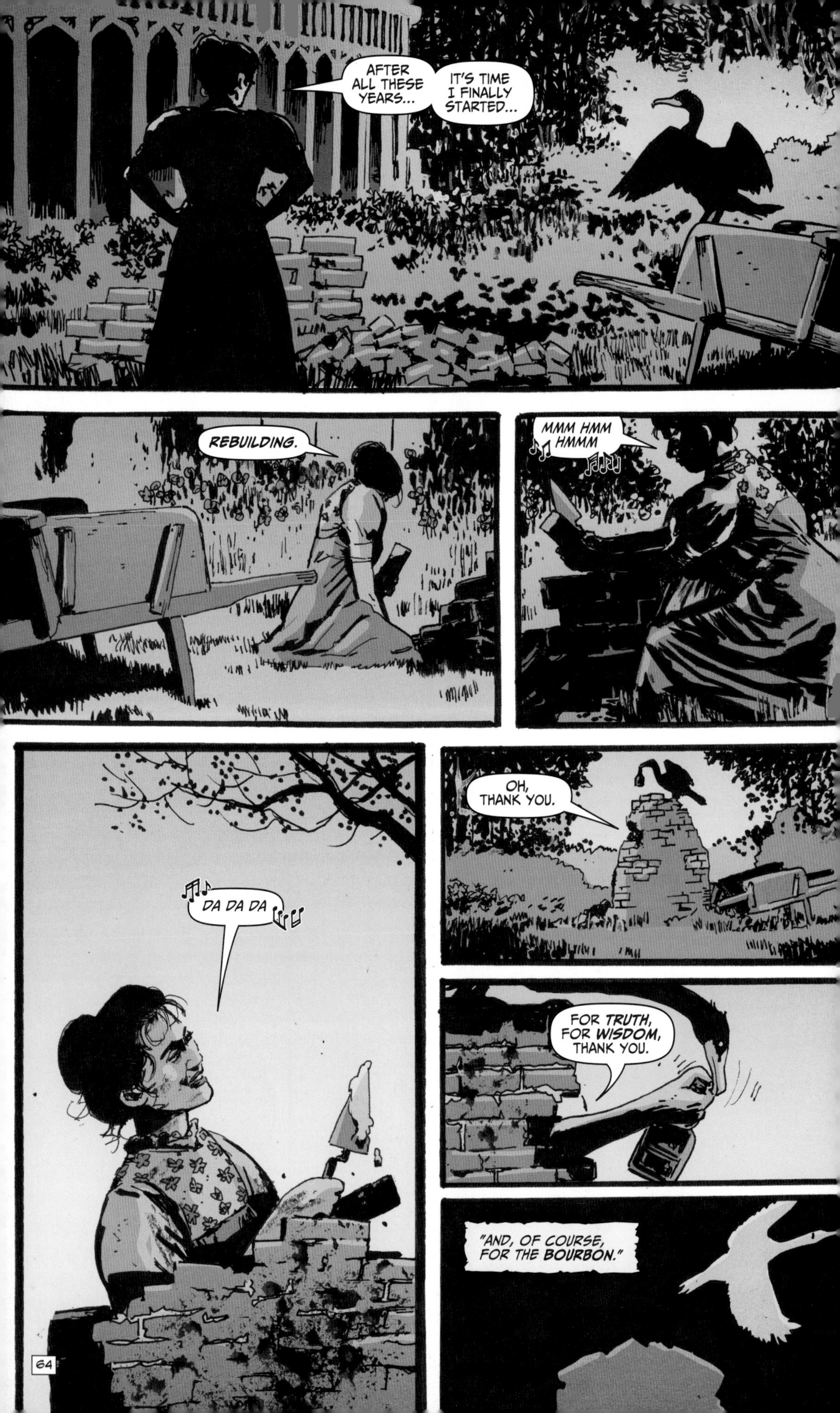

AFTER ALL THESE YEARS...
IT'S TIME I FINALLY STARTED...
REBUILDING.
MMM HMM HMMM
DA DA DA
OH, THANK YOU.
FOR TRUTH, FOR WISDOM, THANK YOU.
"AND, OF COURSE, FOR THE BOURBON."

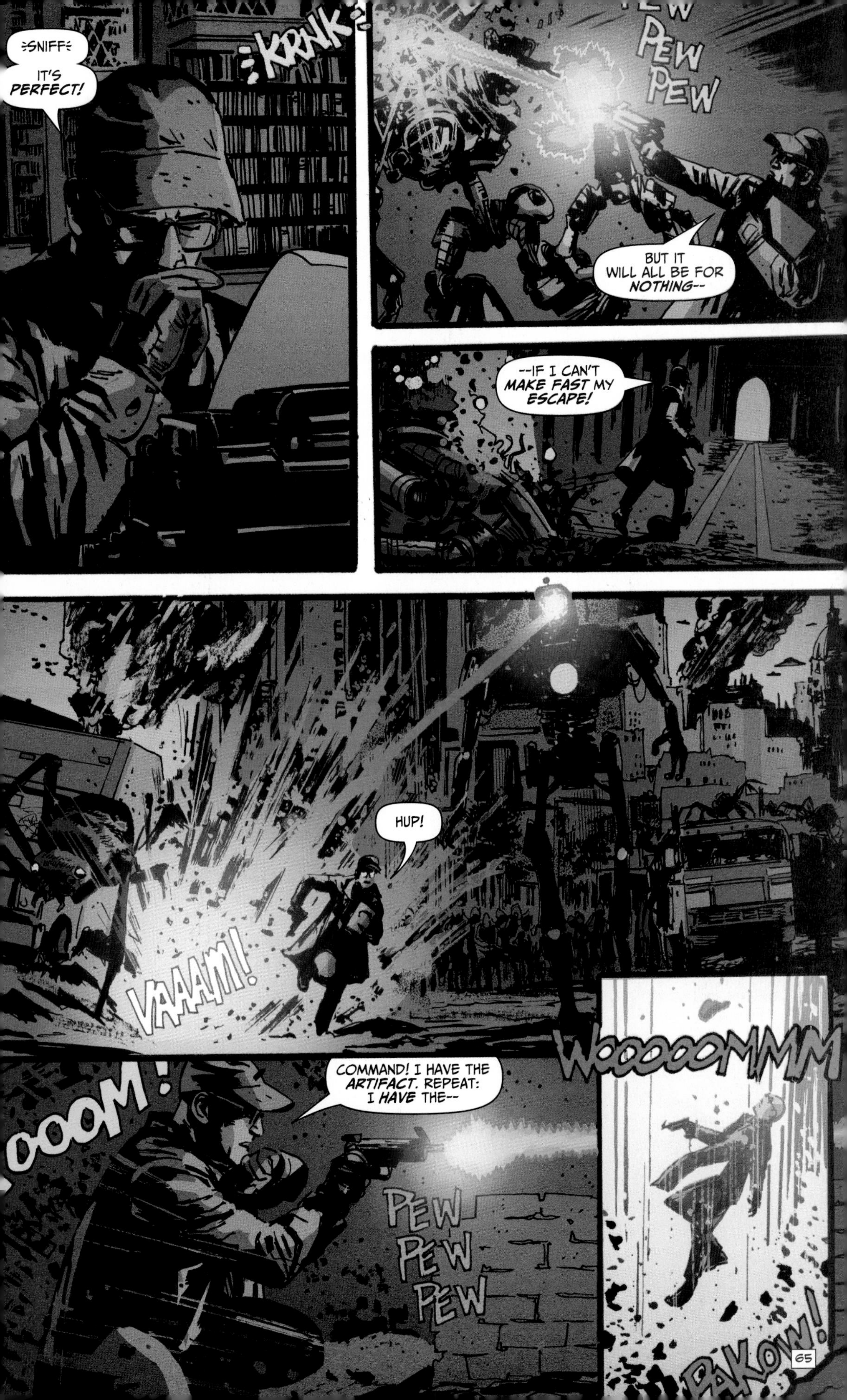

=SNIFF=
IT'S PERFECT!
KRNK
PEW
PEW
BUT IT WILL ALL BE FOR NOTHING--
--IF I CAN'T MAKE FAST MY ESCAPE!
HUP!
VAAAM!
OOOM!
COMMAND! I HAVE THE ARTIFACT. REPEAT: I HAVE THE--
PEW PEW PEW
WOOOOOMMM
BAKOW!

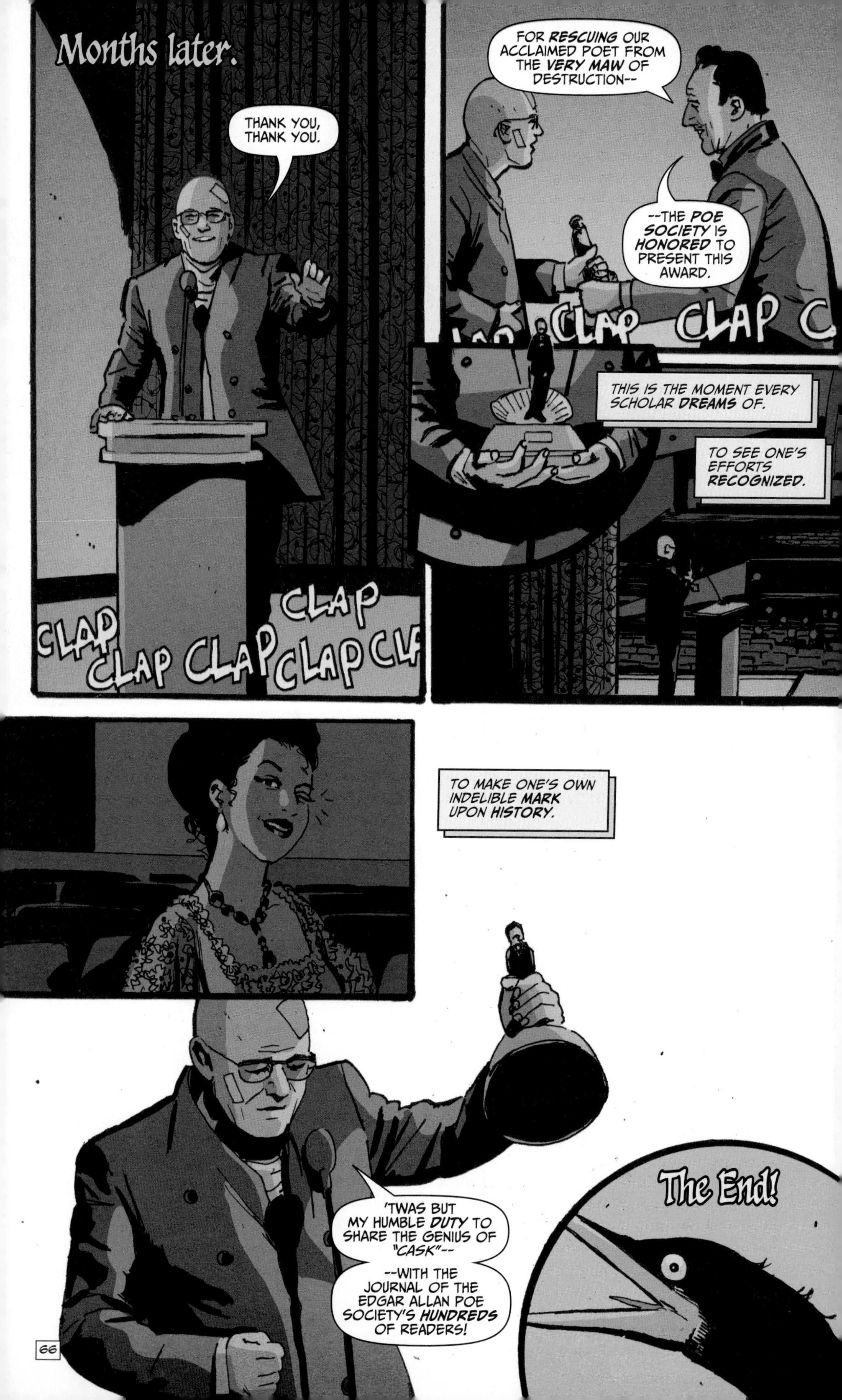
Months later.
THANK YOU, THANK YOU.
CLAP CLAP CLAP CLAP CLAP CLAP CL
FOR RESCUING OUR ACCLAIMED POET FROM THE VERY MAW OF DESTRUCTION--
--THE POE SOCIETY IS HONORED TO PRESENT THIS AWARD.
CLAP CLAP C
THIS IS THE MOMENT EVERY SCHOLAR DREAMS OF.
TO SEE ONE'S EFFORTS RECOGNIZED.
TO MAKE ONE'S OWN INDELIBLE MARK UPON HISTORY.
'TWAS BUT MY HUMBLE DUTY TO SHARE THE GENIUS OF "CASK"--
--WITH THE JOURNAL OF THE EDGAR ALLAN POE SOCIETY'S HUNDREDS OF READERS!
The End!

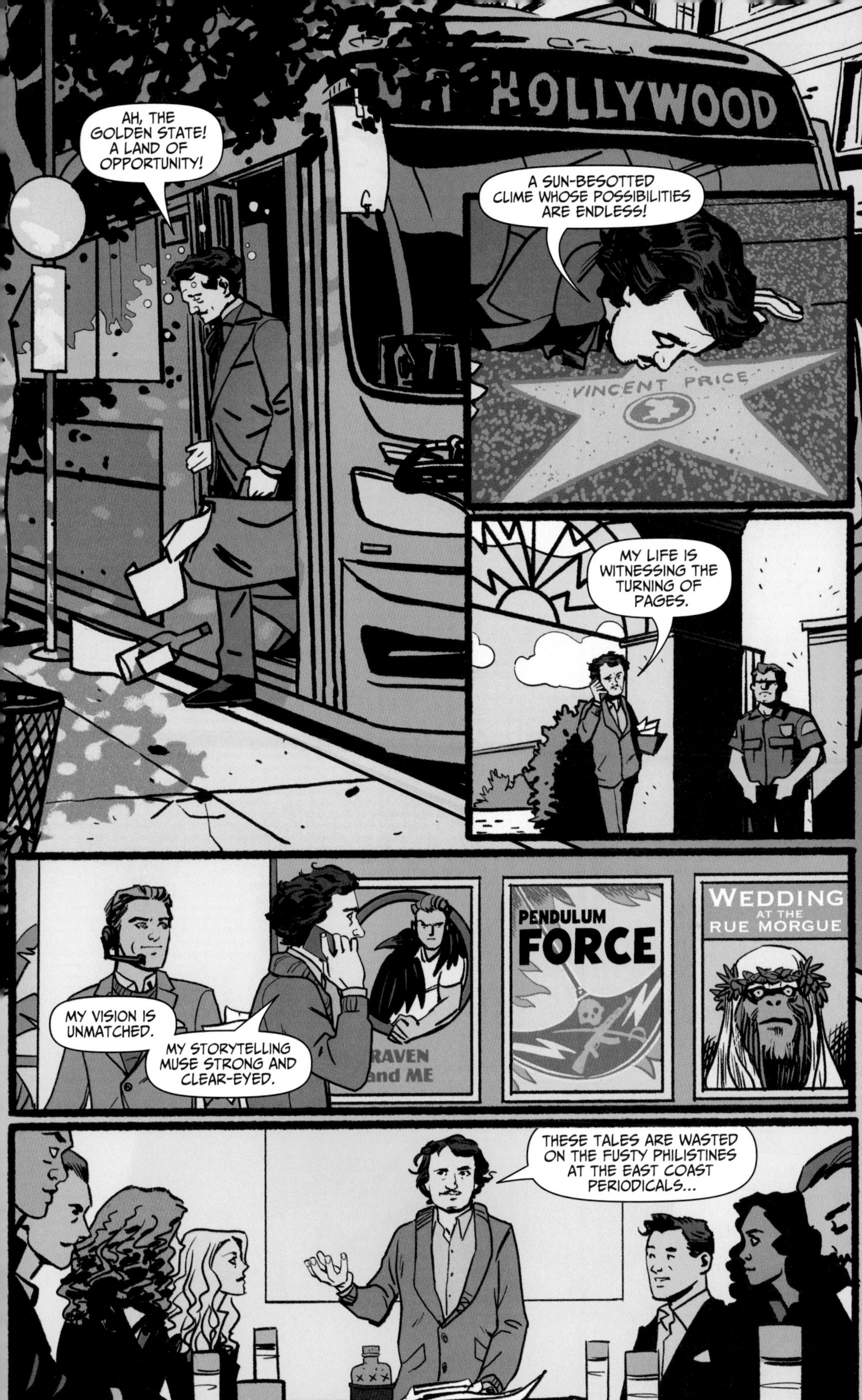
HOLLYWOOD
AH, THE GOLDEN STATE! A LAND OF OPPORTUNITY!
A SUN-BESOTTED CLIME WHOSE POSSIBILITIES ARE ENDLESS!
VINCENT PRICE
MY LIFE IS WITNESSING THE TURNING OF PAGES.
MY VISION IS UNMATCHED.
MY STORYTELLING MUSE STRONG AND CLEAR-EYED.
RAVEN
and ME
PENDULUM FORCE
WEDDING AT THE RUE MORGUE
THESE TALES ARE WASTED ON THE FUSTY PHILISTINES AT THE EAST COAST PERIODICALS...

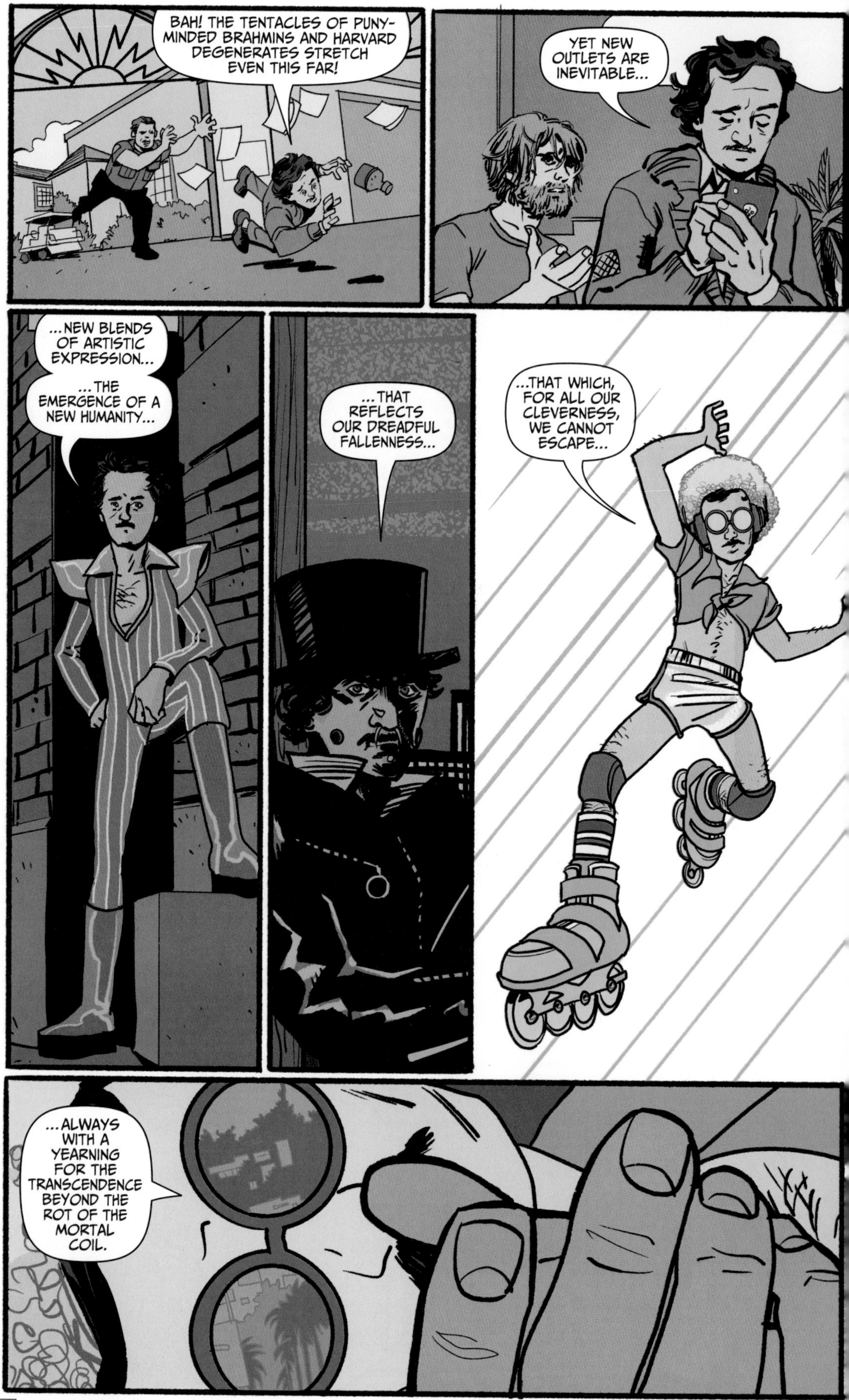

BAH! THE TENTACLES OF PUNY-MINDED BRAHMINS AND HARVARD DEGENERATES STRETCH EVEN THIS FAR!
YET NEW OUTLETS ARE INEVITABLE...
...NEW BLENDS OF ARTISTIC EXPRESSION...
...THE EMERGENCE OF A NEW HUMANITY...
...THAT REFLECTS OUR DREADFUL FALLENNESS...
...THAT WHICH, FOR ALL OUR CLEVERNESS, WE CANNOT ESCAPE...
...ALWAYS WITH A YEARNING FOR THE TRANSCENDENCE BEYOND THE ROT OF THE MORTAL COIL.

The Tell-Tale Heart

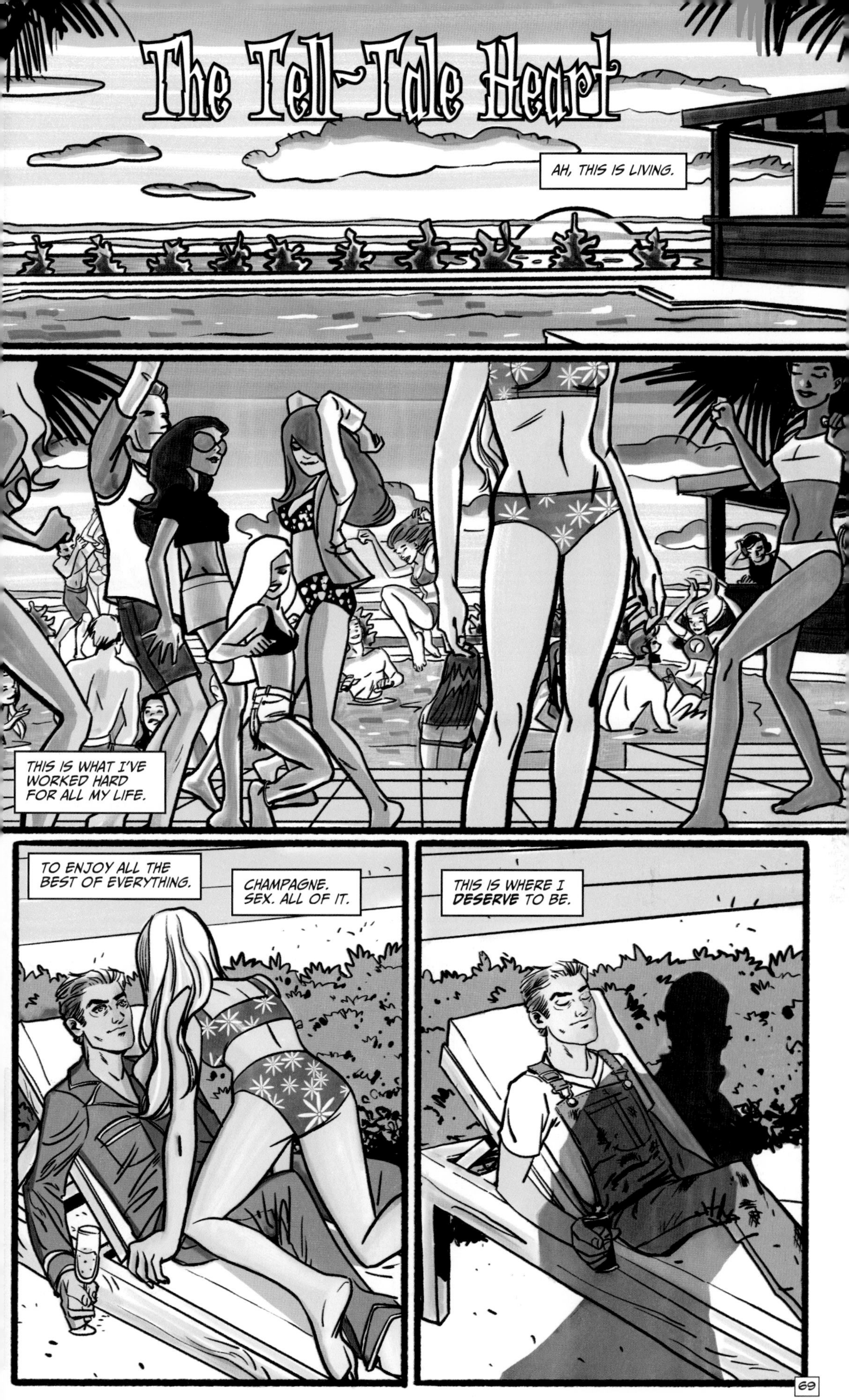
AH, THIS IS LIVING.
THIS IS WHAT I'VE WORKED HARD FOR ALL MY LIFE.
TO ENJOY ALL THE BEST OF EVERYTHING.
CHAMPAGNE. SEX. ALL OF IT.
THIS IS WHERE I **DESERVE** TO BE.

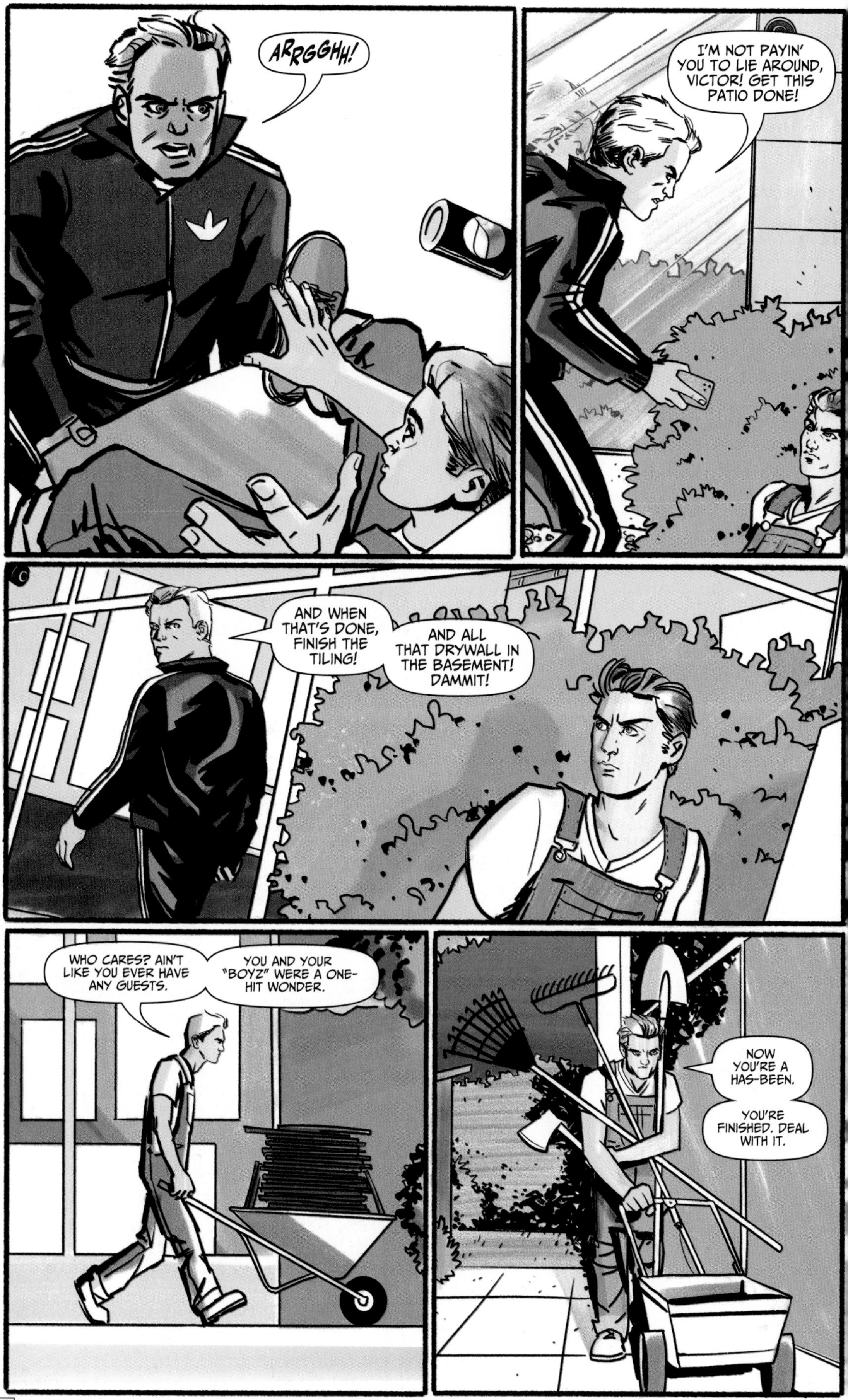
ARRGGHH!
I'M NOT PAYIN' YOU TO LIE AROUND, VICTOR! GET THIS PATIO DONE!
AND WHEN THAT'S DONE, FINISH THE TILING!
AND ALL THAT DRYWALL IN THE BASEMENT! DAMMIT!
WHO CARES? AIN'T LIKE YOU EVER HAVE ANY GUESTS.
YOU AND YOUR "BOYZ" WERE A ONE-HIT WONDER.
NOW YOU'RE A HAS-BEEN.
YOU'RE FINISHED. DEAL WITH IT.

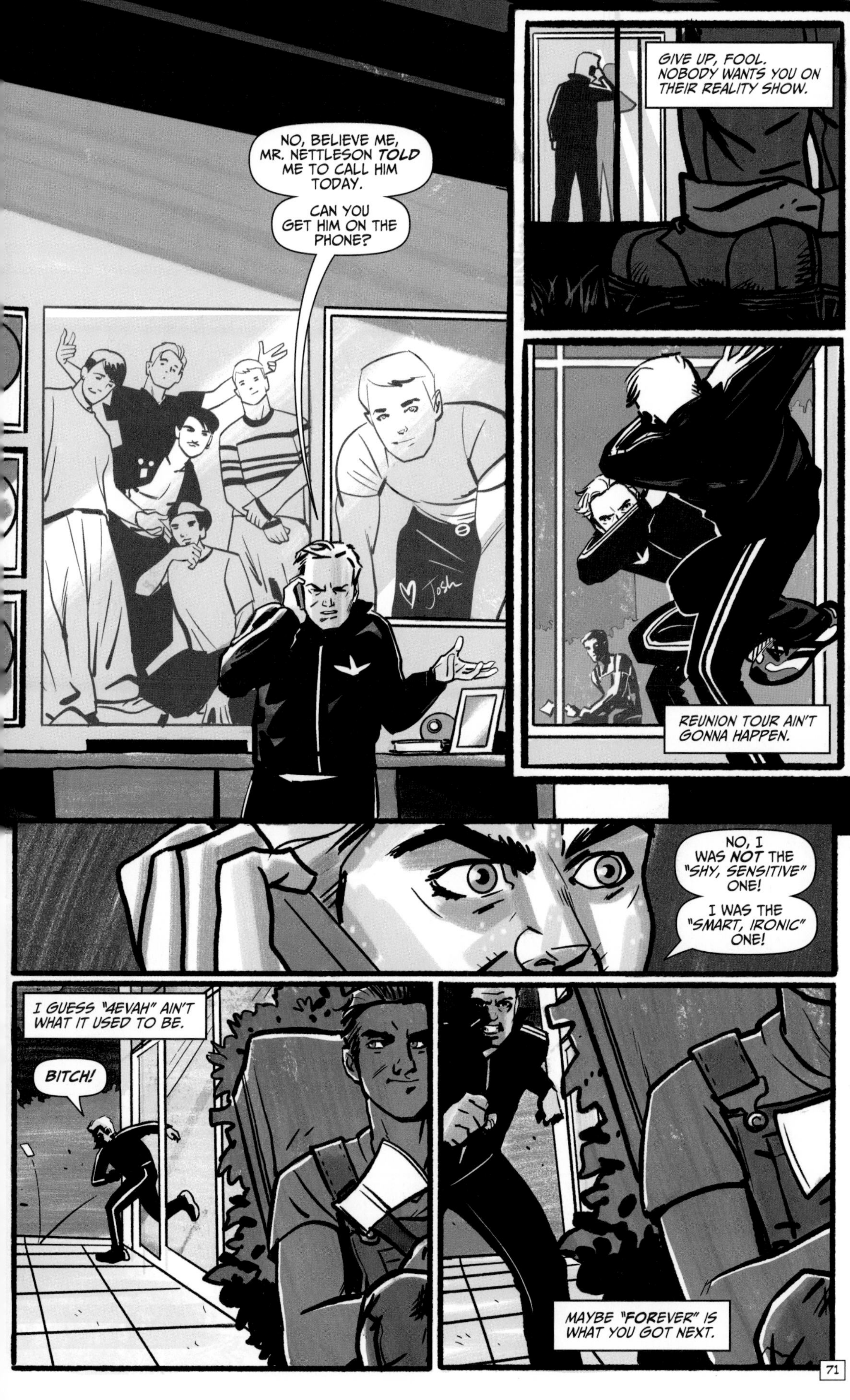
NO, BELIEVE ME, MR. NETTLESON TOLD ME TO CALL HIM TODAY.
CAN YOU GET HIM ON THE PHONE?
Josh
GIVE UP, FOOL. NOBODY WANTS YOU ON THEIR REALITY SHOW.
REUNION TOUR AIN'T GONNA HAPPEN.
NO, I WAS NOT THE "SHY, SENSITIVE" ONE!
I WAS THE "SMART, IRONIC" ONE!
I GUESS "4EVAH" AIN'T WHAT IT USED TO BE.
BITCH!
MAYBE "FOREVER" IS WHAT YOU GOT NEXT.

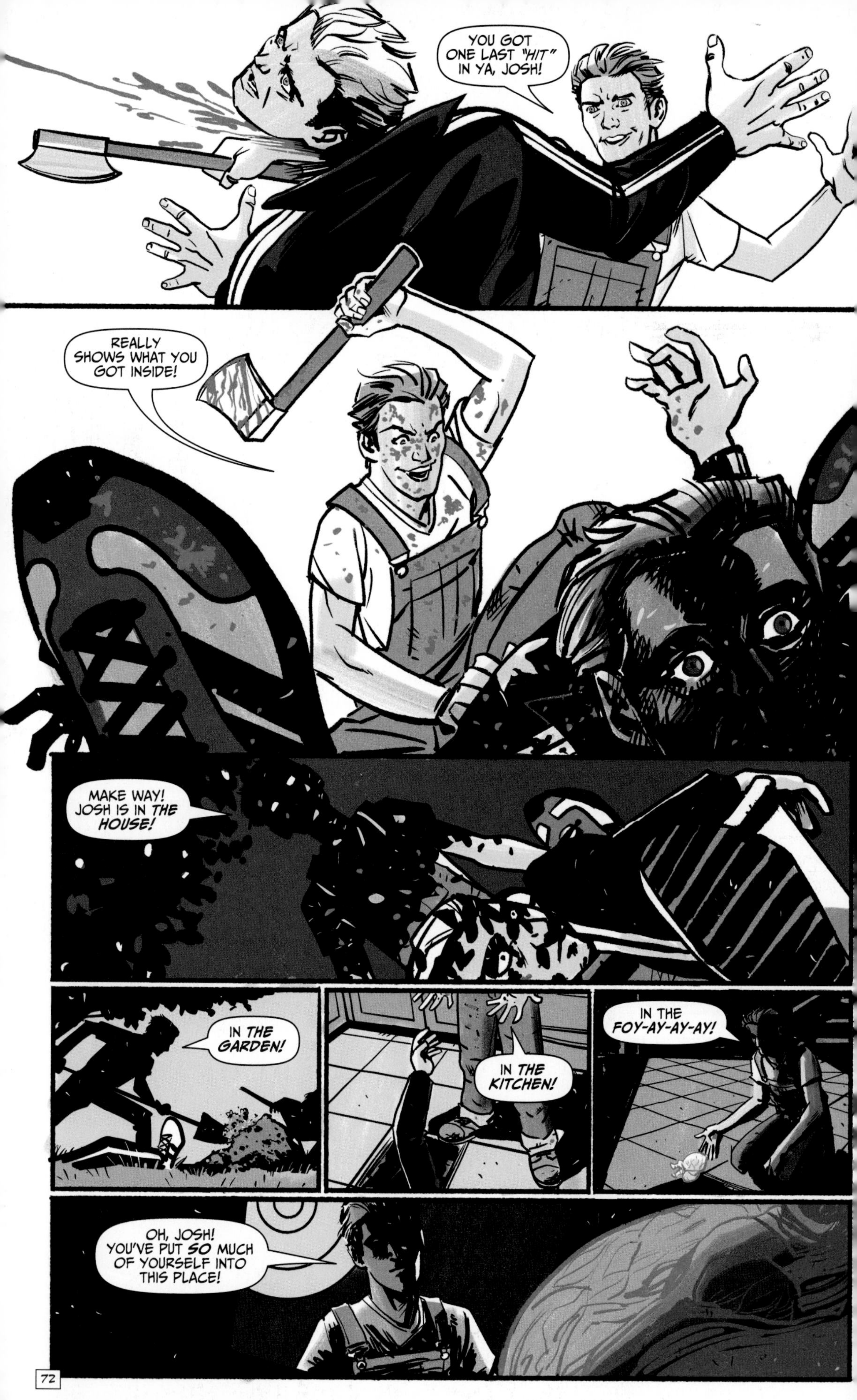
YOU GOT ONE LAST "HIT" IN YA, JOSH!
REALLY SHOWS WHAT YOU GOT INSIDE!
MAKE WAY! JOSH IS IN THE HOUSE!
IN THE GARDEN!
IN THE KITCHEN!
IN THE FOY-AY-AY-AY!
OH, JOSH! YOU'VE PUT SO MUCH OF YOURSELF INTO THIS PLACE!

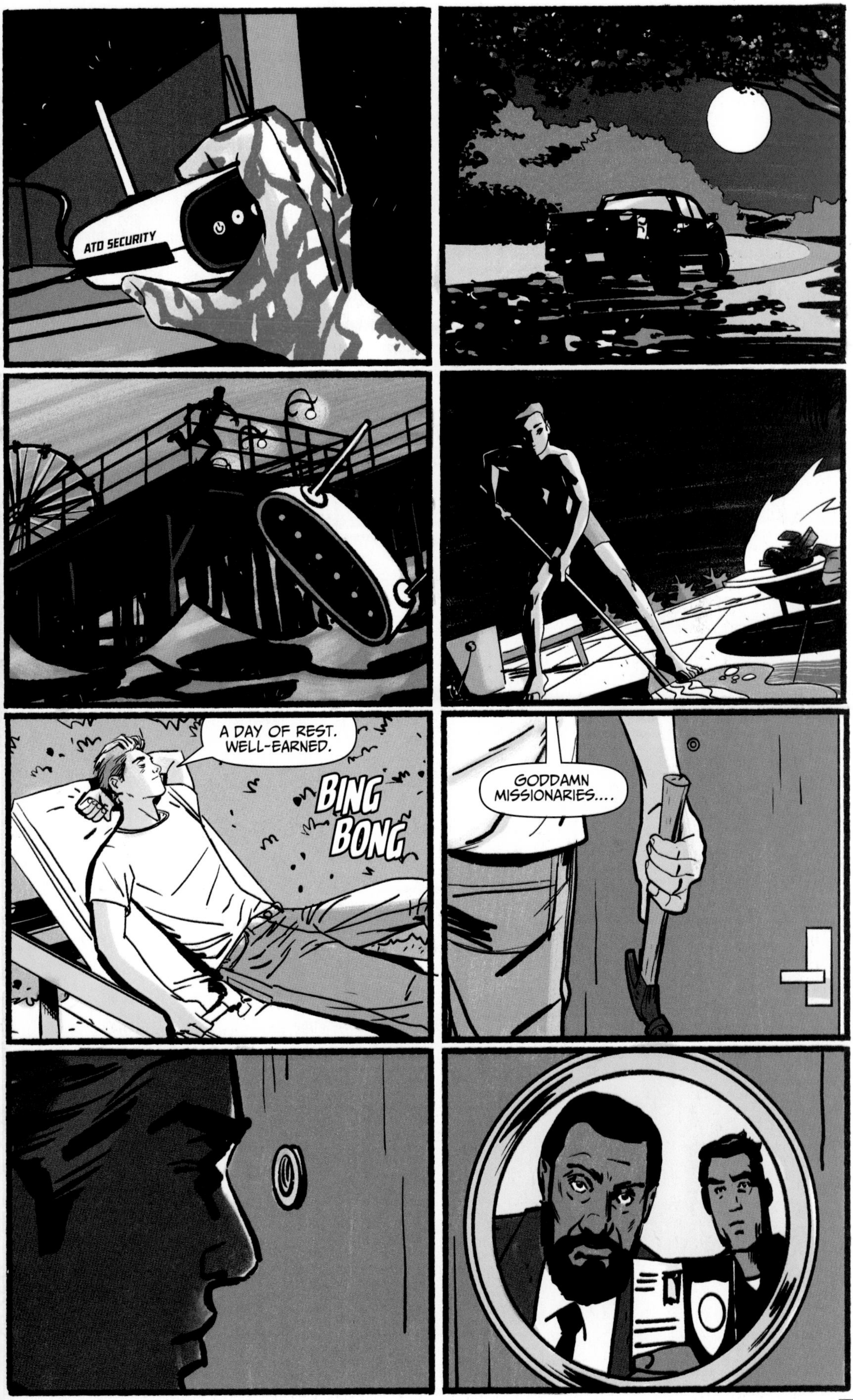
ATO SECURITY
A DAY OF REST. WELL-EARNED.
BING BONG
GODDAMN MISSIONARIES....

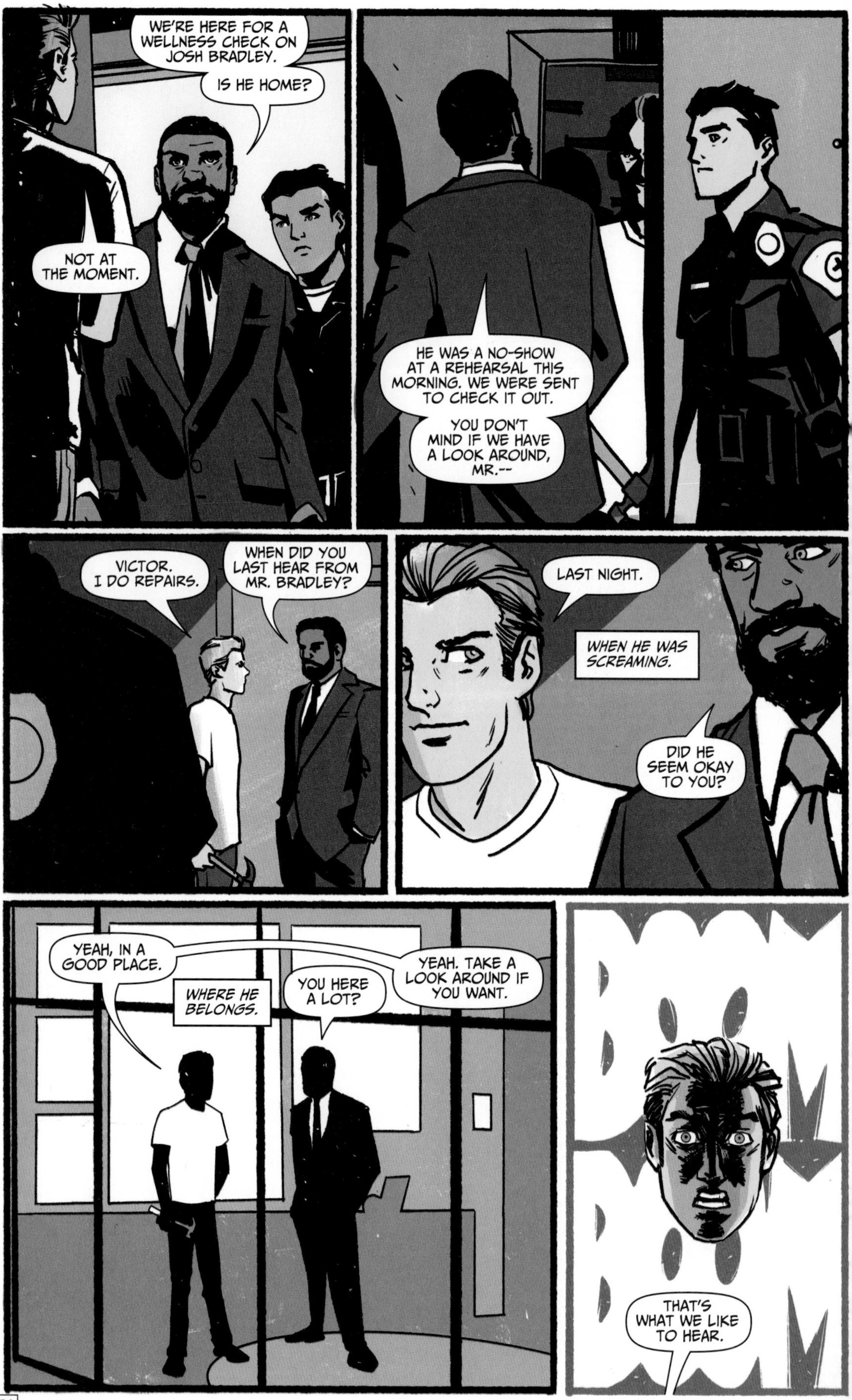
WE'RE HERE FOR A WELLNESS CHECK ON JOSH BRADLEY.
IS HE HOME?
NOT AT THE MOMENT.
HE WAS A NO-SHOW AT A REHEARSAL THIS MORNING. WE WERE SENT TO CHECK IT OUT.
YOU DON'T MIND IF WE HAVE A LOOK AROUND, MR.--
VICTOR. I DO REPAIRS.
WHEN DID YOU LAST HEAR FROM MR. BRADLEY?
LAST NIGHT.
WHEN HE WAS SCREAMING.
DID HE SEEM OKAY TO YOU?
YEAH, IN A GOOD PLACE.
WHERE HE BELONGS.
YOU HERE A LOT?
YEAH. TAKE A LOOK AROUND IF YOU WANT.
BOOM BOOM
THAT'S WHAT WE LIKE TO HEAR.

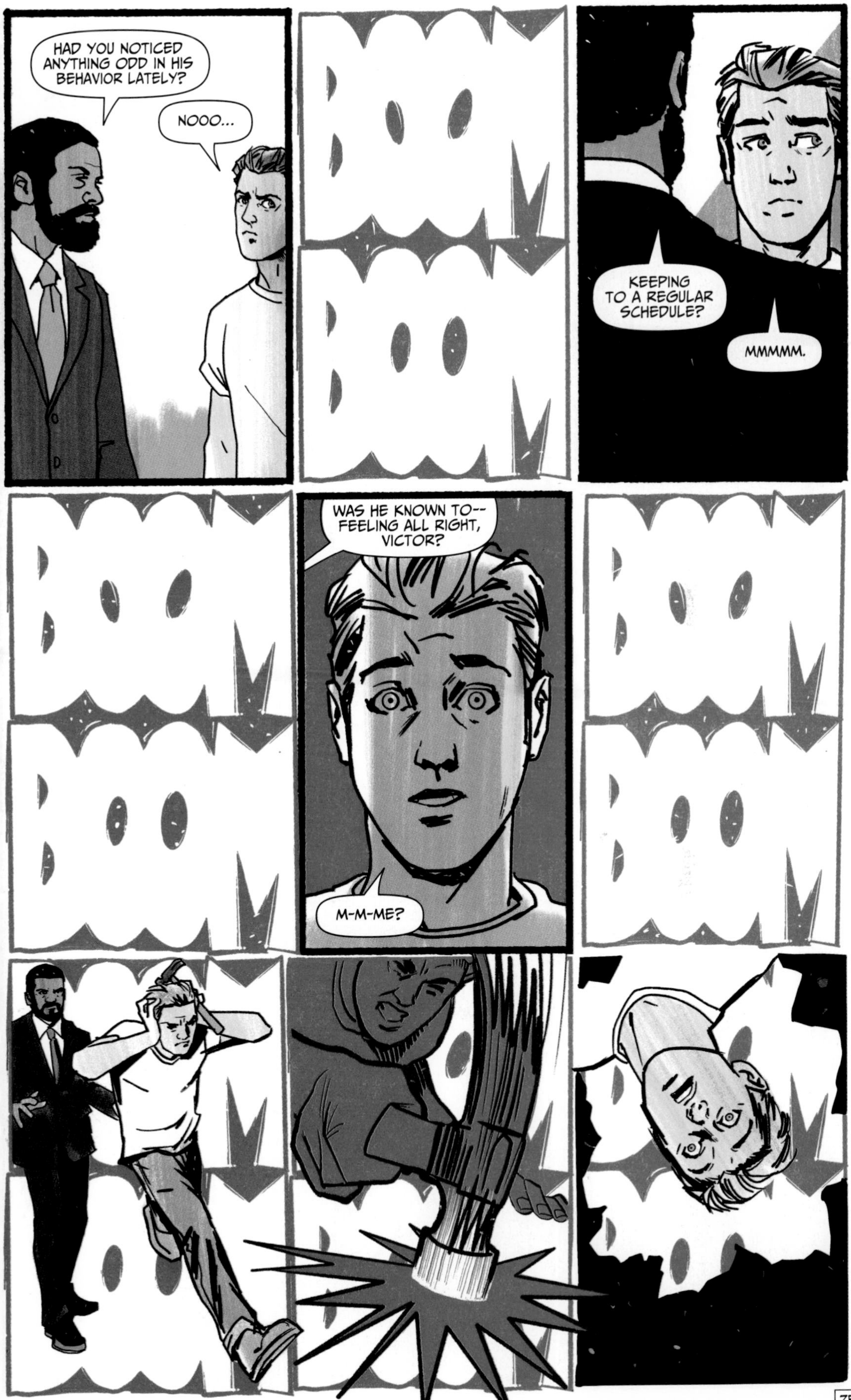
HAD YOU NOTICED ANYTHING ODD IN HIS BEHAVIOR LATELY?
NOOO...
BOOM
BOOM
KEEPING TO A REGULAR SCHEDULE?
MMMMM.
BOOM
BOOM
WAS HE KNOWN TO-- FEELING ALL RIGHT, VICTOR?
M-M-ME?
BOOM
BOOM

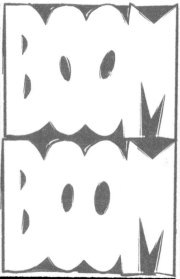

BOOM
BOOM
LOOKS LIKE YOU'RE COMING DOWNTOWN WITH--
BOOM
BOOM
DELGADO! TURN THAT MUSIC OFF!
BOOM
BOOM
CLOWN...
REMEMBER, THIS IS A CRIME SCENE, A-HOLE?
SORRY, COULDN'T HELP MYSELF. THAT'S ONE SICK SOUND SYSTEM YOU INSTALLED, MAN!
DELGADO KNOWS WHAT HE'S TALKING ABOUT.
HE'S A WEDDING DJ ON THE WEEKENDS.

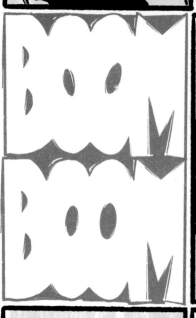

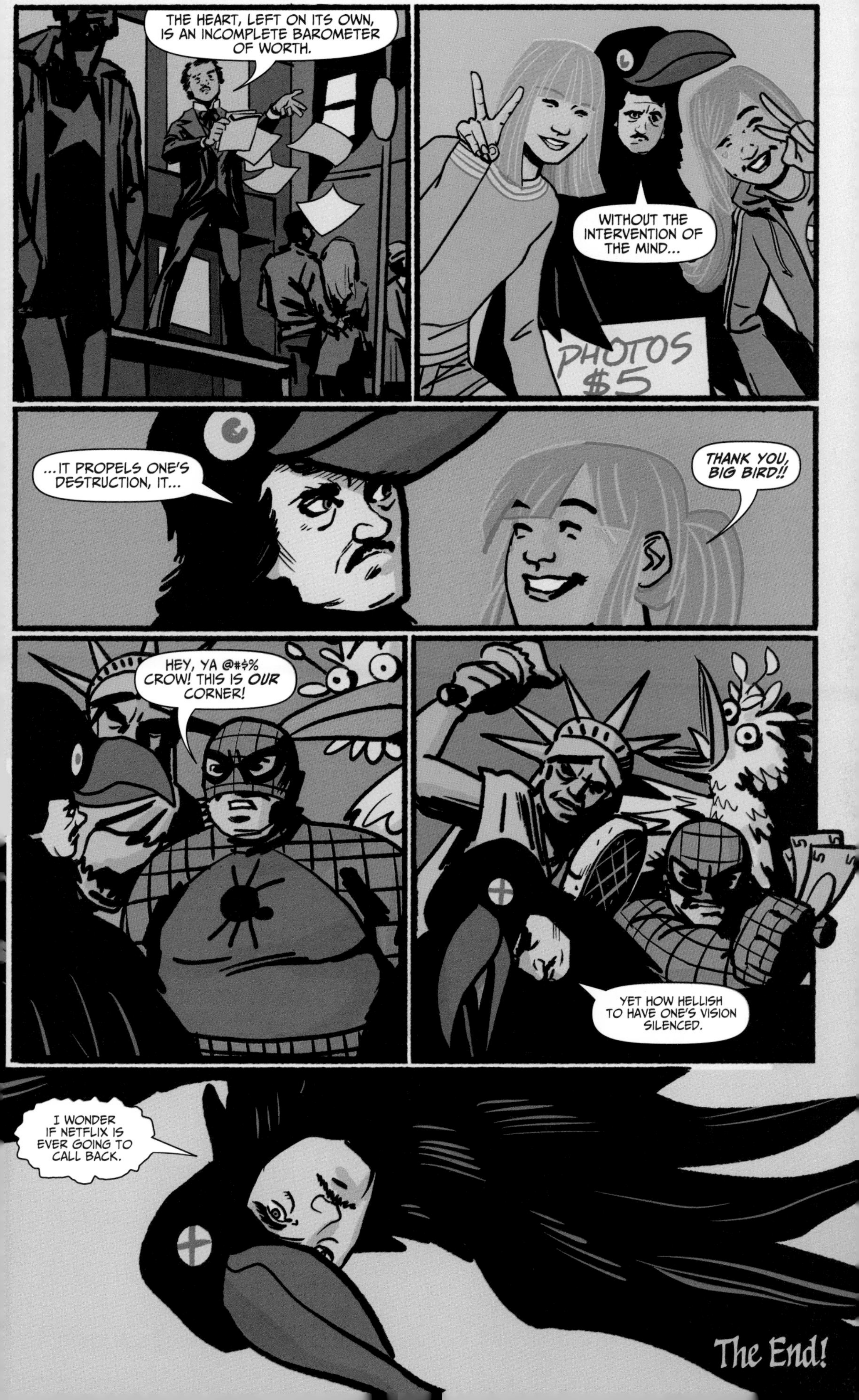
THE HEART, LEFT ON ITS OWN, IS AN INCOMPLETE BAROMETER OF WORTH.
WITHOUT THE INTERVENTION OF THE MIND...
PHOTOS $5
...IT PROPELS ONE'S DESTRUCTION, IT...
THANK YOU, BIG BIRD!!
HEY, YA @#$% CROW! THIS IS *OUR* CORNER!
YET HOW HELLISH TO HAVE ONE'S VISION SILENCED.
I WONDER IF NETFLIX IS EVER GOING TO CALL BACK.
The End!

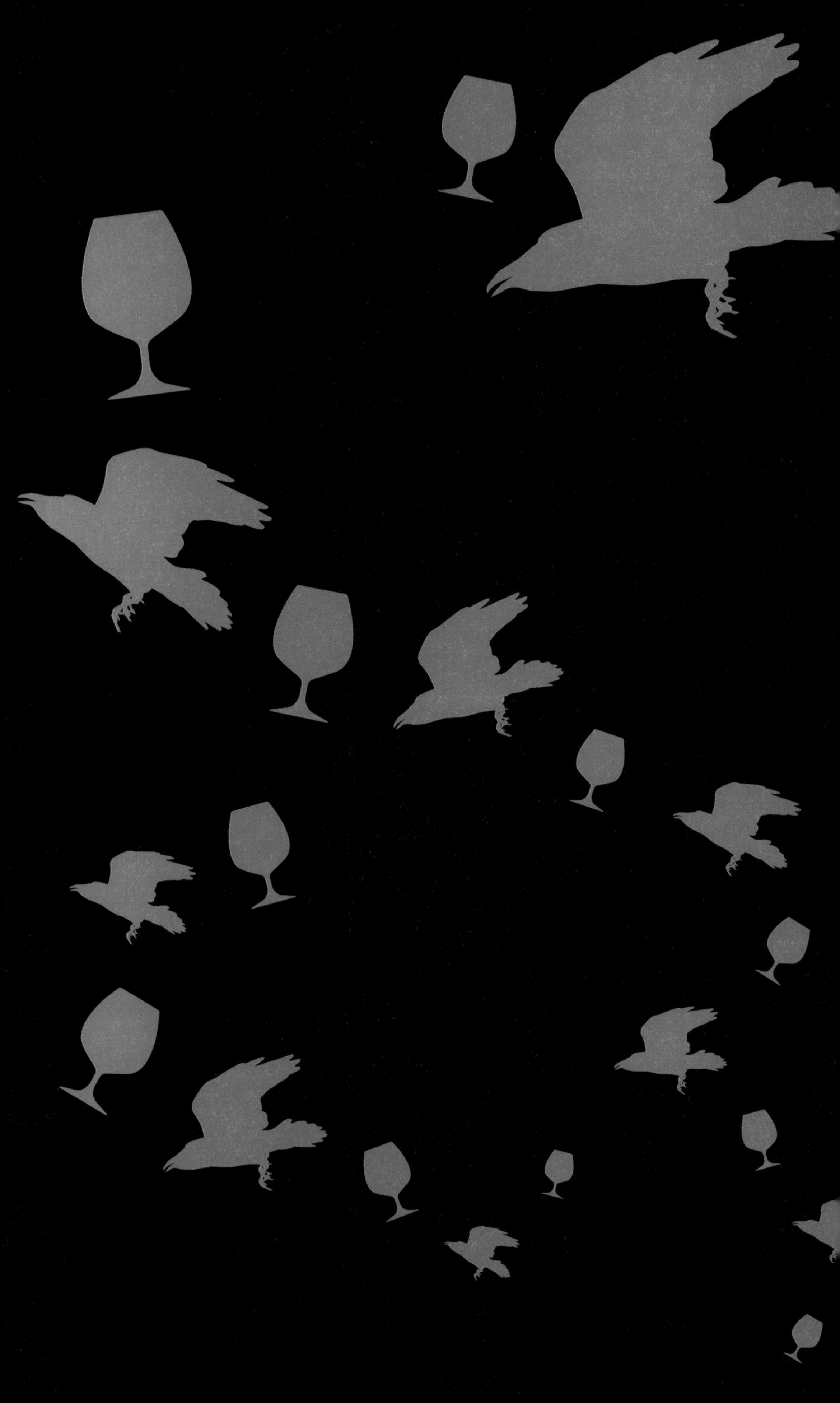

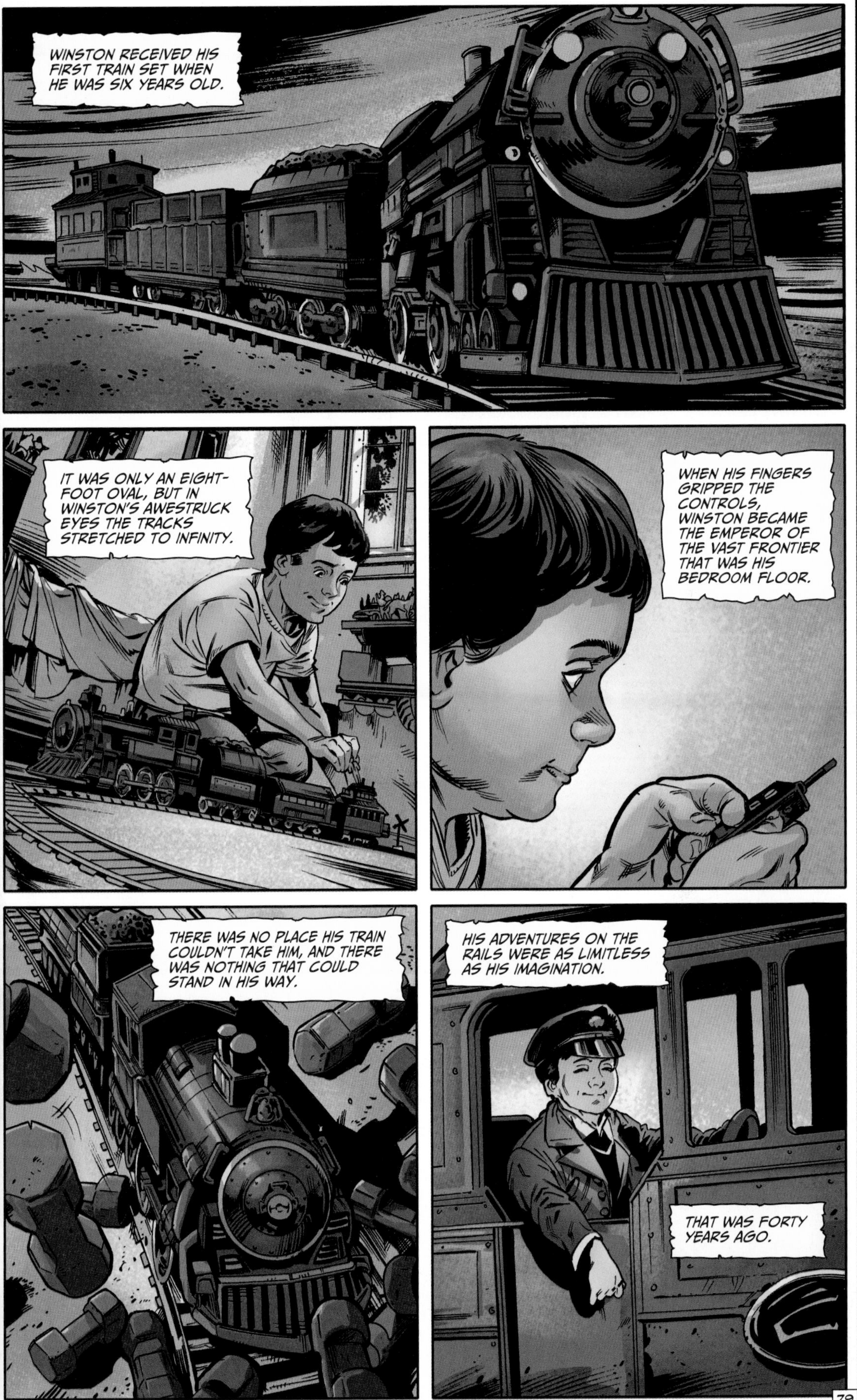
WINSTON RECEIVED HIS FIRST TRAIN SET WHEN HE WAS SIX YEARS OLD.
IT WAS ONLY AN EIGHT-FOOT OVAL, BUT IN WINSTON'S AWESTRUCK EYES THE TRACKS STRETCHED TO INFINITY.
WHEN HIS FINGERS GRIPPED THE CONTROLS, WINSTON BECAME THE EMPEROR OF THE VAST FRONTIER THAT WAS HIS BEDROOM FLOOR.
THERE WAS NO PLACE HIS TRAIN COULDN'T TAKE HIM, AND THERE WAS NOTHING THAT COULD STAND IN HIS WAY.
HIS ADVENTURES ON THE RAILS WERE AS LIMITLESS AS HIS IMAGINATION.
THAT WAS FORTY YEARS AGO.

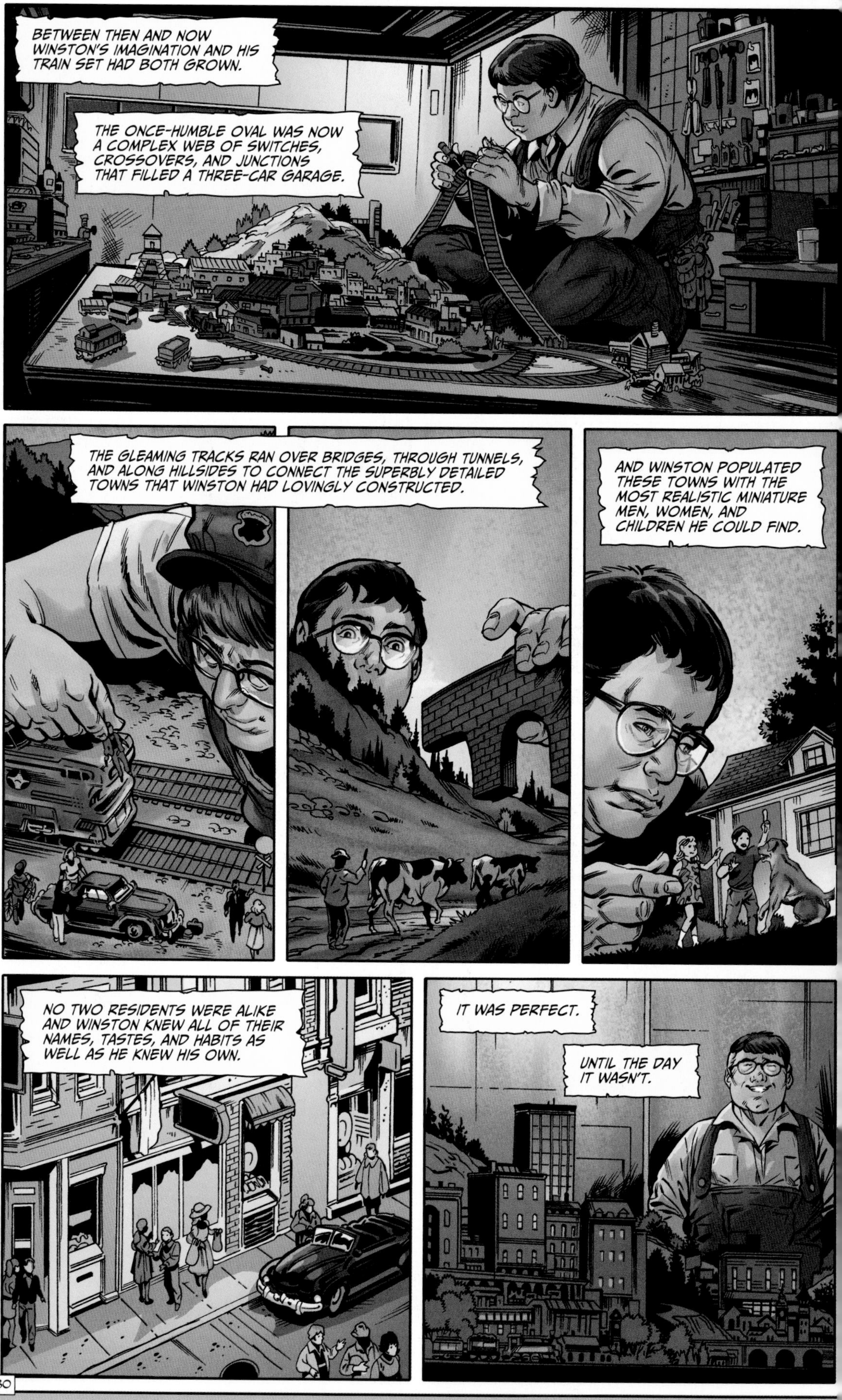
BETWEEN THEN AND NOW WINSTON'S IMAGINATION AND HIS TRAIN SET HAD BOTH GROWN.
THE ONCE-HUMBLE OVAL WAS NOW A COMPLEX WEB OF SWITCHES, CROSSOVERS, AND JUNCTIONS THAT FILLED A THREE-CAR GARAGE.
THE GLEAMING TRACKS RAN OVER BRIDGES, THROUGH TUNNELS, AND ALONG HILLSIDES TO CONNECT THE SUPERBLY DETAILED TOWNS THAT WINSTON HAD LOVINGLY CONSTRUCTED.
AND WINSTON POPULATED THESE TOWNS WITH THE MOST REALISTIC MINIATURE MEN, WOMEN, AND CHILDREN HE COULD FIND.
NO TWO RESIDENTS WERE ALIKE AND WINSTON KNEW ALL OF THEIR NAMES, TASTES, AND HABITS AS WELL AS HE KNEW HIS OWN.
IT WAS PERFECT.
UNTIL THE DAY IT WASN'T.

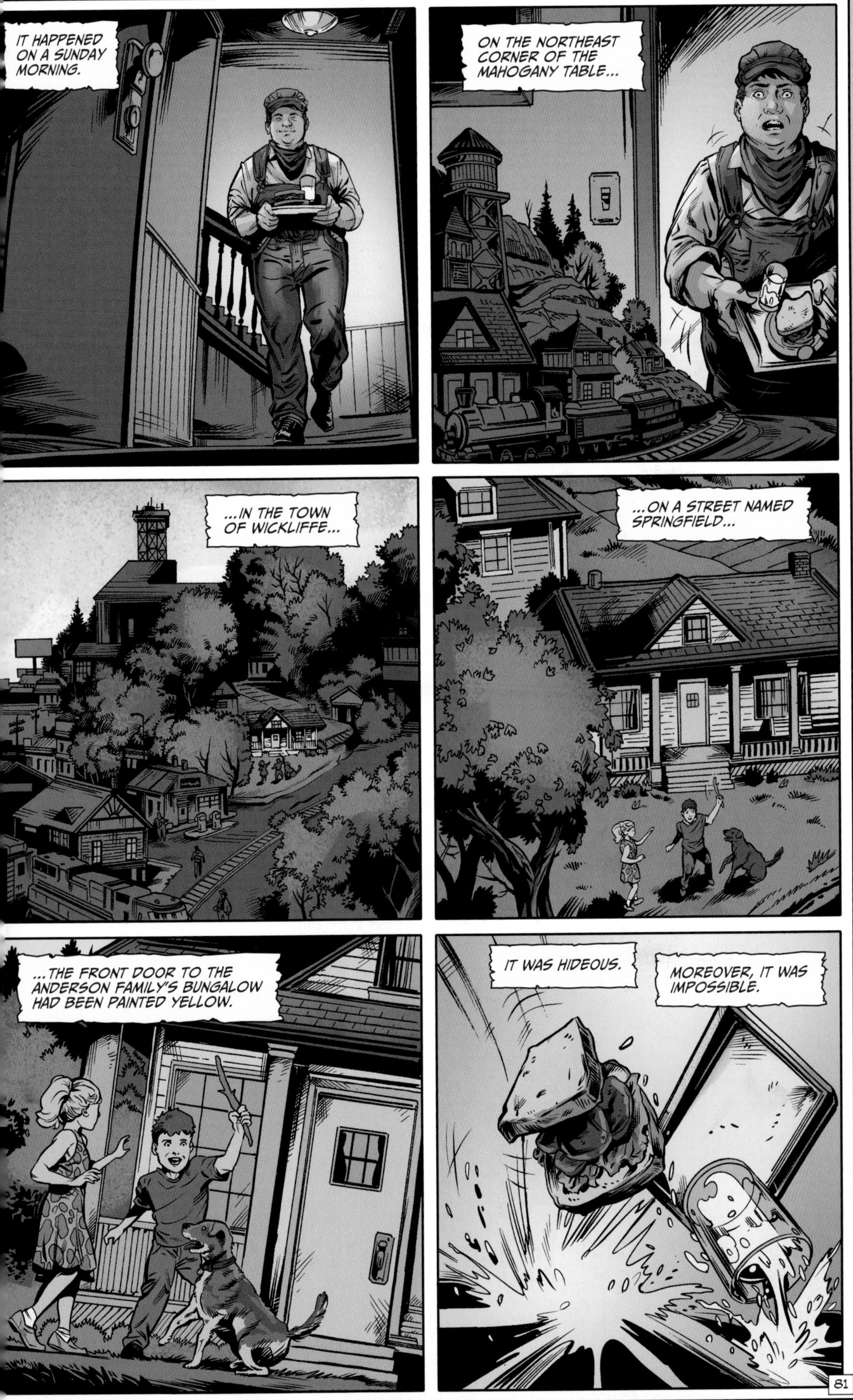
IT HAPPENED ON A SUNDAY MORNING.
ON THE NORTHEAST CORNER OF THE MAHOGANY TABLE...
...IN THE TOWN OF WICKLIFFE...
...ON A STREET NAMED SPRINGFIELD...
...THE FRONT DOOR TO THE ANDERSON FAMILY'S BUNGALOW HAD BEEN PAINTED YELLOW.
IT WAS HIDEOUS.
MOREOVER, IT WAS IMPOSSIBLE.

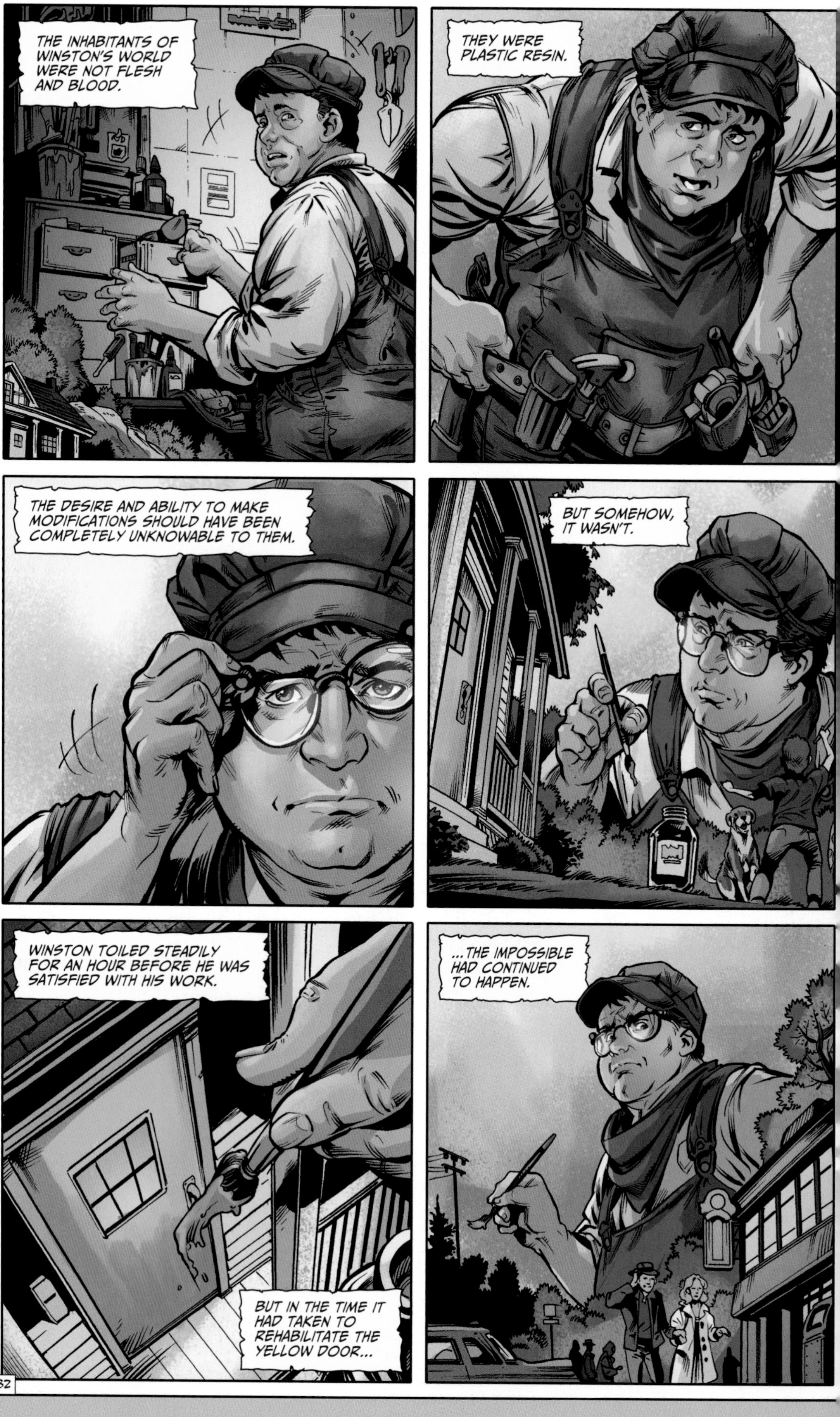
THE INHABITANTS OF WINSTON'S WORLD WERE NOT FLESH AND BLOOD.
THEY WERE PLASTIC RESIN.
THE DESIRE AND ABILITY TO MAKE MODIFICATIONS SHOULD HAVE BEEN COMPLETELY UNKNOWABLE TO THEM.
BUT SOMEHOW, IT WASN'T.
WINSTON TOILED STEADILY FOR AN HOUR BEFORE HE WAS SATISFIED WITH HIS WORK.
BUT IN THE TIME IT HAD TAKEN TO REHABILITATE THE YELLOW DOOR...
...THE IMPOSSIBLE HAD CONTINUED TO HAPPEN.

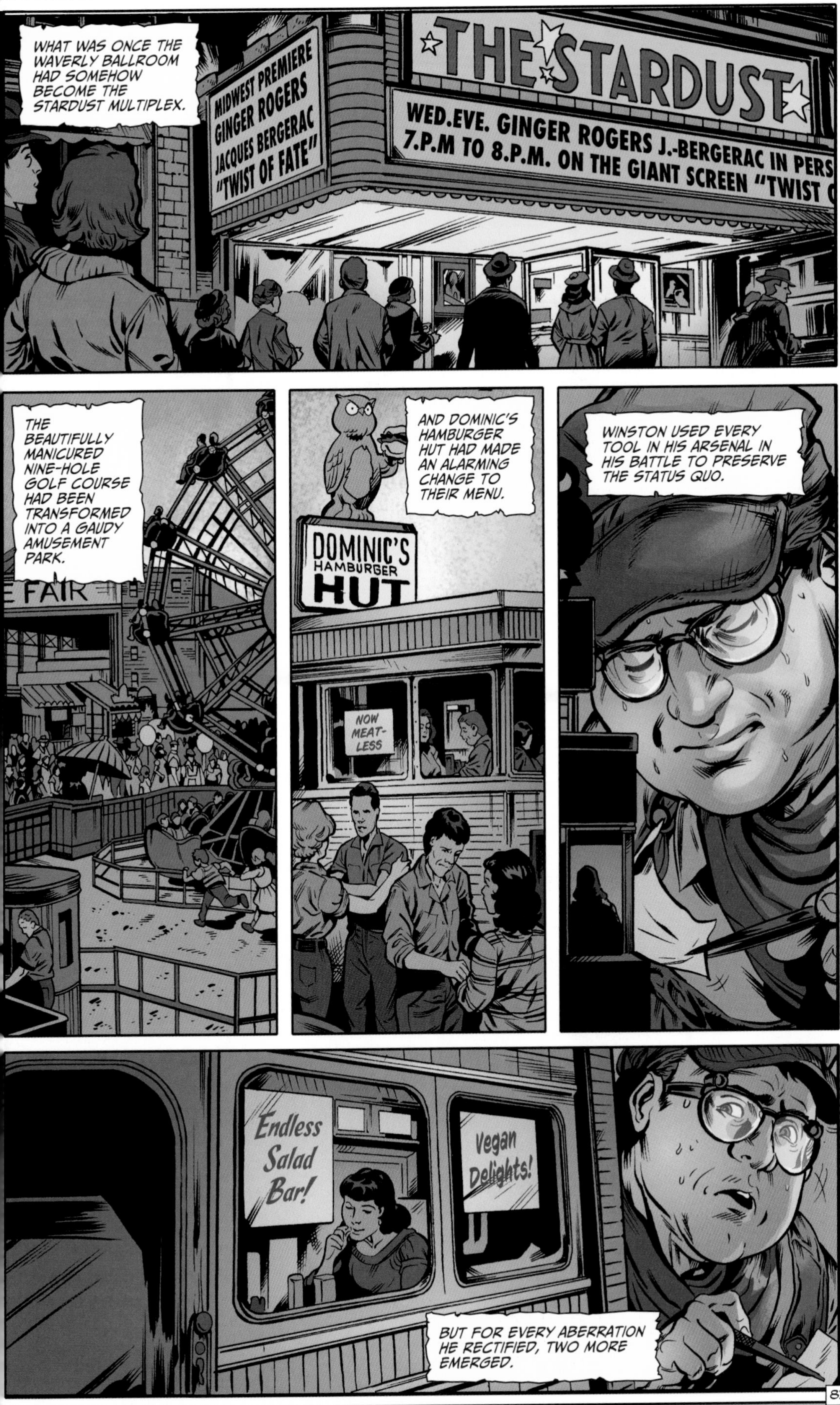
WHAT WAS ONCE THE WAVERLY BALLROOM HAD SOMEHOW BECOME THE STARDUST MULTIPLEX.
MIDWEST PREMIERE GINGER ROGERS JACQUES BERGERAC "TWIST OF FATE"
THE STARDUST
WED.EVE. GINGER ROGERS J.-BERGERAC IN PERS
7.P.M TO 8.P.M. ON THE GIANT SCREEN "TWIST
THE BEAUTIFULLY MANICURED NINE-HOLE GOLF COURSE HAD BEEN TRANSFORMED INTO A GAUDY AMUSEMENT PARK.
E FAIR
AND DOMINIC'S HAMBURGER HUT HAD MADE AN ALARMING CHANGE TO THEIR MENU.
DOMINIC'S HAMBURGER HUT
NOW MEAT-LESS
WINSTON USED EVERY TOOL IN HIS ARSENAL IN HIS BATTLE TO PRESERVE THE STATUS QUO.
Endless Salad Bar!
Vegan Delights!
BUT FOR EVERY ABERRATION HE RECTIFIED, TWO MORE EMERGED.

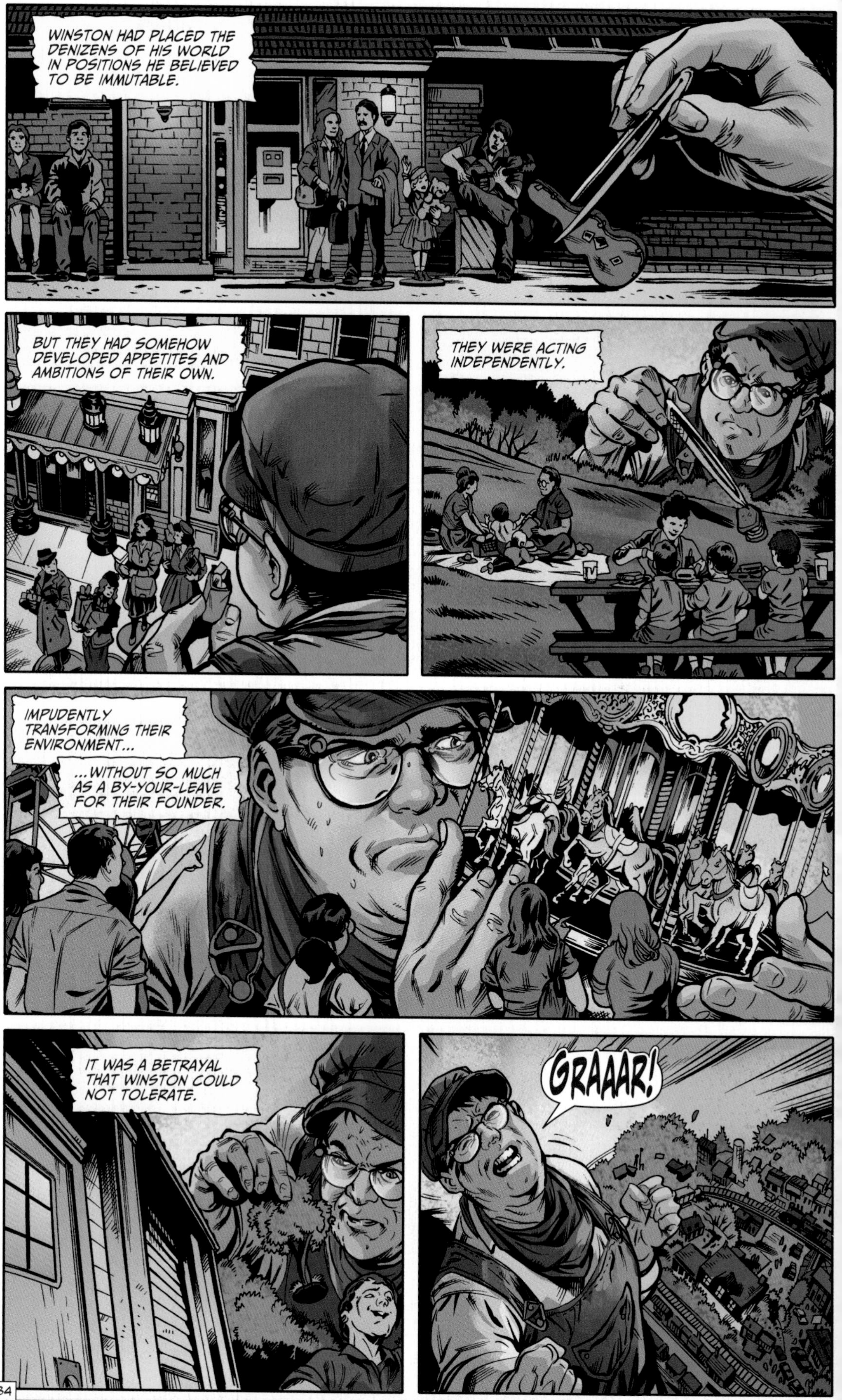
WINSTON HAD PLACED THE DENIZENS OF HIS WORLD IN POSITIONS HE BELIEVED TO BE IMMUTABLE.
BUT THEY HAD SOMEHOW DEVELOPED APPETITES AND AMBITIONS OF THEIR OWN.
THEY WERE ACTING INDEPENDENTLY.
TV
IMPUDENTLY TRANSFORMING THEIR ENVIRONMENT...
...WITHOUT SO MUCH AS A BY-YOUR-LEAVE FOR THEIR FOUNDER.
IT WAS A BETRAYAL THAT WINSTON COULD NOT TOLERATE.
GRAAAR!

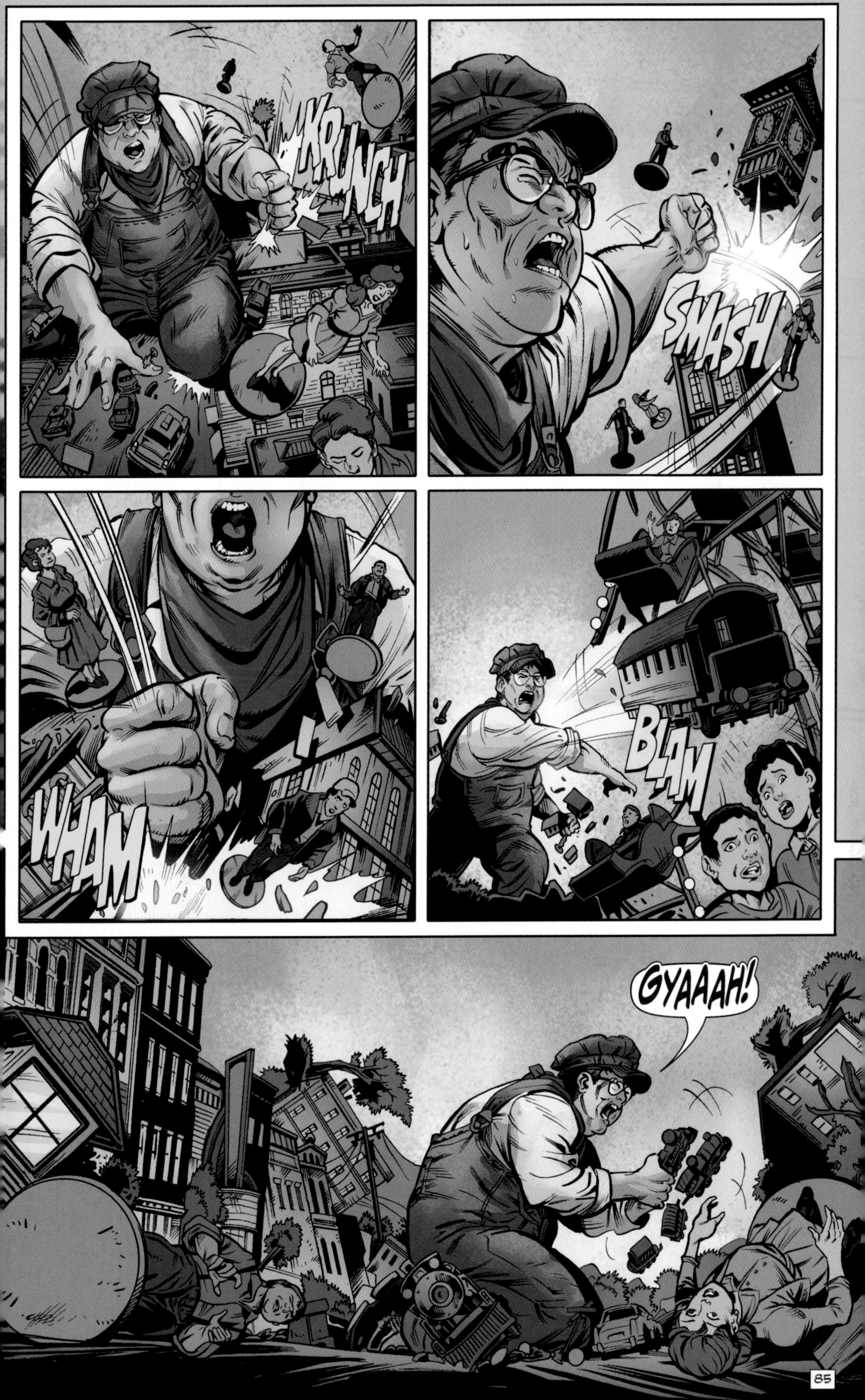
KRUNCH
SMASH
WHAM
BLAM
GYAAAH!

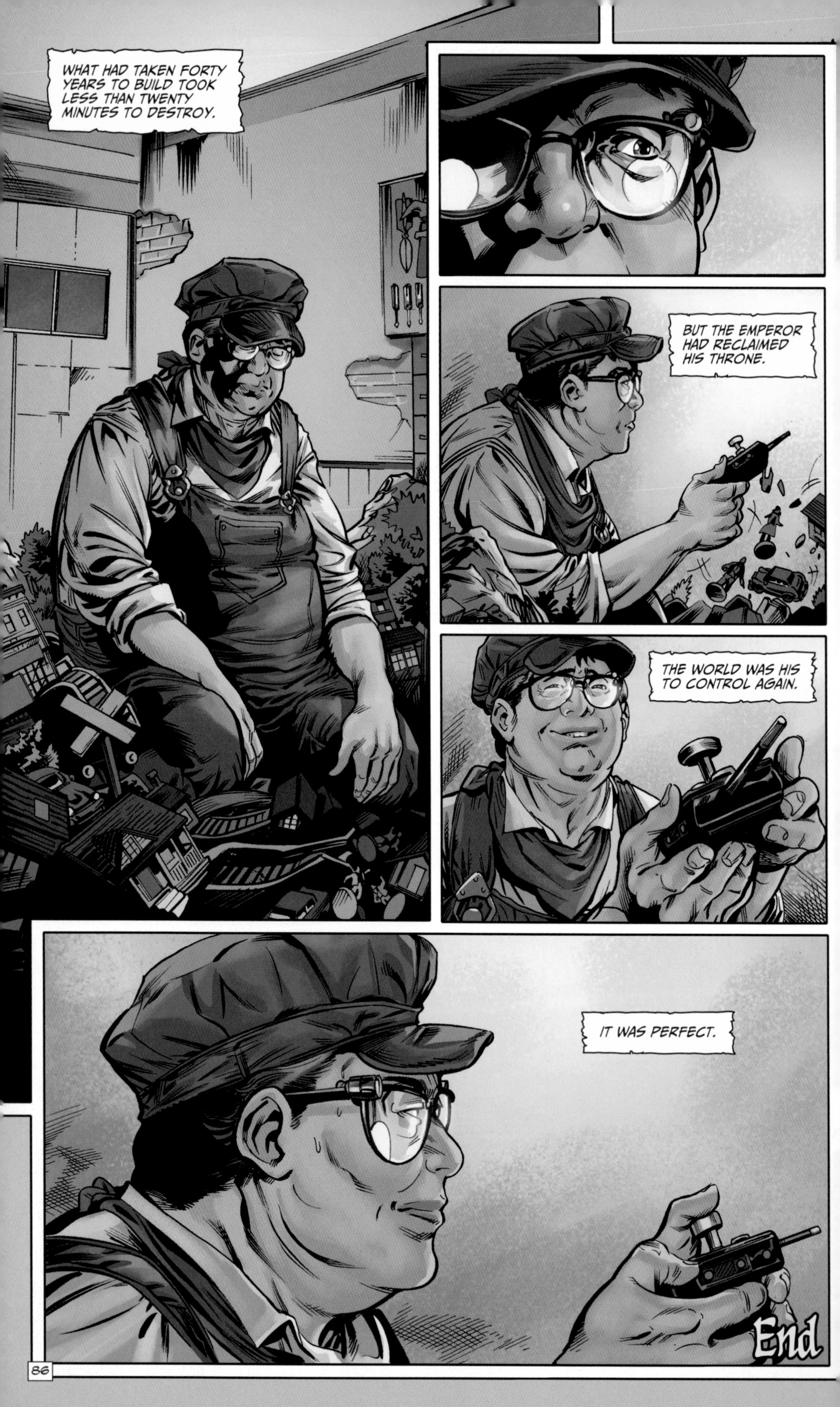
WHAT HAD TAKEN FORTY YEARS TO BUILD TOOK LESS THAN TWENTY MINUTES TO DESTROY.
BUT THE EMPEROR HAD RECLAIMED HIS THRONE.
THE WORLD WAS HIS TO CONTROL AGAIN.
IT WAS PERFECT.
End

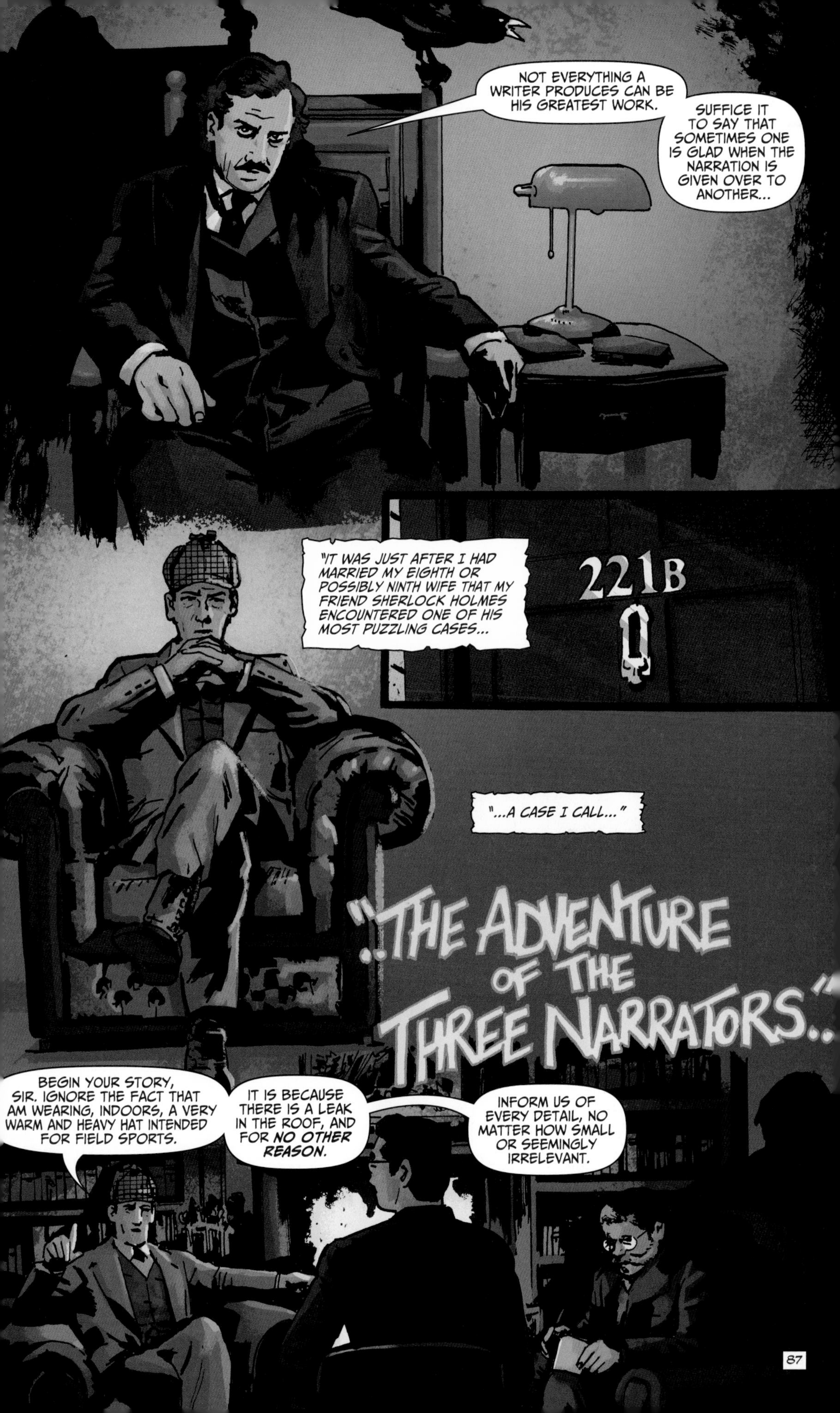

NOT EVERYTHING A WRITER PRODUCES CAN BE HIS GREATEST WORK.
SUFFICE IT TO SAY THAT SOMETIMES ONE IS GLAD WHEN THE NARRATION IS GIVEN OVER TO ANOTHER...
"IT WAS JUST AFTER I HAD MARRIED MY EIGHTH OR POSSIBLY NINTH WIFE THAT MY FRIEND SHERLOCK HOLMES ENCOUNTERED ONE OF HIS MOST PUZZLING CASES...
221B
"...A CASE I CALL..."
"...THE ADVENTURE OF THE THREE NARRATORS..."
BEGIN YOUR STORY, SIR. IGNORE THE FACT THAT AM WEARING, INDOORS, A VERY WARM AND HEAVY HAT INTENDED FOR FIELD SPORTS.
IT IS BECAUSE THERE IS A LEAK IN THE ROOF, AND FOR ***NO OTHER REASON***.
INFORM US OF EVERY DETAIL, NO MATTER HOW SMALL OR SEEMINGLY IRRELEVANT.

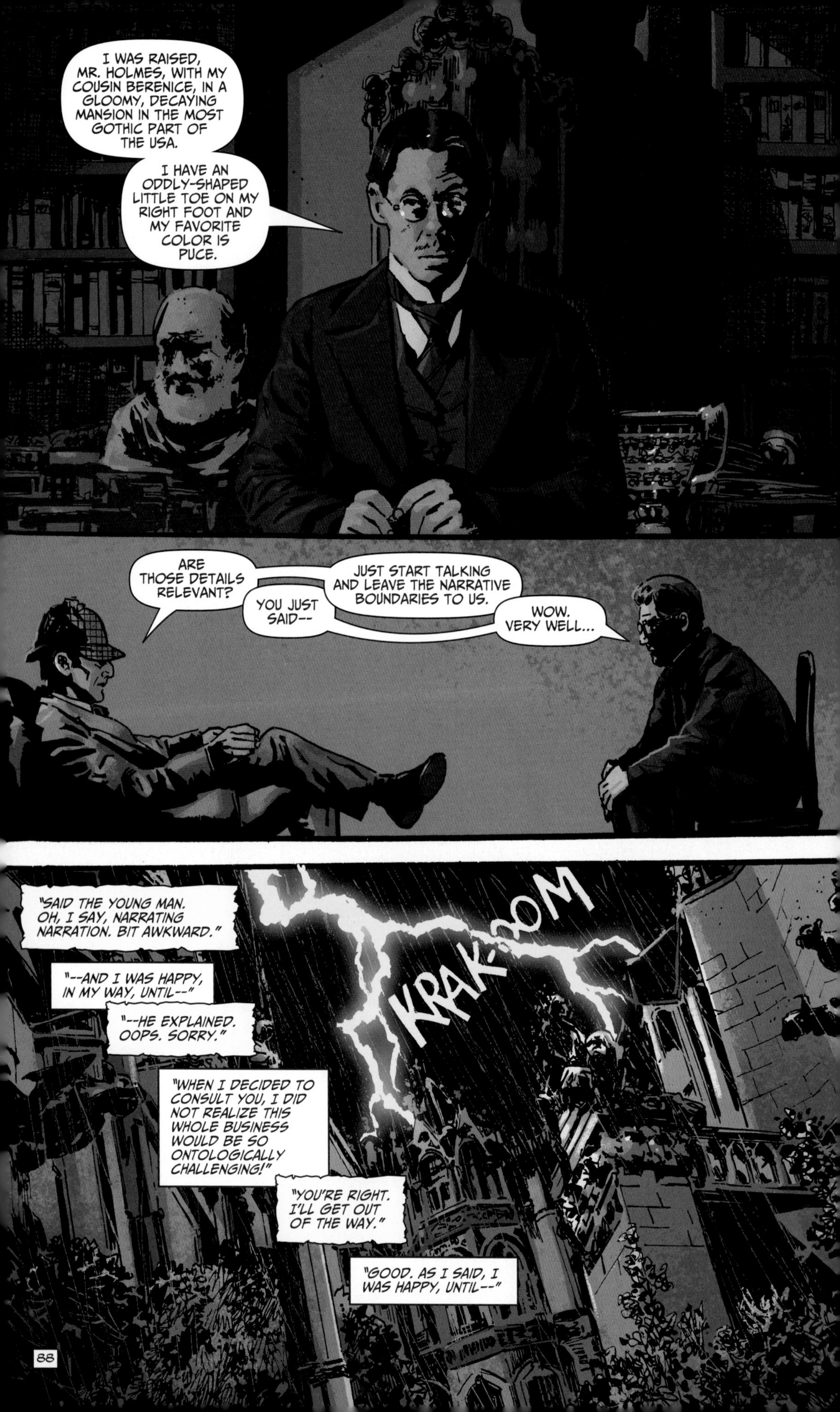
I WAS RAISED, MR. HOLMES, WITH MY COUSIN BERENICE, IN A GLOOMY, DECAYING MANSION IN THE MOST GOTHIC PART OF THE USA.
I HAVE AN ODDLY-SHAPED LITTLE TOE ON MY RIGHT FOOT AND MY FAVORITE COLOR IS PUCE.
ARE THOSE DETAILS RELEVANT?
YOU JUST SAID--
JUST START TALKING AND LEAVE THE NARRATIVE BOUNDARIES TO US.
WOW. VERY WELL...
"SAID THE YOUNG MAN. OH, I SAY, NARRATING NARRATION. BIT AWKWARD."
"--AND I WAS HAPPY, IN MY WAY, UNTIL--"
"--HE EXPLAINED. OOPS. SORRY."
"WHEN I DECIDED TO CONSULT YOU, I DID NOT REALIZE THIS WHOLE BUSINESS WOULD BE SO ONTOLOGICALLY CHALLENGING!"
"YOU'RE RIGHT. I'LL GET OUT OF THE WAY."
KRAK-BOOM
"GOOD. AS I SAID, I WAS HAPPY, UNTIL--"

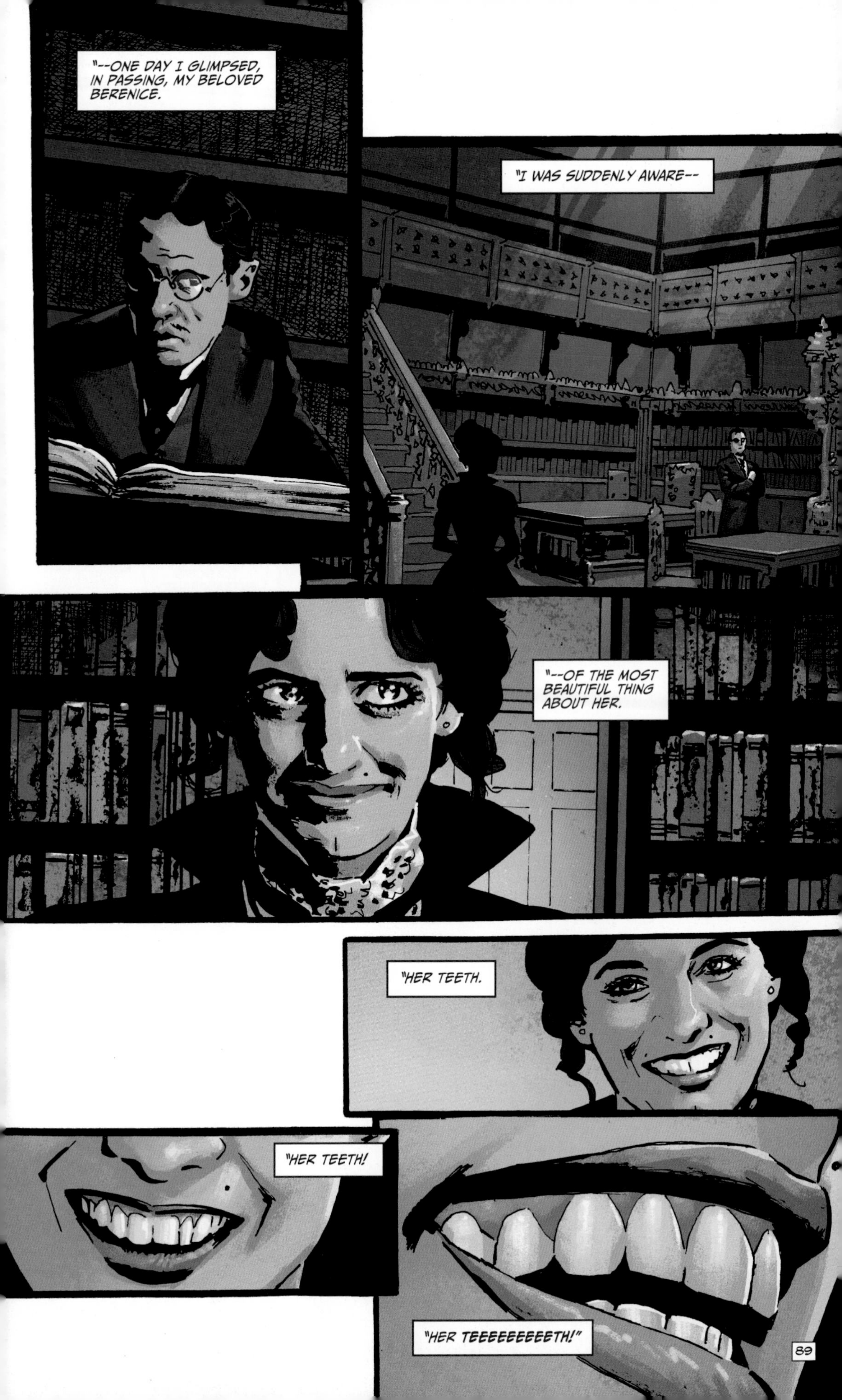
"--ONE DAY I GLIMPSED, IN PASSING, MY BELOVED BERENICE.
"I WAS SUDDENLY AWARE--
"--OF THE MOST BEAUTIFUL THING ABOUT HER.
"HER TEETH.
"HER TEETH!
"HER TEEEEEEEEETH!"

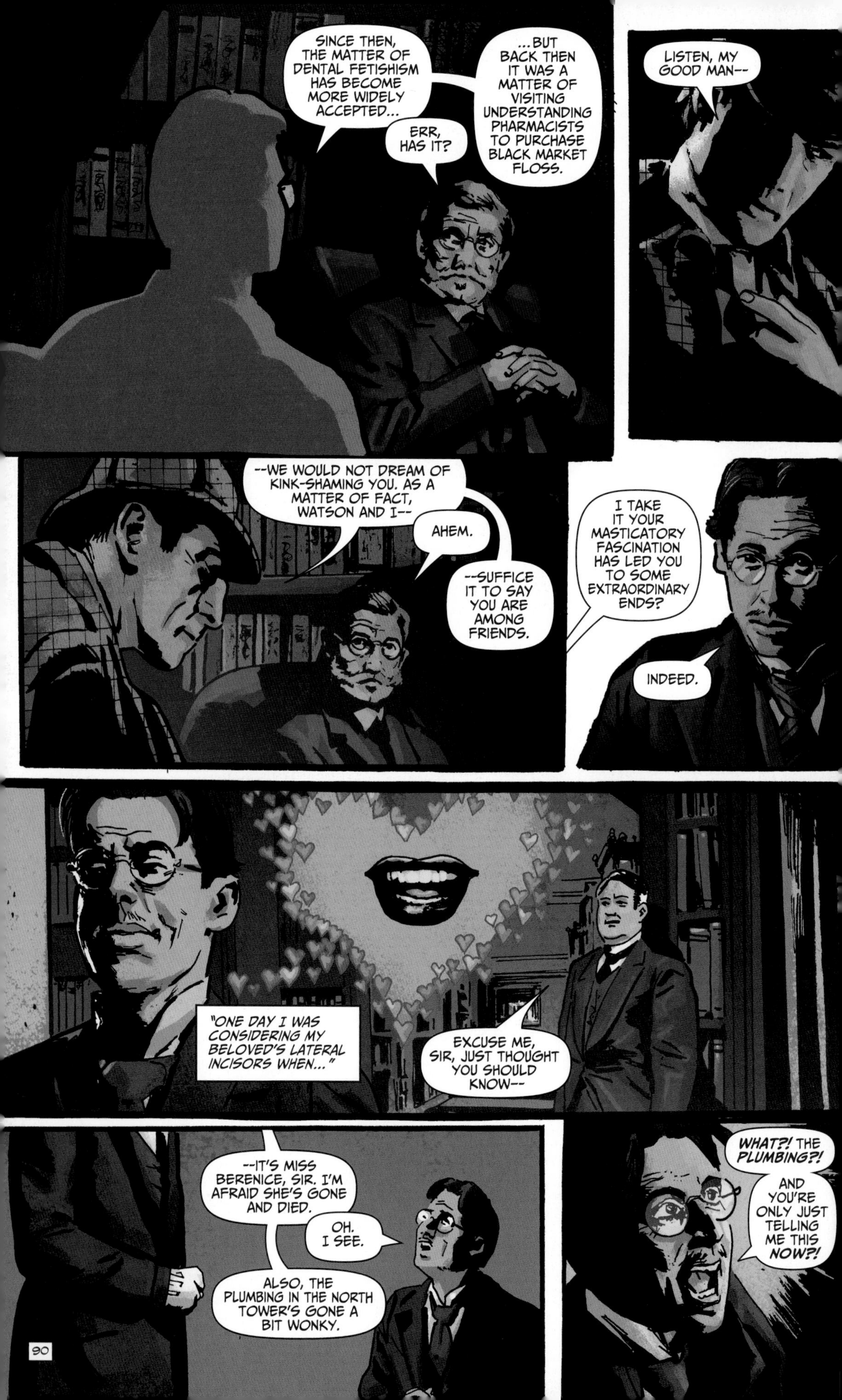
SINCE THEN, THE MATTER OF DENTAL FETISHISM HAS BECOME MORE WIDELY ACCEPTED...
...BUT BACK THEN IT WAS A MATTER OF VISITING UNDERSTANDING PHARMACISTS TO PURCHASE BLACK MARKET FLOSS.
ERR, HAS IT?
LISTEN, MY GOOD MAN--
--WE WOULD NOT DREAM OF KINK-SHAMING YOU. AS A MATTER OF FACT, WATSON AND I--
AHEM.
--SUFFICE IT TO SAY YOU ARE AMONG FRIENDS.
I TAKE IT YOUR MASTICATORY FASCINATION HAS LED YOU TO SOME EXTRAORDINARY ENDS?
INDEED.
"ONE DAY I WAS CONSIDERING MY BELOVED'S LATERAL INCISORS WHEN..."
EXCUSE ME, SIR, JUST THOUGHT YOU SHOULD KNOW--
--IT'S MISS BERENICE, SIR. I'M AFRAID SHE'S GONE AND DIED.
OH. I SEE.
ALSO, THE PLUMBING IN THE NORTH TOWER'S GONE A BIT WONKY.
WHAT?! THE PLUMBING?!
AND YOU'RE ONLY JUST TELLING ME THIS NOW?!

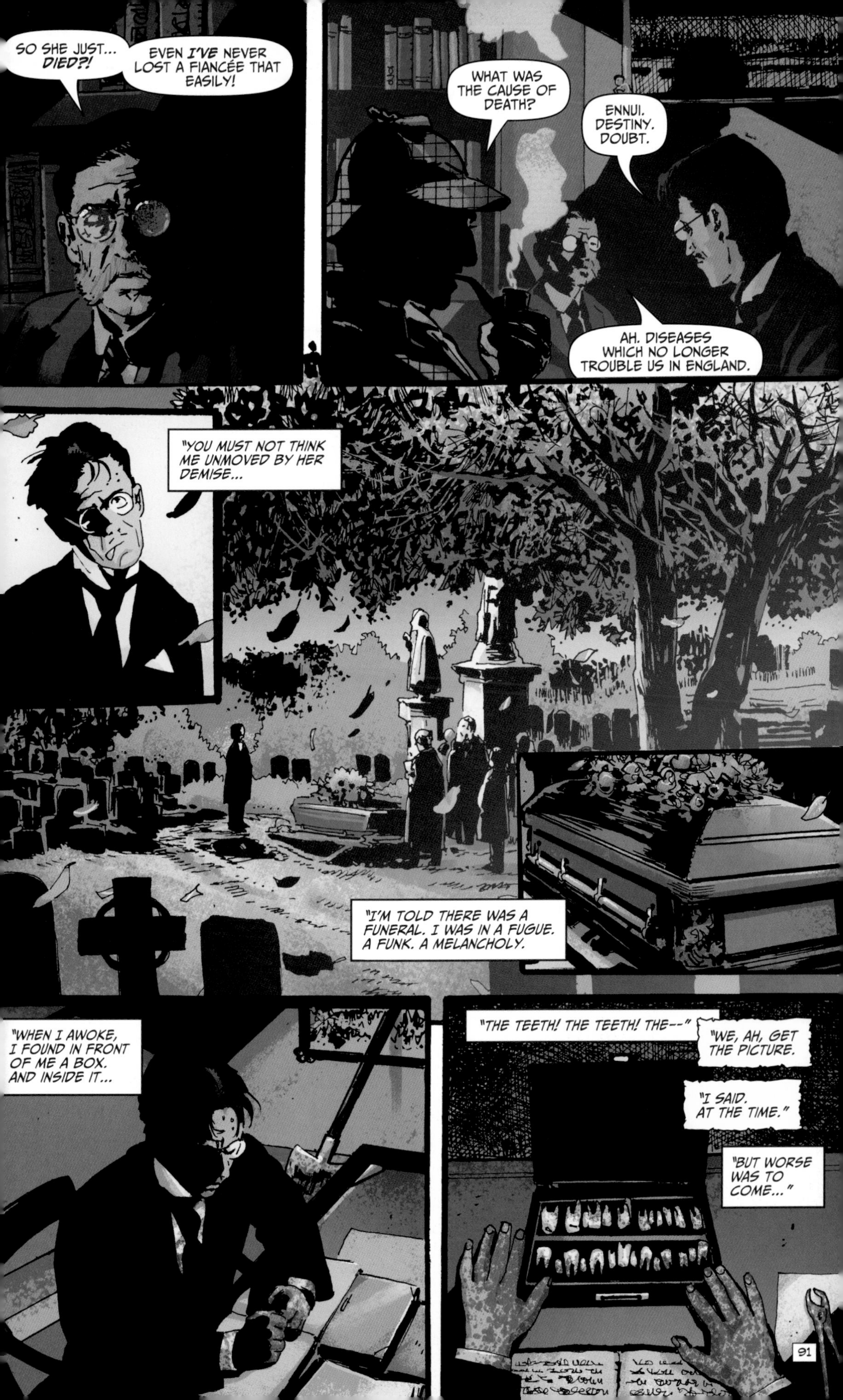
SO SHE JUST... DIED?!
EVEN I'VE NEVER LOST A FIANCÉE THAT EASILY!
WHAT WAS THE CAUSE OF DEATH?
ENNUI. DESTINY. DOUBT.
AH. DISEASES WHICH NO LONGER TROUBLE US IN ENGLAND.
"YOU MUST NOT THINK ME UNMOVED BY HER DEMISE...
"I'M TOLD THERE WAS A FUNERAL. I WAS IN A FUGUE. A FUNK. A MELANCHOLY.
"WHEN I AWOKE, I FOUND IN FRONT OF ME A BOX. AND INSIDE IT...
"THE TEETH! THE TEETH! THE--"
"WE, AH, GET THE PICTURE.
"I SAID. AT THE TIME."
"BUT WORSE WAS TO COME..."

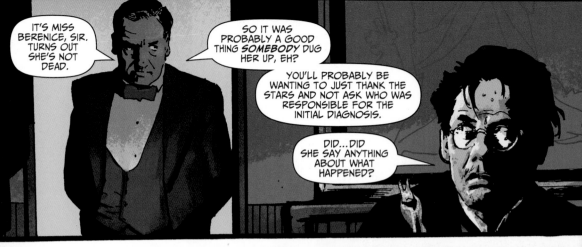

IT'S MISS BERENICE, SIR. TURNS OUT SHE'S NOT DEAD.

SO IT WAS PROBABLY A GOOD THING *SOMEBODY* DUG HER UP, EH?

YOU'LL PROBABLY BE WANTING TO JUST THANK THE STARS AND NOT ASK WHO WAS RESPONSIBLE FOR THE INITIAL DIAGNOSIS.

DID...DID SHE SAY ANYTHING ABOUT WHAT HAPPENED?

YES, SHE SAID SHE HAD A MESSAGE FOR YOU. I WROTE IT DOWN.

AHEM.

"MEFFEER UGHHER! MEW FFOLE MEEF UGHING TEEEEFFF!"

"OF COURSE, I DID NOT INQUIRE FURTHER AS TO HER LOCATION OR SITUATION.

"I CAME STRAIGHT TO YOU, MR. HOLMES.

"ONLY YOU CAN SOLVE THE MYSTERY OF WHAT HAPPENED."

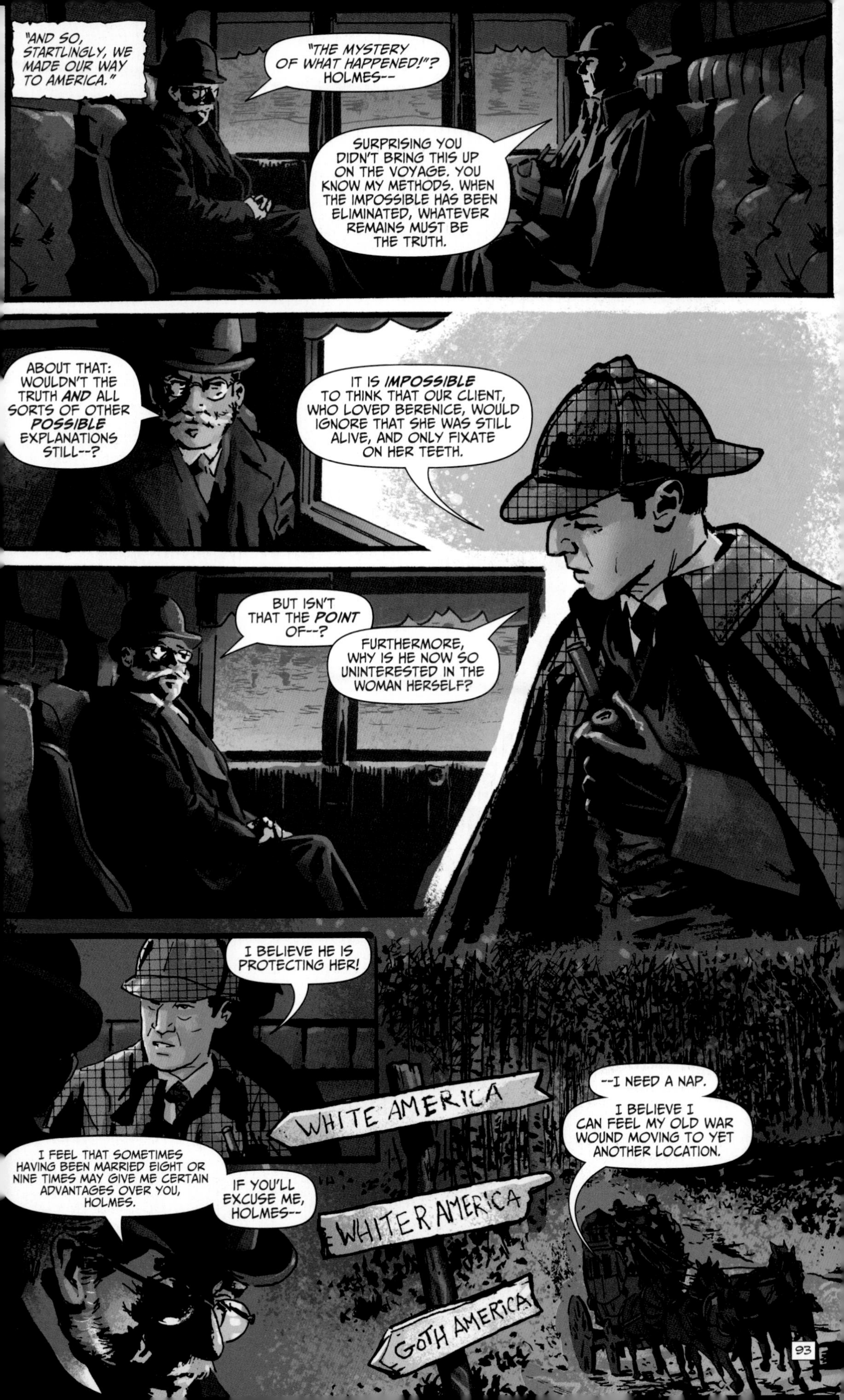
"AND SO, STARTLINGLY, WE MADE OUR WAY TO AMERICA."
"THE MYSTERY OF WHAT HAPPENED!"? HOLMES--
SURPRISING YOU DIDN'T BRING THIS UP ON THE VOYAGE. YOU KNOW MY METHODS. WHEN THE IMPOSSIBLE HAS BEEN ELIMINATED, WHATEVER REMAINS MUST BE THE TRUTH.
ABOUT THAT: WOULDN'T THE TRUTH AND ALL SORTS OF OTHER POSSIBLE EXPLANATIONS STILL--?
IT IS IMPOSSIBLE TO THINK THAT OUR CLIENT, WHO LOVED BERENICE, WOULD IGNORE THAT SHE WAS STILL ALIVE, AND ONLY FIXATE ON HER TEETH.
BUT ISN'T THAT THE POINT OF--?
FURTHERMORE, WHY IS HE NOW SO UNINTERESTED IN THE WOMAN HERSELF?
I BELIEVE HE IS PROTECTING HER!
I FEEL THAT SOMETIMES HAVING BEEN MARRIED EIGHT OR NINE TIMES MAY GIVE ME CERTAIN ADVANTAGES OVER YOU, HOLMES.
IF YOU'LL EXCUSE ME, HOLMES--
WHITE AMERICA
WHITER AMERICA
GOTH AMERICA
--I NEED A NAP.
I BELIEVE I CAN FEEL MY OLD WAR WOUND MOVING TO YET ANOTHER LOCATION.

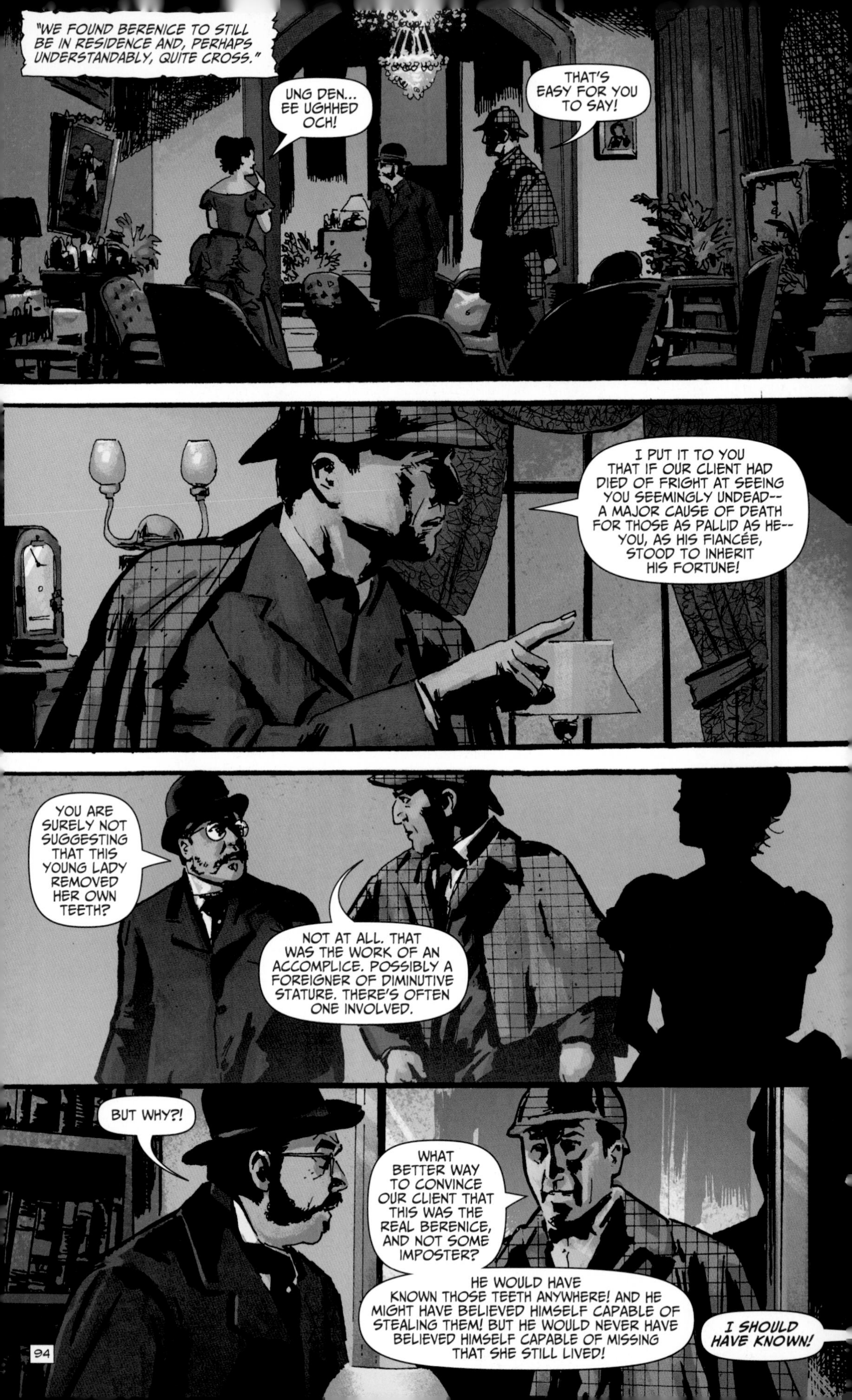
"WE FOUND BERENICE TO STILL BE IN RESIDENCE AND, PERHAPS UNDERSTANDABLY, QUITE CROSS."
UNG DEN... EE UGHHED OCH!
THAT'S EASY FOR YOU TO SAY!
I PUT IT TO YOU THAT IF OUR CLIENT HAD DIED OF FRIGHT AT SEEING YOU SEEMINGLY UNDEAD-- A MAJOR CAUSE OF DEATH FOR THOSE AS PALLID AS HE-- YOU, AS HIS FIANCÉE, STOOD TO INHERIT HIS FORTUNE!
YOU ARE SURELY NOT SUGGESTING THAT THIS YOUNG LADY REMOVED HER OWN TEETH?
NOT AT ALL. THAT WAS THE WORK OF AN ACCOMPLICE. POSSIBLY A FOREIGNER OF DIMINUTIVE STATURE. THERE'S OFTEN ONE INVOLVED.
BUT WHY?!
WHAT BETTER WAY TO CONVINCE OUR CLIENT THAT THIS WAS THE REAL BERENICE, AND NOT SOME IMPOSTER?
HE WOULD HAVE KNOWN THOSE TEETH ANYWHERE! AND HE MIGHT HAVE BELIEVED HIMSELF CAPABLE OF STEALING THEM! BUT HE WOULD NEVER HAVE BELIEVED HIMSELF CAPABLE OF MISSING THAT SHE STILL LIVED!
I SHOULD HAVE KNOWN!

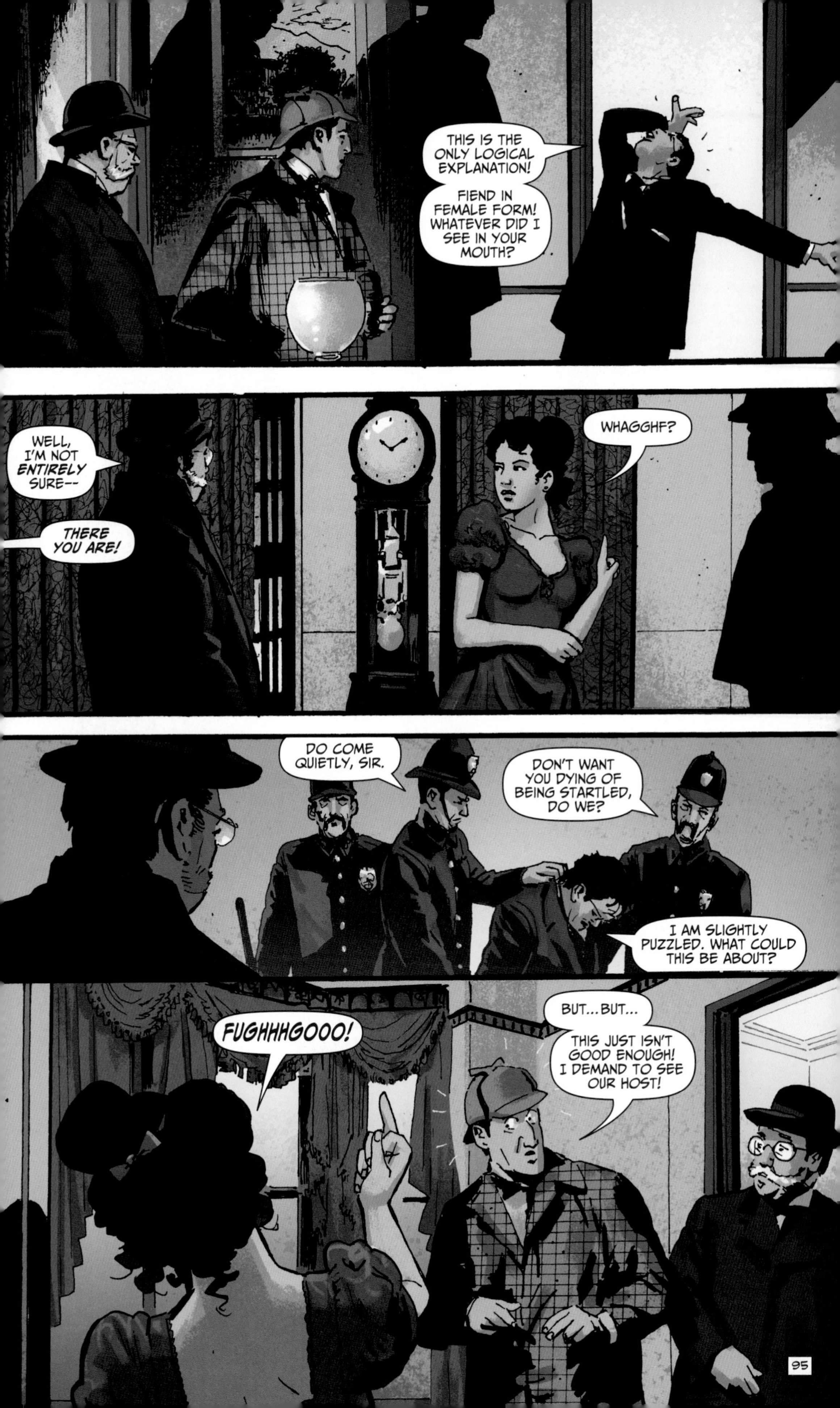
THIS IS THE ONLY LOGICAL EXPLANATION!
FIEND IN FEMALE FORM! WHATEVER DID I SEE IN YOUR MOUTH?
WELL, I'M NOT *ENTIRELY* SURE--
THERE YOU ARE!
WHAGGHF?
DO COME QUIETLY, SIR.
DON'T WANT YOU DYING OF BEING STARTLED, DO WE?
I AM SLIGHTLY PUZZLED. WHAT COULD THIS BE ABOUT?
FUGHHHGOOO!
BUT... BUT...
THIS JUST ISN'T GOOD ENOUGH! I DEMAND TO SEE OUR HOST!

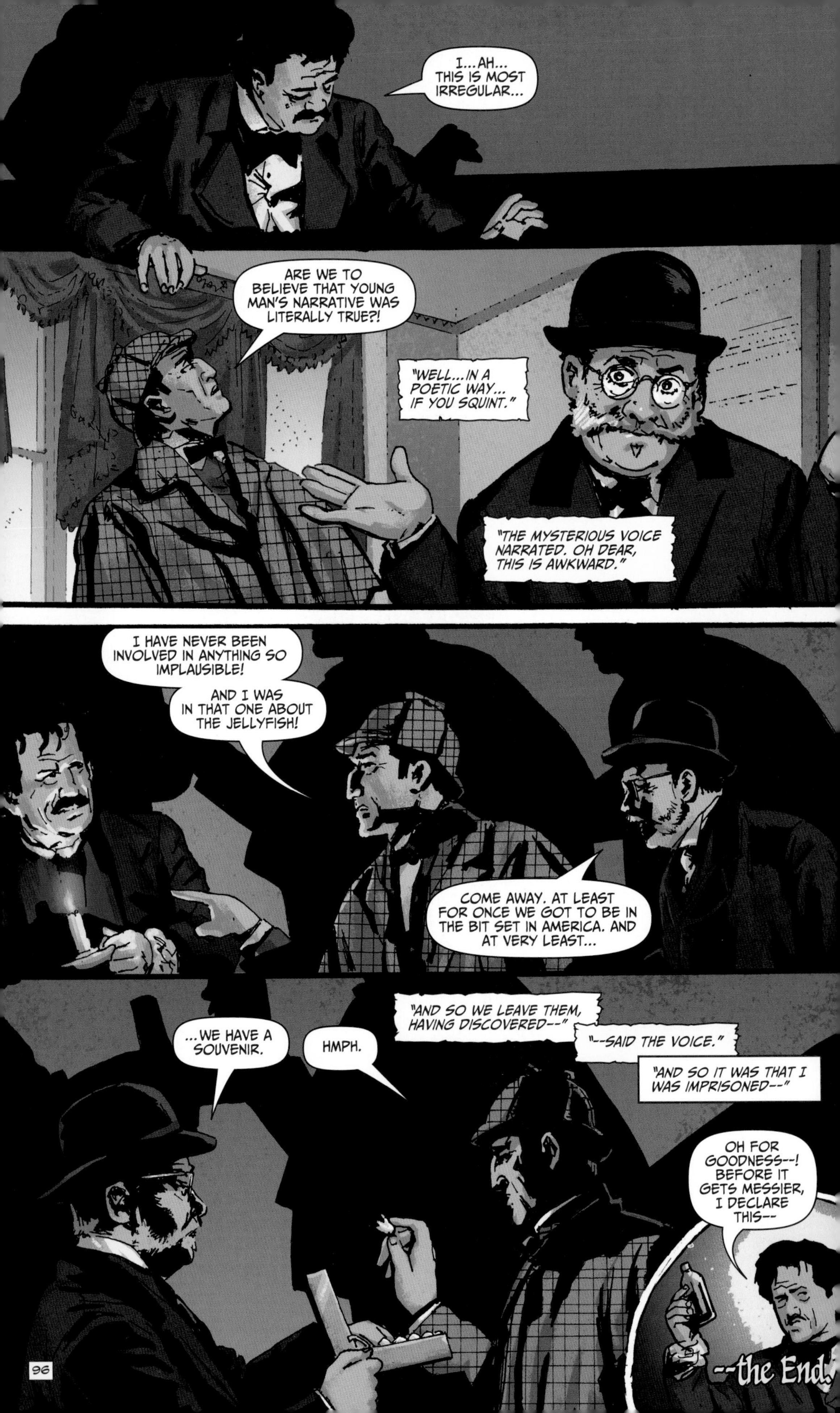
I...AH... THIS IS MOST IRREGULAR...
ARE WE TO BELIEVE THAT YOUNG MAN'S NARRATIVE WAS LITERALLY TRUE?!
"WELL...IN A POETIC WAY... IF YOU SQUINT."
"THE MYSTERIOUS VOICE NARRATED. OH DEAR, THIS IS AWKWARD."
I HAVE NEVER BEEN INVOLVED IN ANYTHING SO IMPLAUSIBLE!
AND I WAS IN THAT ONE ABOUT THE JELLYFISH!
COME AWAY. AT LEAST FOR ONCE WE GOT TO BE IN THE BIT SET IN AMERICA. AND AT VERY LEAST...
...WE HAVE A SOUVENIR.
HMPH.
"AND SO WE LEAVE THEM, HAVING DISCOVERED--"
"--SAID THE VOICE."
"AND SO IT WAS THAT I WAS IMPRISONED--"
OH FOR GOODNESS--! BEFORE IT GETS MESSIER, I DECLARE THIS--
--the End.

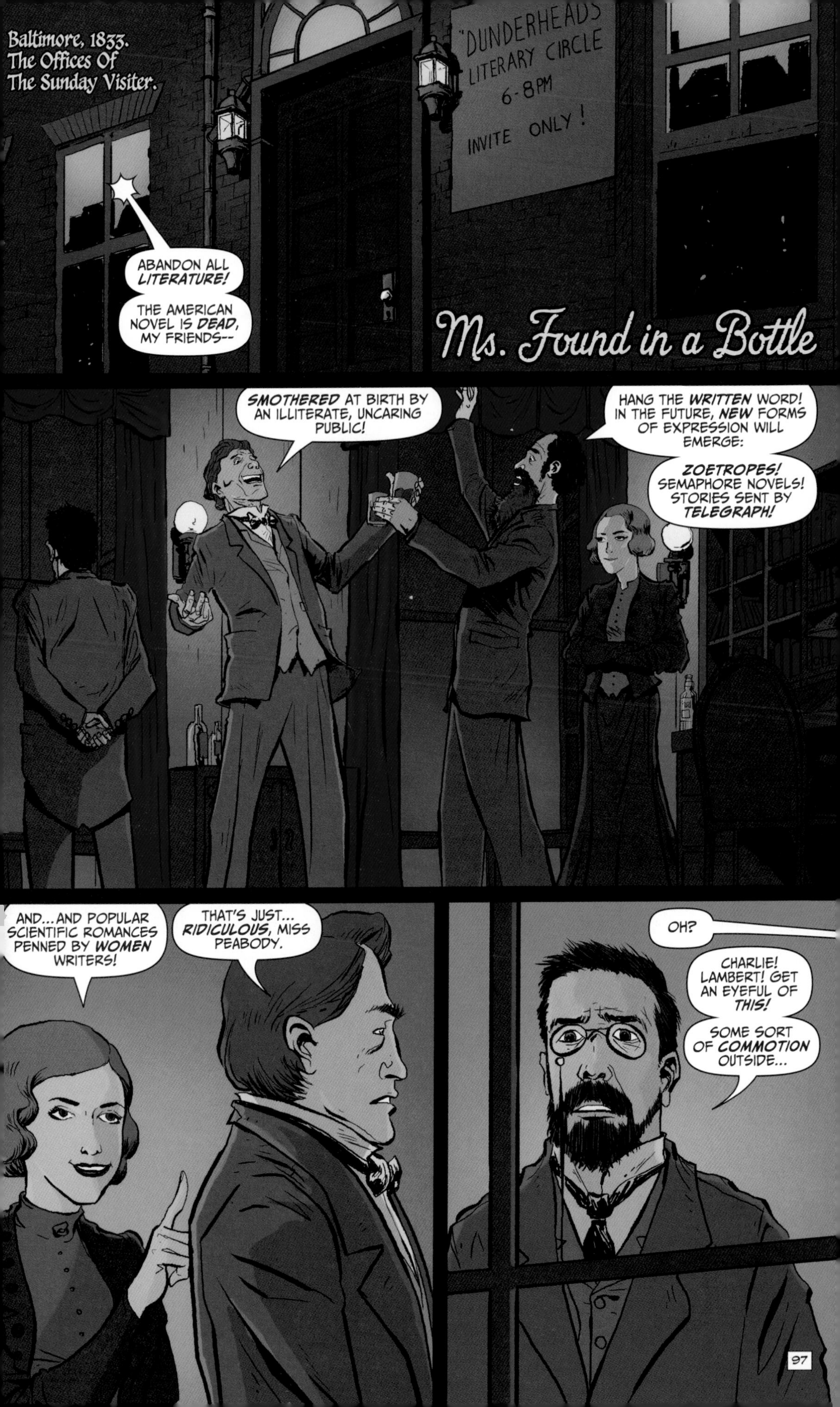
Baltimore, 1833. The Offices Of The Sunday Visiter.
"DUNDERHEADS" LITERARY CIRCLE 6-8PM INVITE ONLY!
ABANDON ALL LITERATURE!
THE AMERICAN NOVEL IS DEAD, MY FRIENDS--
Ms. Found in a Bottle
SMOTHERED AT BIRTH BY AN ILLITERATE, UNCARING PUBLIC!
HANG THE WRITTEN WORD! IN THE FUTURE, NEW FORMS OF EXPRESSION WILL EMERGE:
ZOETROPES! SEMAPHORE NOVELS! STORIES SENT BY TELEGRAPH!
AND...AND POPULAR SCIENTIFIC ROMANCES PENNED BY WOMEN WRITERS!
THAT'S JUST... RIDICULOUS, MISS PEABODY.
OH?
CHARLIE! LAMBERT! GET AN EYEFUL OF THIS!
SOME SORT OF COMMOTION OUTSIDE...

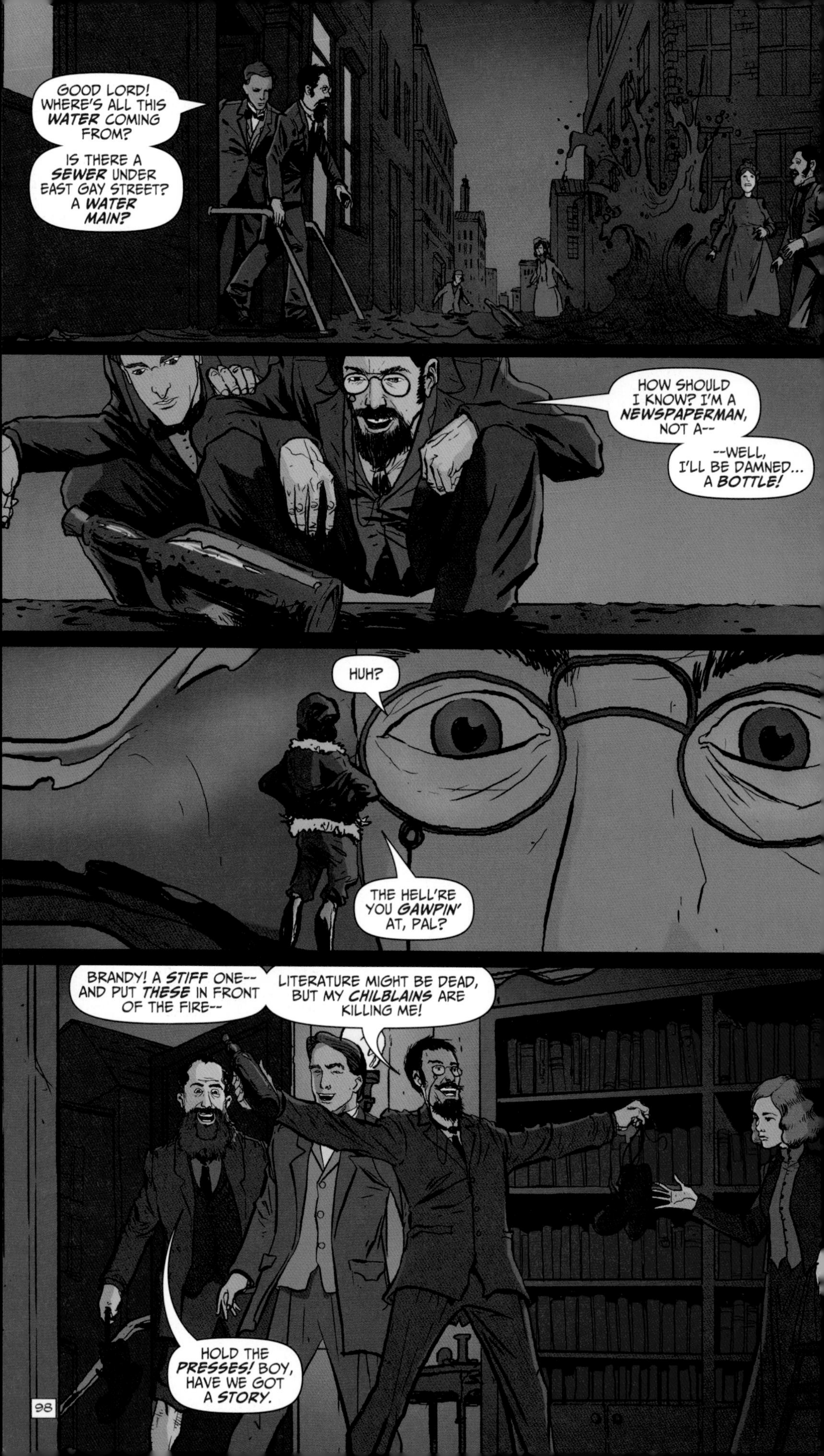
GOOD LORD! WHERE'S ALL THIS *WATER* COMING FROM?
IS THERE A *SEWER* UNDER EAST GAY STREET? A *WATER MAIN?*
HOW SHOULD I KNOW? I'M A *NEWSPAPERMAN,* NOT A--
--WELL, I'LL BE DAMNED... A *BOTTLE!*
HUH?
THE HELL'RE YOU *GAWPIN'* AT, PAL?
BRANDY! A *STIFF* ONE-- AND PUT *THESE* IN FRONT OF THE FIRE--
LITERATURE MIGHT BE DEAD, BUT MY *CHILBLAINS* ARE KILLING ME!
HOLD THE *PRESSES!* BOY, HAVE WE GOT A *STORY.*

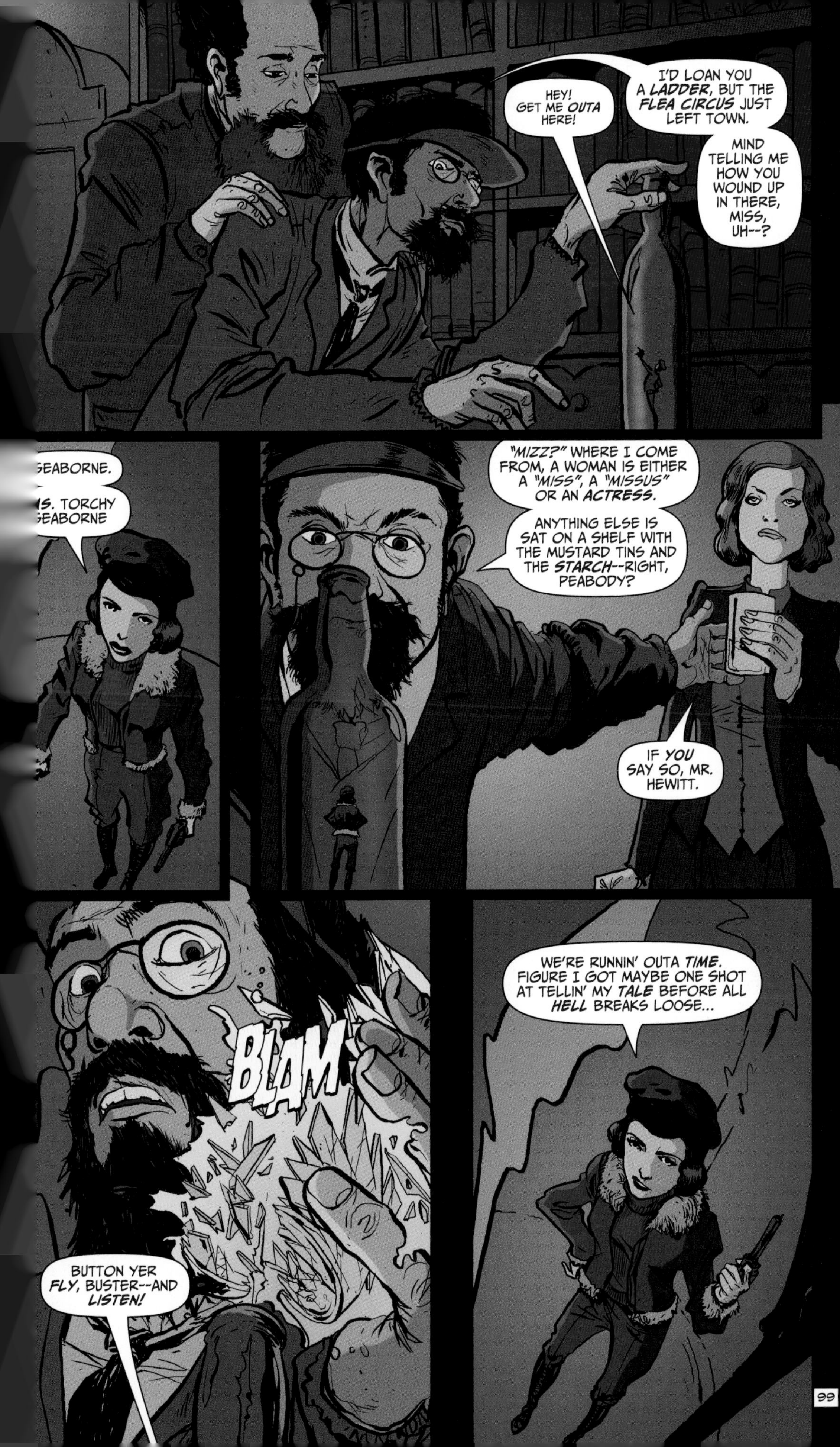
HEY! GET ME OUTA HERE!
I'D LOAN YOU A LADDER, BUT THE FLEA CIRCUS JUST LEFT TOWN.
MIND TELLING ME HOW YOU WOUND UP IN THERE, MISS, UH--?
EABORNE.
S. TORCHY EABORNE
"MIZZ?" WHERE I COME FROM, A WOMAN IS EITHER A "MISS", A "MISSUS" OR AN ACTRESS.
ANYTHING ELSE IS SAT ON A SHELF WITH THE MUSTARD TINS AND THE STARCH--RIGHT, PEABODY?
IF YOU SAY SO, MR. HEWITT.
BLAM
BUTTON YER FLY, BUSTER--AND LISTEN!
WE'RE RUNNIN' OUTA TIME. FIGURE I GOT MAYBE ONE SHOT AT TELLIN' MY TALE BEFORE ALL HELL BREAKS LOOSE...

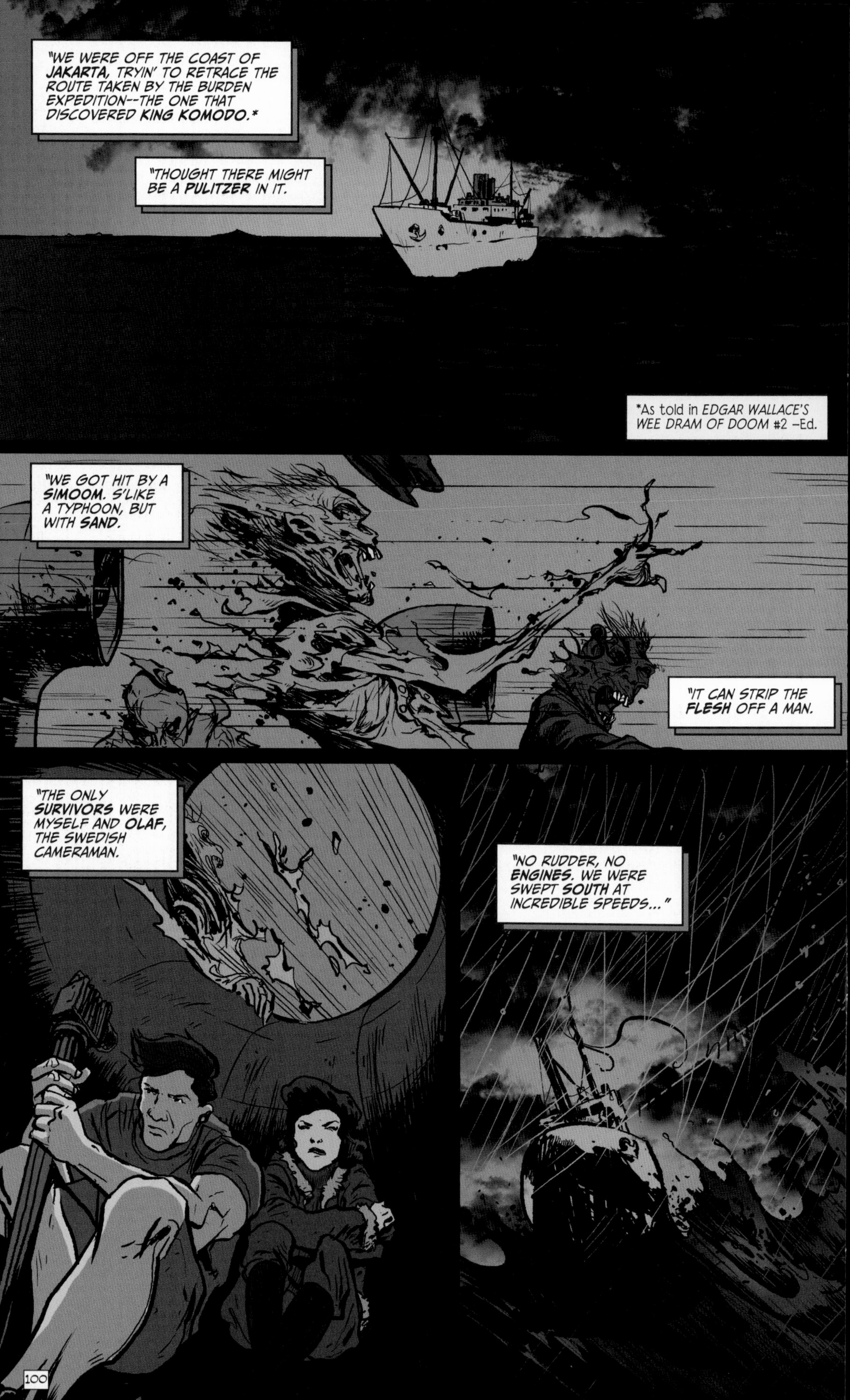
"WE WERE OFF THE COAST OF JAKARTA, TRYIN' TO RETRACE THE ROUTE TAKEN BY THE BURDEN EXPEDITION--THE ONE THAT DISCOVERED KING KOMODO.*
"THOUGHT THERE MIGHT BE A PULITZER IN IT.
*As told in EDGAR WALLACE'S WEE DRAM OF DOOM #2 –Ed.
"WE GOT HIT BY A SIMOOM. S'LIKE A TYPHOON, BUT WITH SAND.
"IT CAN STRIP THE FLESH OFF A MAN.
"THE ONLY SURVIVORS WERE MYSELF AND OLAF, THE SWEDISH CAMERAMAN.
"NO RUDDER, NO ENGINES. WE WERE SWEPT SOUTH AT INCREDIBLE SPEEDS..."

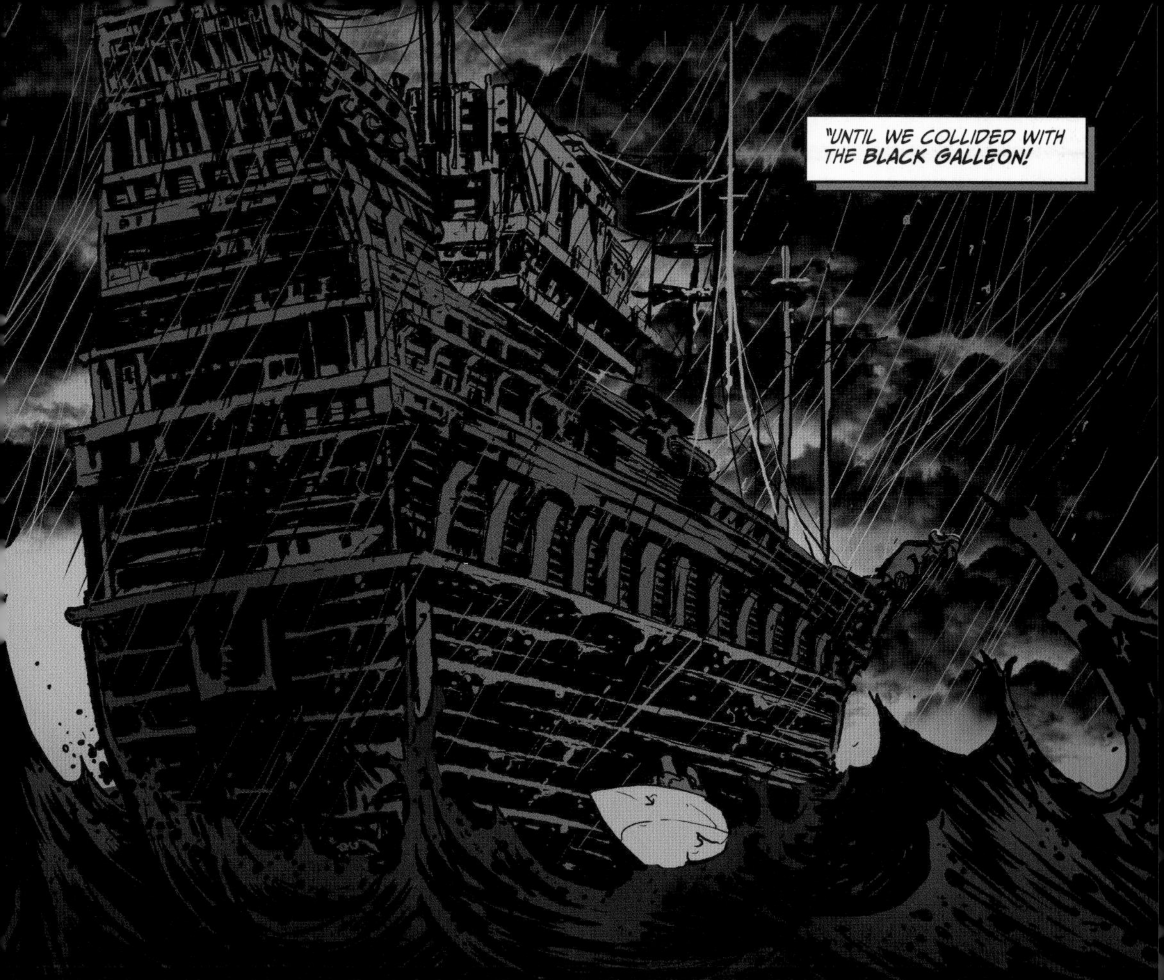
"UNTIL WE COLLIDED WITH THE BLACK GALLEON!

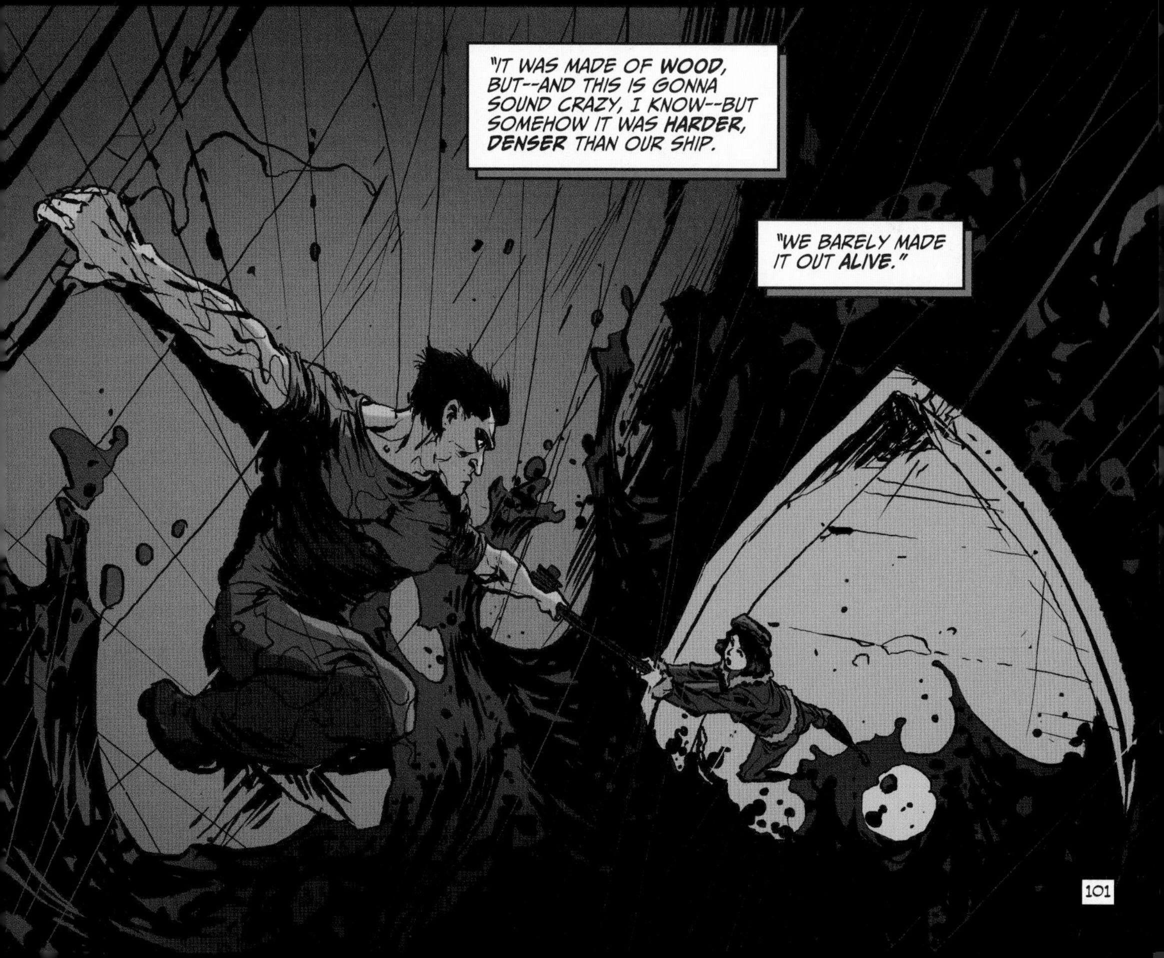
"IT WAS MADE OF WOOD, BUT--AND THIS IS GONNA SOUND CRAZY, I KNOW--BUT SOMEHOW IT WAS HARDER, DENSER THAN OUR SHIP.
"WE BARELY MADE IT OUT ALIVE."

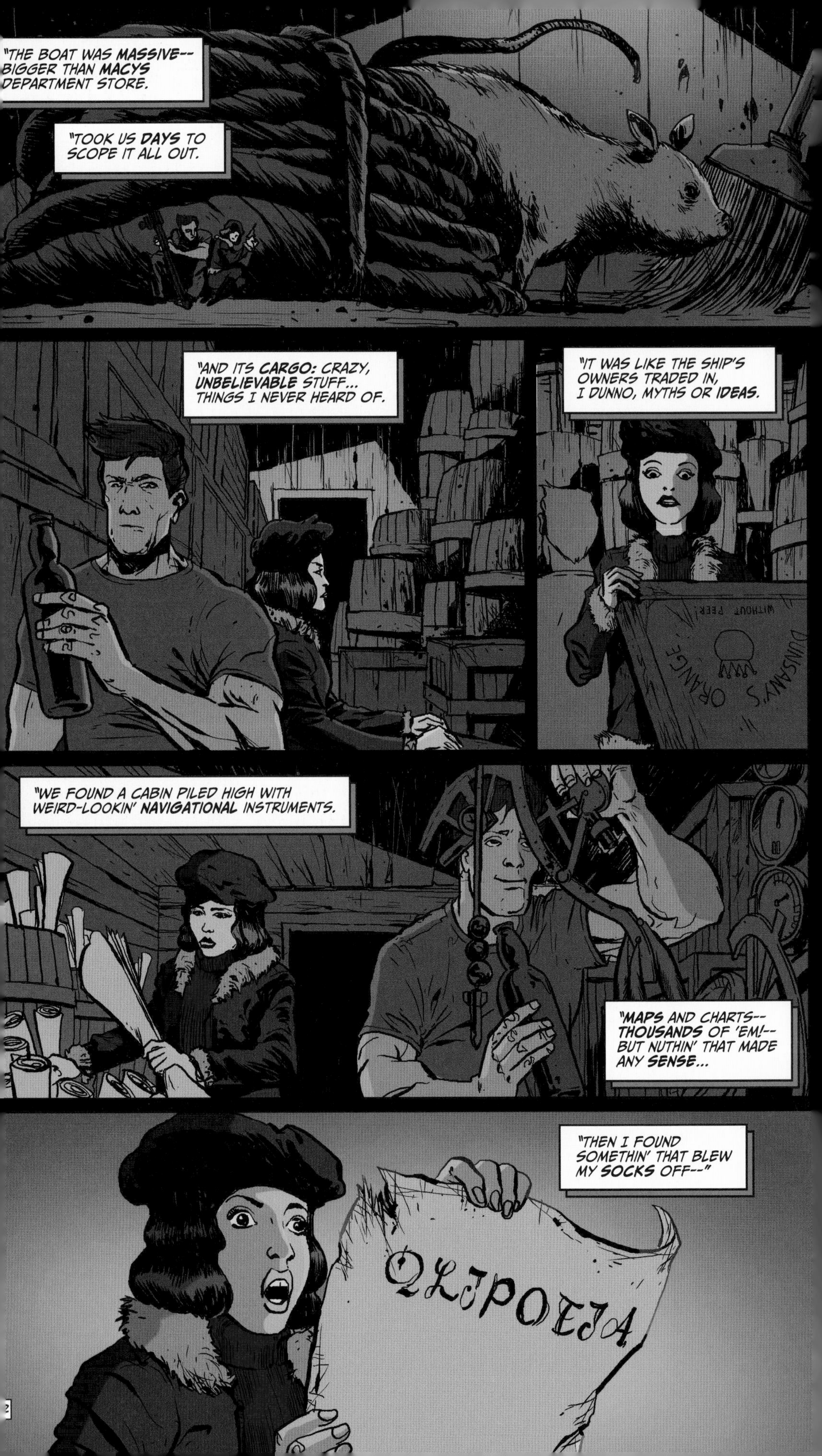
"THE BOAT WAS **MASSIVE**-- BIGGER THAN **MACYS** DEPARTMENT STORE.
"TOOK US **DAYS** TO SCOPE IT ALL OUT.
"AND ITS **CARGO:** CRAZY, **UNBELIEVABLE** STUFF... THINGS I NEVER HEARD OF.
"IT WAS LIKE THE SHIP'S OWNERS TRADED IN, I DUNNO, MYTHS OR **IDEAS**.
WITHOUT PEER!
DUNSANY'S ORANGE
"WE FOUND A CABIN PILED HIGH WITH WEIRD-LOOKIN' **NAVIGATIONAL** INSTRUMENTS.
"**MAPS** AND CHARTS-- **THOUSANDS** OF 'EM!-- BUT NUTHIN' THAT MADE ANY **SENSE**...
"THEN I FOUND SOMETHIN' THAT BLEW MY **SOCKS** OFF--"

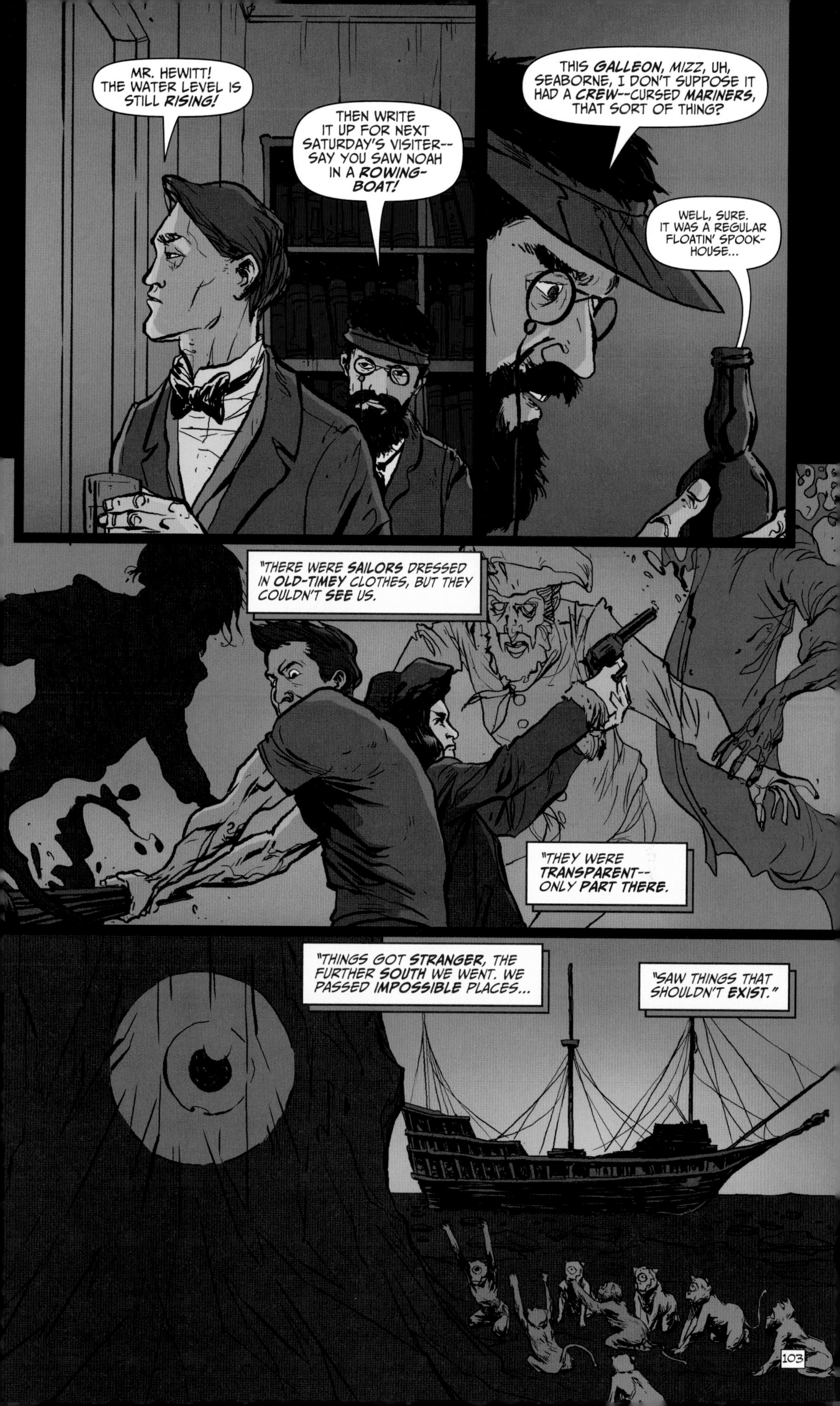
MR. HEWITT! THE WATER LEVEL IS STILL RISING!
THEN WRITE IT UP FOR NEXT SATURDAY'S VISITER-- SAY YOU SAW NOAH IN A ROWING-BOAT!
THIS GALLEON, MIZZ, UH, SEABORNE, I DON'T SUPPOSE IT HAD A CREW--CURSED MARINERS, THAT SORT OF THING?
WELL, SURE. IT WAS A REGULAR FLOATIN' SPOOK-HOUSE...
"THERE WERE SAILORS DRESSED IN OLD-TIMEY CLOTHES, BUT THEY COULDN'T SEE US.
"THEY WERE TRANSPARENT-- ONLY PART THERE.
"THINGS GOT STRANGER, THE FURTHER SOUTH WE WENT. WE PASSED IMPOSSIBLE PLACES...
"SAW THINGS THAT SHOULDN'T EXIST."

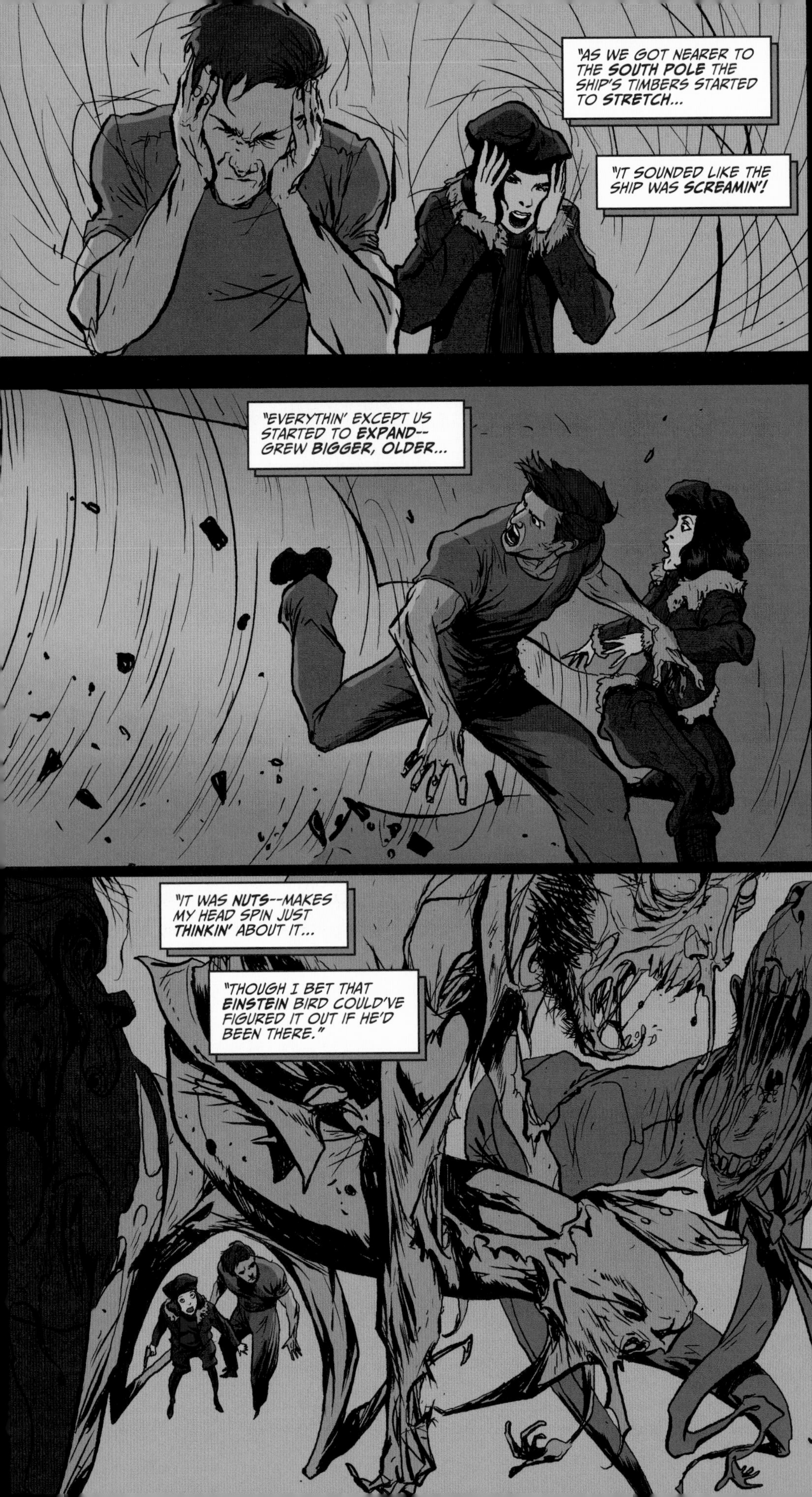
"AS WE GOT NEARER TO THE SOUTH POLE THE SHIP'S TIMBERS STARTED TO STRETCH...
"IT SOUNDED LIKE THE SHIP WAS SCREAMIN'!
"EVERYTHIN' EXCEPT US STARTED TO EXPAND-- GREW BIGGER, OLDER...
"IT WAS NUTS--MAKES MY HEAD SPIN JUST THINKIN' ABOUT IT...
"THOUGH I BET THAT EINSTEIN BIRD COULD'VE FIGURED IT OUT IF HE'D BEEN THERE."

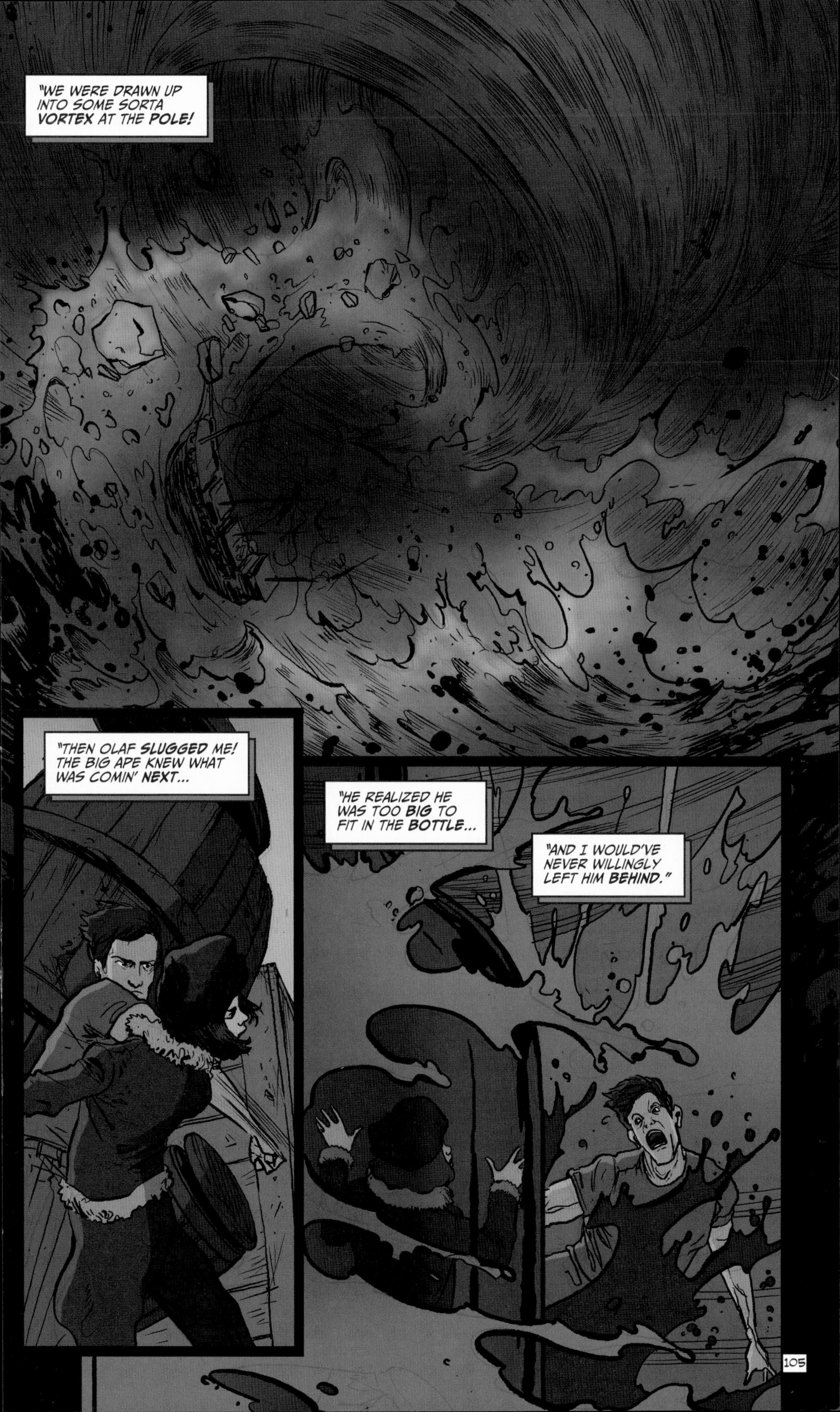
"WE WERE DRAWN UP INTO SOME SORTA VORTEX AT THE POLE!
"THEN OLAF SLUGGED ME! THE BIG APE KNEW WHAT WAS COMIN' NEXT...
"HE REALIZED HE WAS TOO BIG TO FIT IN THE BOTTLE...
"AND I WOULD'VE NEVER WILLINGLY LEFT HIM BEHIND."

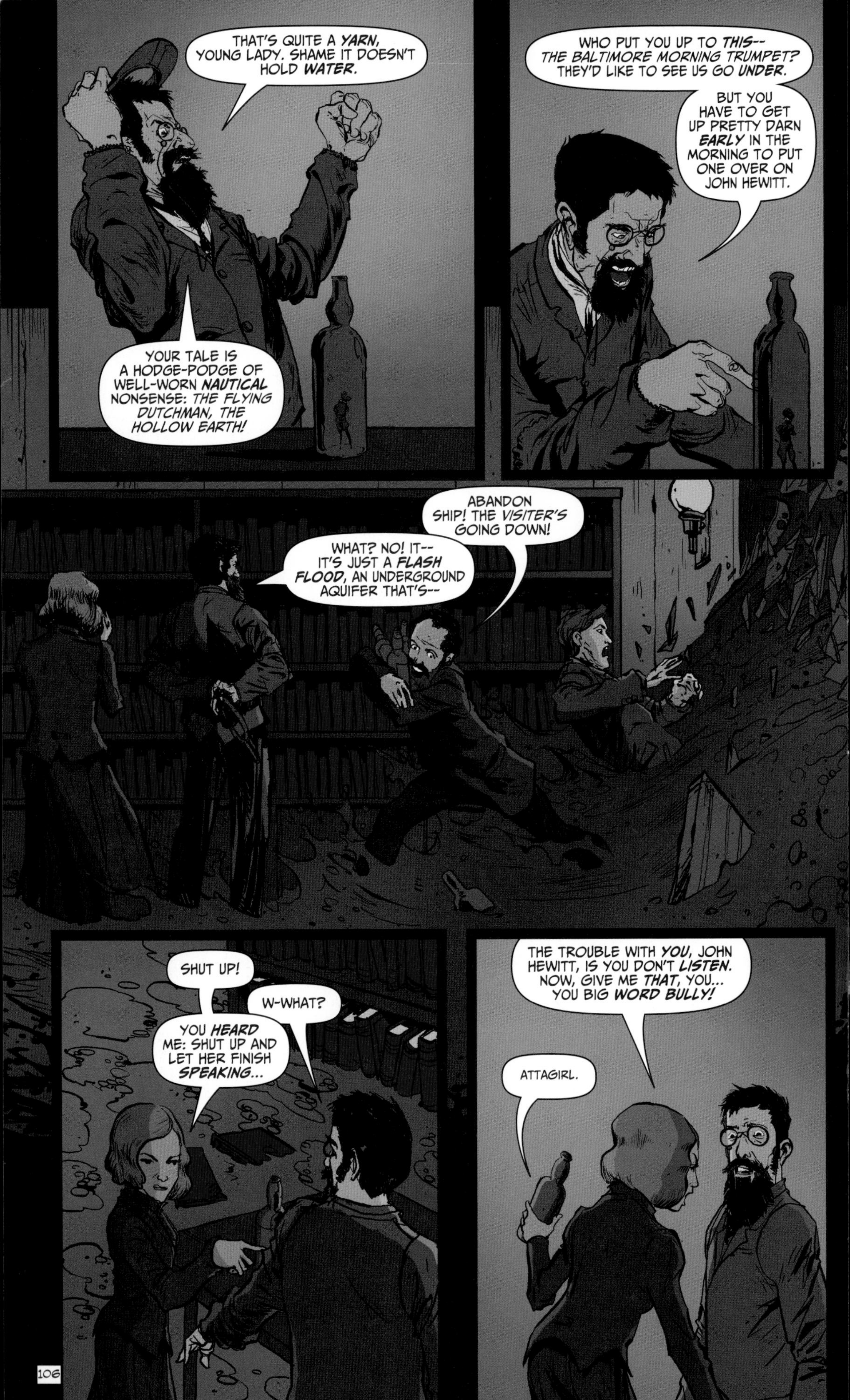
THAT'S QUITE A YARN, YOUNG LADY. SHAME IT DOESN'T HOLD WATER.
YOUR TALE IS A HODGE-PODGE OF WELL-WORN NAUTICAL NONSENSE: THE FLYING DUTCHMAN, THE HOLLOW EARTH!
WHO PUT YOU UP TO THIS-- THE BALTIMORE MORNING TRUMPET? THEY'D LIKE TO SEE US GO UNDER.
BUT YOU HAVE TO GET UP PRETTY DARN EARLY IN THE MORNING TO PUT ONE OVER ON JOHN HEWITT.
WHAT? NO! IT-- IT'S JUST A FLASH FLOOD, AN UNDERGROUND AQUIFER THAT'S--
ABANDON SHIP! THE VISITER'S GOING DOWN!
SHUT UP!
W-WHAT?
YOU HEARD ME: SHUT UP AND LET HER FINISH SPEAKING...
THE TROUBLE WITH YOU, JOHN HEWITT, IS YOU DON'T LISTEN. NOW, GIVE ME THAT, YOU... YOU BIG WORD BULLY!
ATTAGIRL.

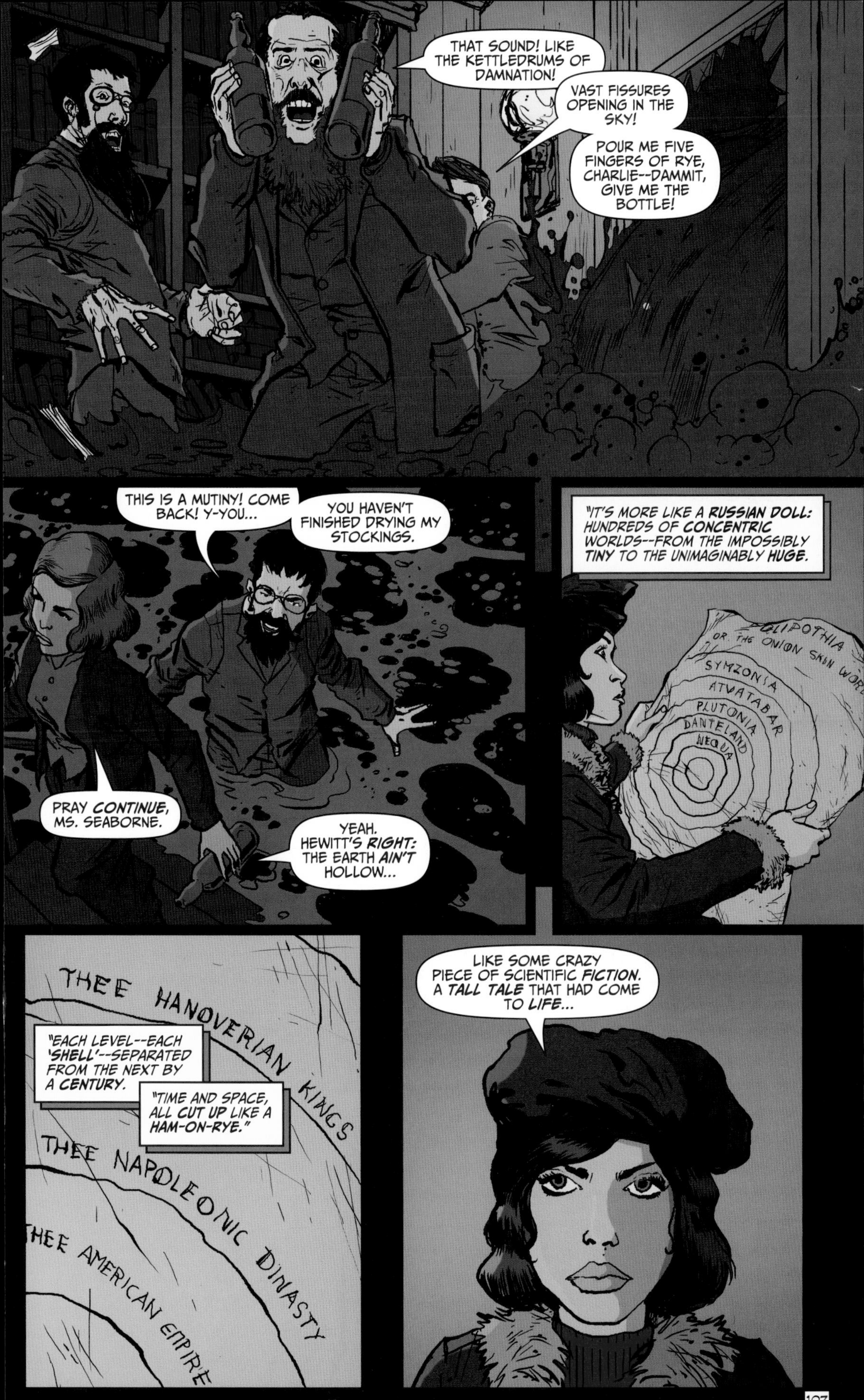

THAT SOUND! LIKE THE KETTLEDRUMS OF DAMNATION!
VAST FISSURES OPENING IN THE SKY!
POUR ME FIVE FINGERS OF RYE, CHARLIE--DAMMIT, GIVE ME THE BOTTLE!
THIS IS A MUTINY! COME BACK! Y-YOU...
YOU HAVEN'T FINISHED DRYING MY STOCKINGS.
PRAY ***CONTINUE***, MS. SEABORNE.
YEAH. HEWITT'S ***RIGHT:*** THE EARTH ***AIN'T*** HOLLOW...
"IT'S MORE LIKE A ***RUSSIAN DOLL:*** HUNDREDS OF ***CONCENTRIC*** WORLDS--FROM THE IMPOSSIBLY ***TINY*** TO THE UNIMAGINABLY ***HUGE***.
OR THE ONION SKIN
SYMZONIA
ATVATABAR
PLUTONIA
DANTELAND
NEQUA
THEE HANOVERIAN KINGS
"EACH LEVEL--EACH '***SHELL***'--SEPARATED FROM THE NEXT BY A ***CENTURY***.
"TIME AND SPACE, ALL ***CUT UP*** LIKE A ***HAM-ON-RYE***."
THEE NAPOLEONIC DINASTY
THEE AMERICAN EMPIRE
LIKE SOME CRAZY PIECE OF SCIENTIFIC ***FICTION***. A ***TALL TALE*** THAT HAD COME TO ***LIFE***...

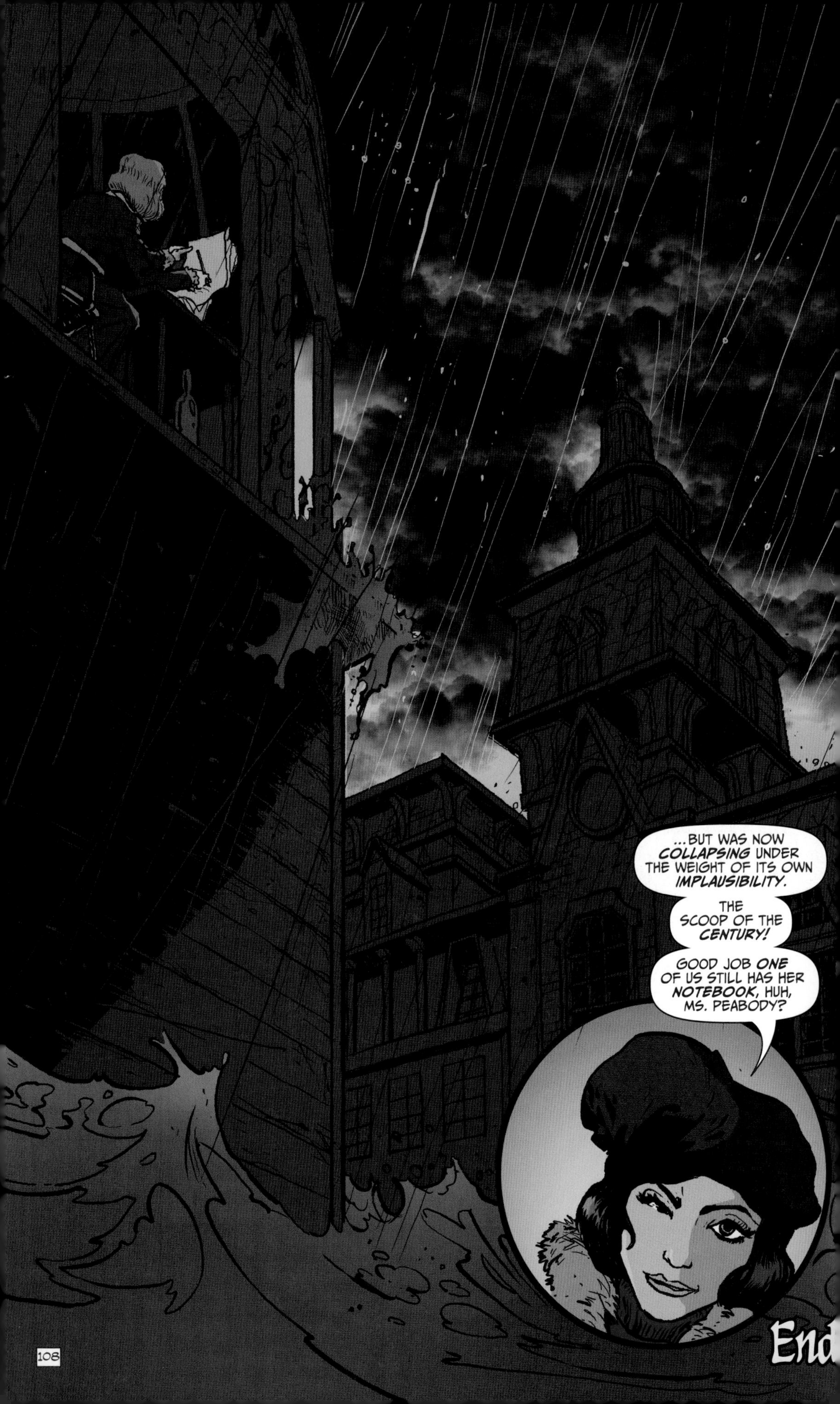
...BUT WAS NOW COLLAPSING UNDER THE WEIGHT OF ITS OWN IMPLAUSIBILITY.
THE SCOOP OF THE CENTURY!
GOOD JOB ONE OF US STILL HAS HER NOTEBOOK, HUH, MS. PEABODY?
End

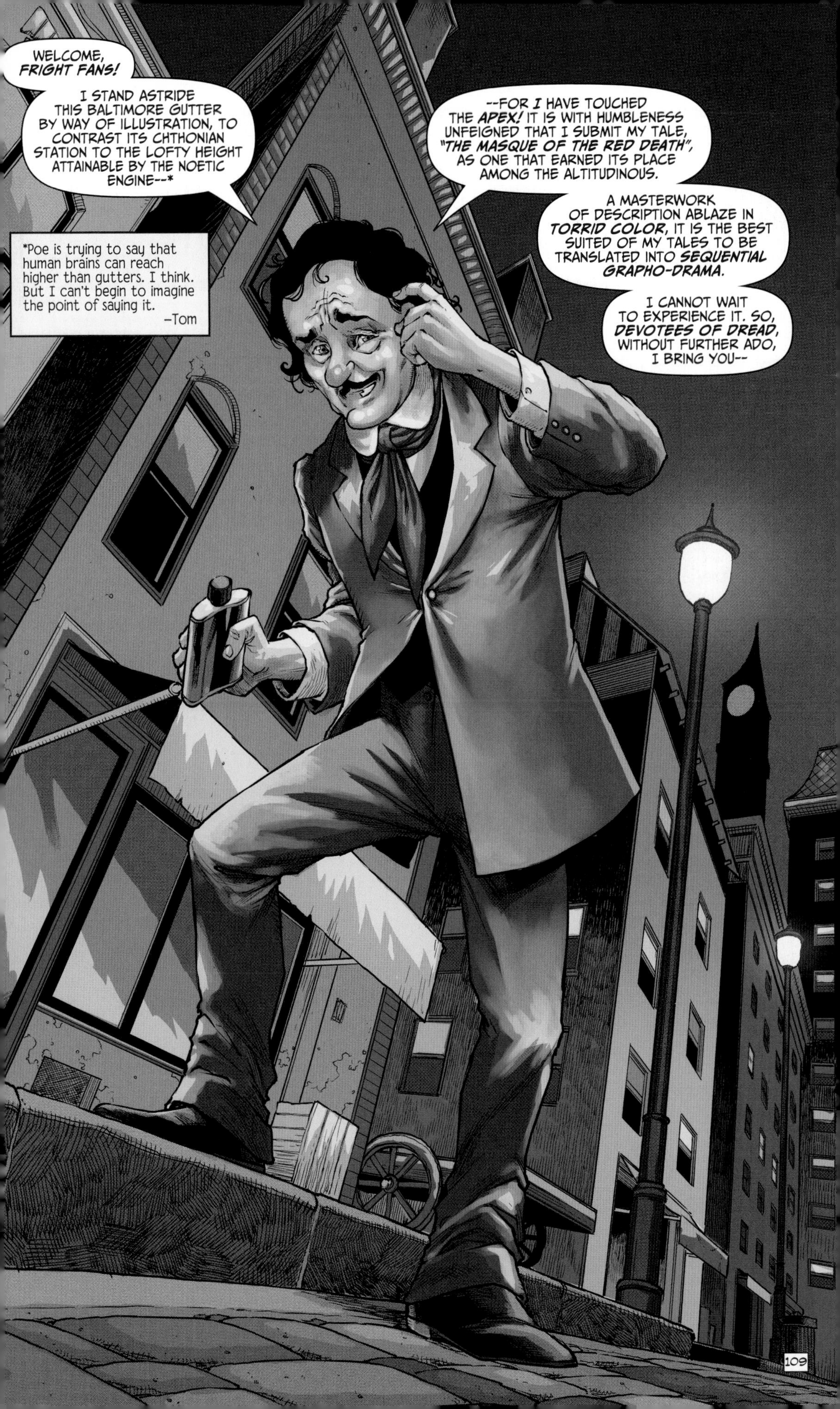
WELCOME, FRIGHT FANS!
I STAND ASTRIDE THIS BALTIMORE GUTTER BY WAY OF ILLUSTRATION, TO CONTRAST ITS CHTHONIAN STATION TO THE LOFTY HEIGHT ATTAINABLE BY THE NOETIC ENGINE--*
*Poe is trying to say that human brains can reach higher than gutters. I think. But I can't begin to imagine the point of saying it. –Tom
--FOR I HAVE TOUCHED THE APEX! IT IS WITH HUMBLENESS UNFEIGNED THAT I SUBMIT MY TALE, "THE MASQUE OF THE RED DEATH", AS ONE THAT EARNED ITS PLACE AMONG THE ALTITUDINOUS.
A MASTERWORK OF DESCRIPTION ABLAZE IN TORRID COLOR, IT IS THE BEST SUITED OF MY TALES TO BE TRANSLATED INTO SEQUENTIAL GRAPHO-DRAMA.
I CANNOT WAIT TO EXPERIENCE IT. SO, DEVOTEES OF DREAD, WITHOUT FURTHER ADO, I BRING YOU--

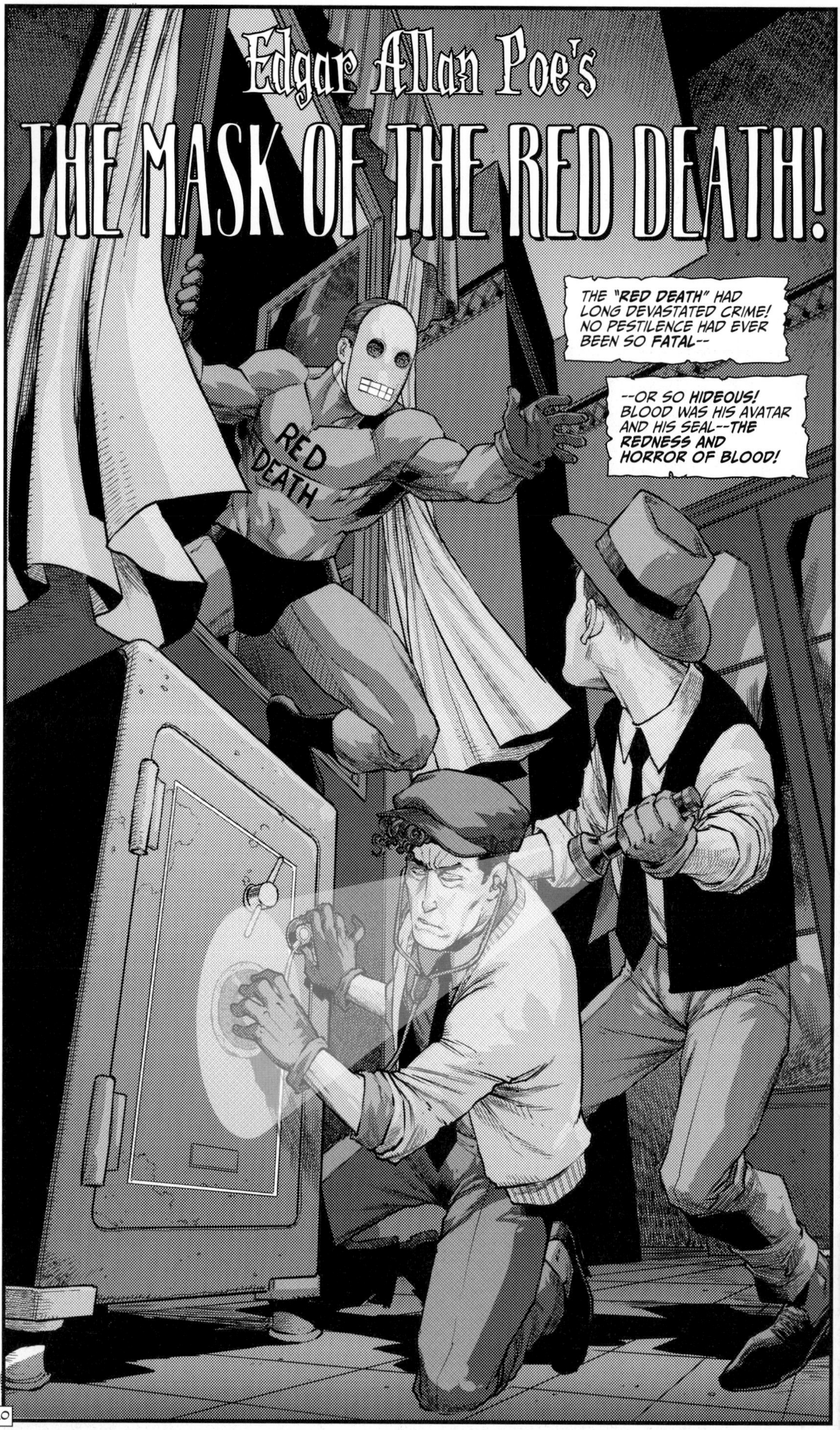
Edgar Allan Poe's
THE MASK OF THE RED DEATH!
THE "RED DEATH" HAD LONG DEVASTATED CRIME! NO PESTILENCE HAD EVER BEEN SO FATAL--
--OR SO HIDEOUS! BLOOD WAS HIS AVATAR AND HIS SEAL--THE REDNESS AND HORROR OF BLOOD!
RED DEATH

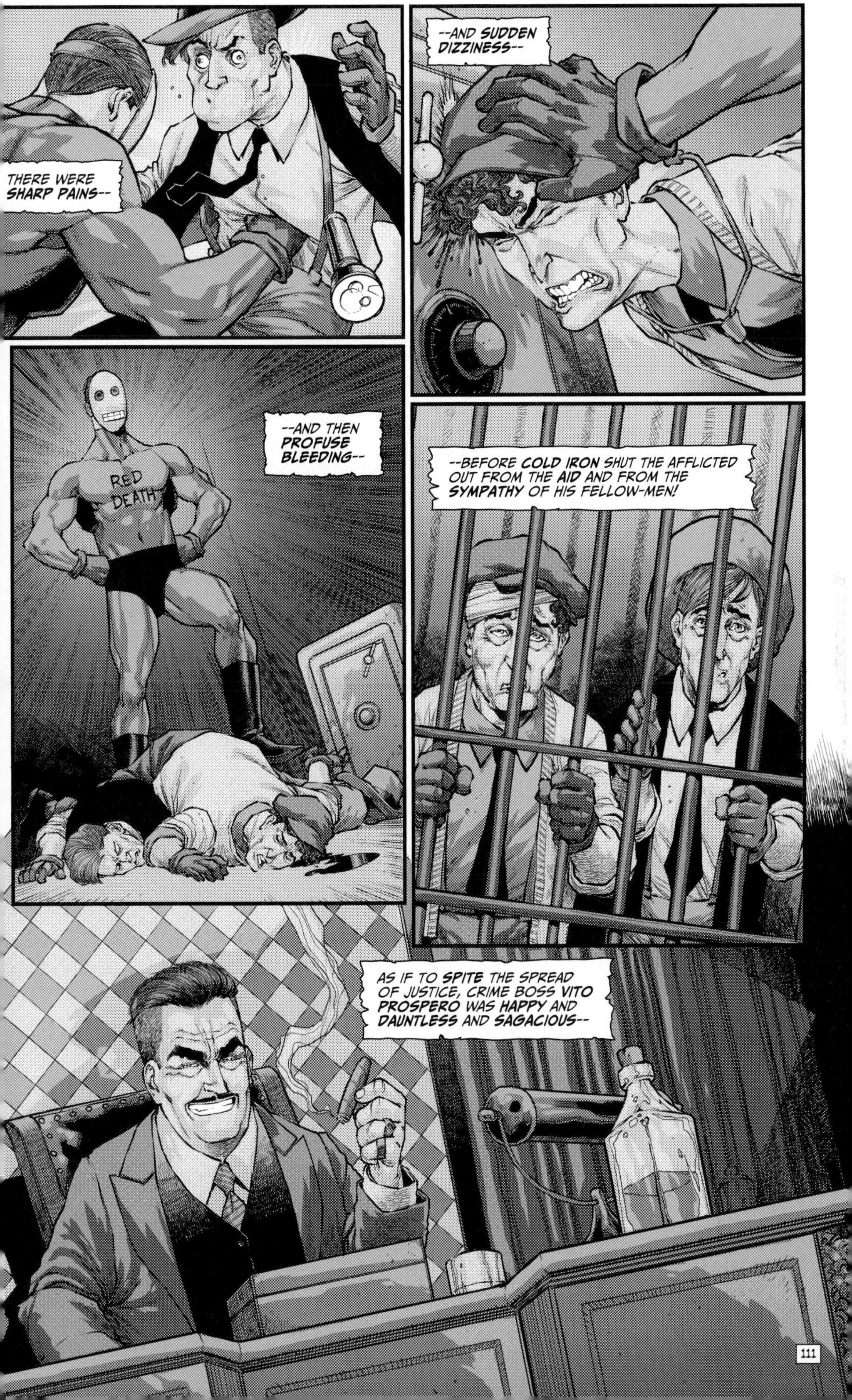
THERE WERE SHARP PAINS--
--AND SUDDEN DIZZINESS--
--AND THEN PROFUSE BLEEDING--
RED DEATH
--BEFORE COLD IRON SHUT THE AFFLICTED OUT FROM THE AID AND FROM THE SYMPATHY OF HIS FELLOW-MEN!
AS IF TO SPITE THE SPREAD OF JUSTICE, CRIME BOSS VITO PROSPERO WAS HAPPY AND DAUNTLESS AND SAGACIOUS--

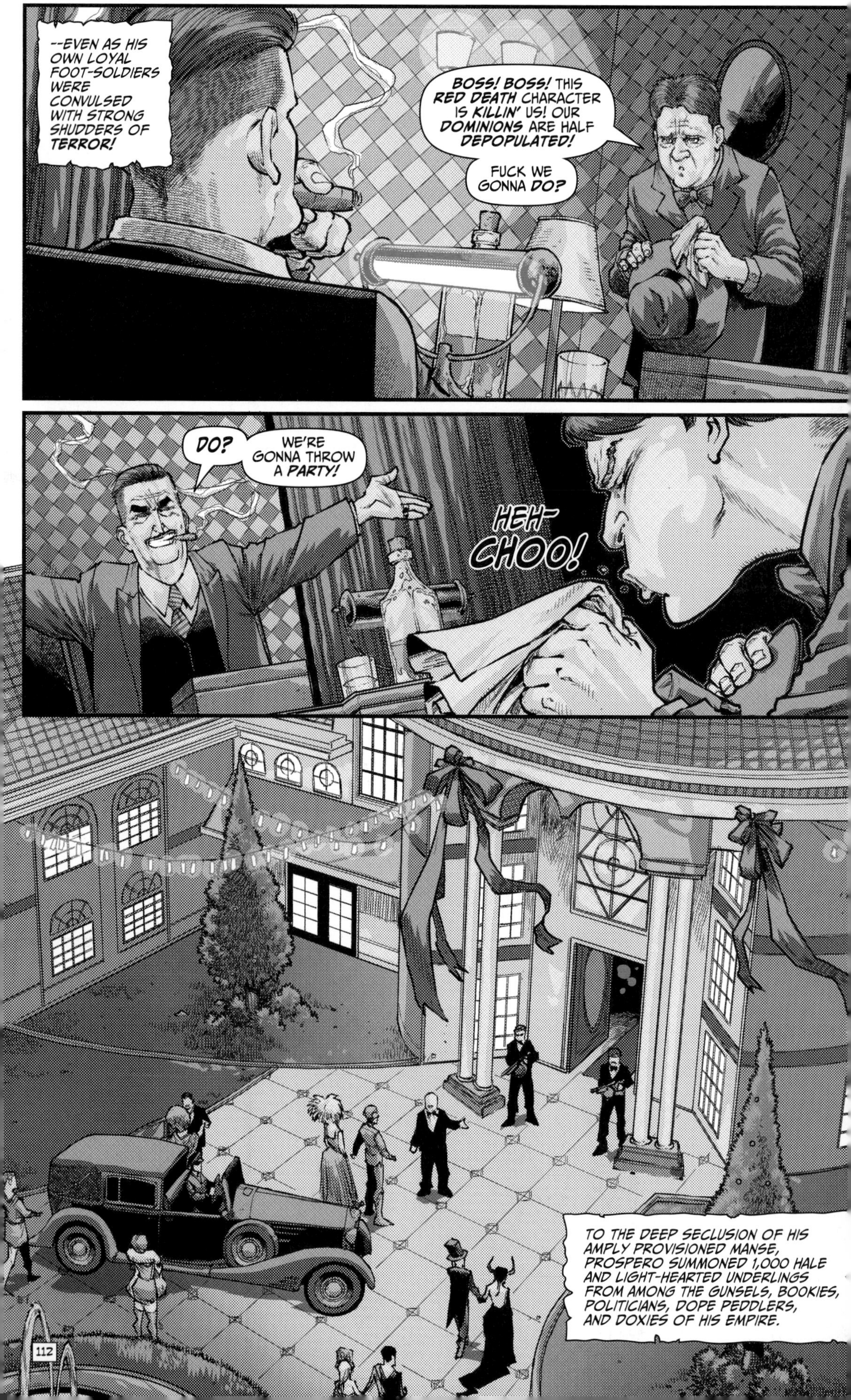
--EVEN AS HIS OWN LOYAL FOOT-SOLDIERS WERE CONVULSED WITH STRONG SHUDDERS OF TERROR!
BOSS! BOSS! THIS RED DEATH CHARACTER IS KILLIN' US! OUR DOMINIONS ARE HALF DEPOPULATED!
FUCK WE GONNA DO?
DO?
WE'RE GONNA THROW A PARTY!
HEH-CHOO!
TO THE DEEP SECLUSION OF HIS AMPLY PROVISIONED MANSE, PROSPERO SUMMONED 1,000 HALE AND LIGHT-HEARTED UNDERLINGS FROM AMONG THE GUNSELS, BOOKIES, POLITICIANS, DOPE PEDDLERS, AND DOXIES OF HIS EMPIRE.

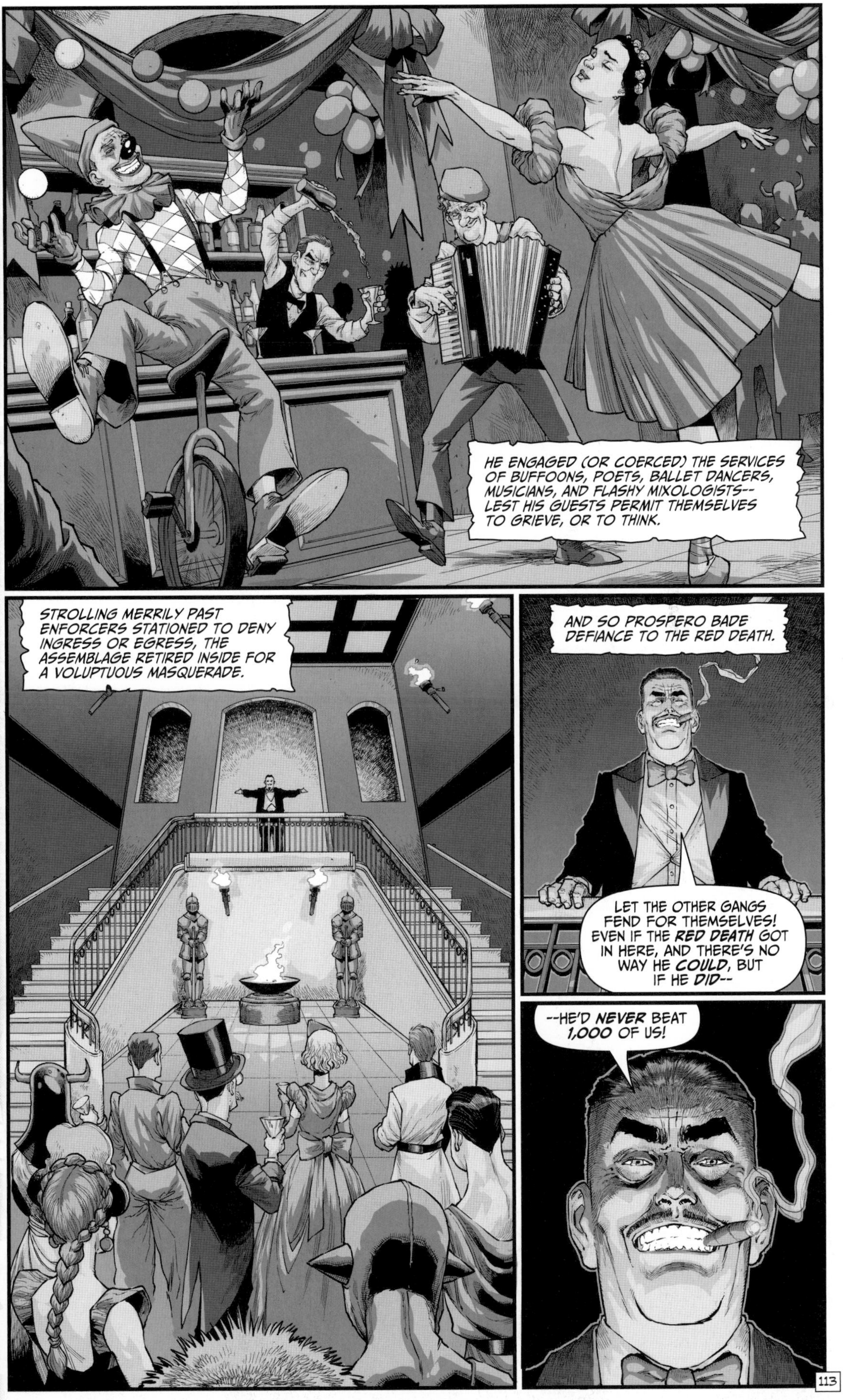
HE ENGAGED (OR COERCED) THE SERVICES OF BUFFOONS, POETS, BALLET DANCERS, MUSICIANS, AND FLASHY MIXOLOGISTS-- LEST HIS GUESTS PERMIT THEMSELVES TO GRIEVE, OR TO THINK.
STROLLING MERRILY PAST ENFORCERS STATIONED TO DENY INGRESS OR EGRESS, THE ASSEMBLAGE RETIRED INSIDE FOR A VOLUPTUOUS MASQUERADE.
AND SO PROSPERO BADE DEFIANCE TO THE RED DEATH.
LET THE OTHER GANGS FEND FOR THEMSELVES! EVEN IF THE RED DEATH GOT IN HERE, AND THERE'S NO WAY HE COULD, BUT IF HE DID--
--HE'D NEVER BEAT 1,000 OF US!

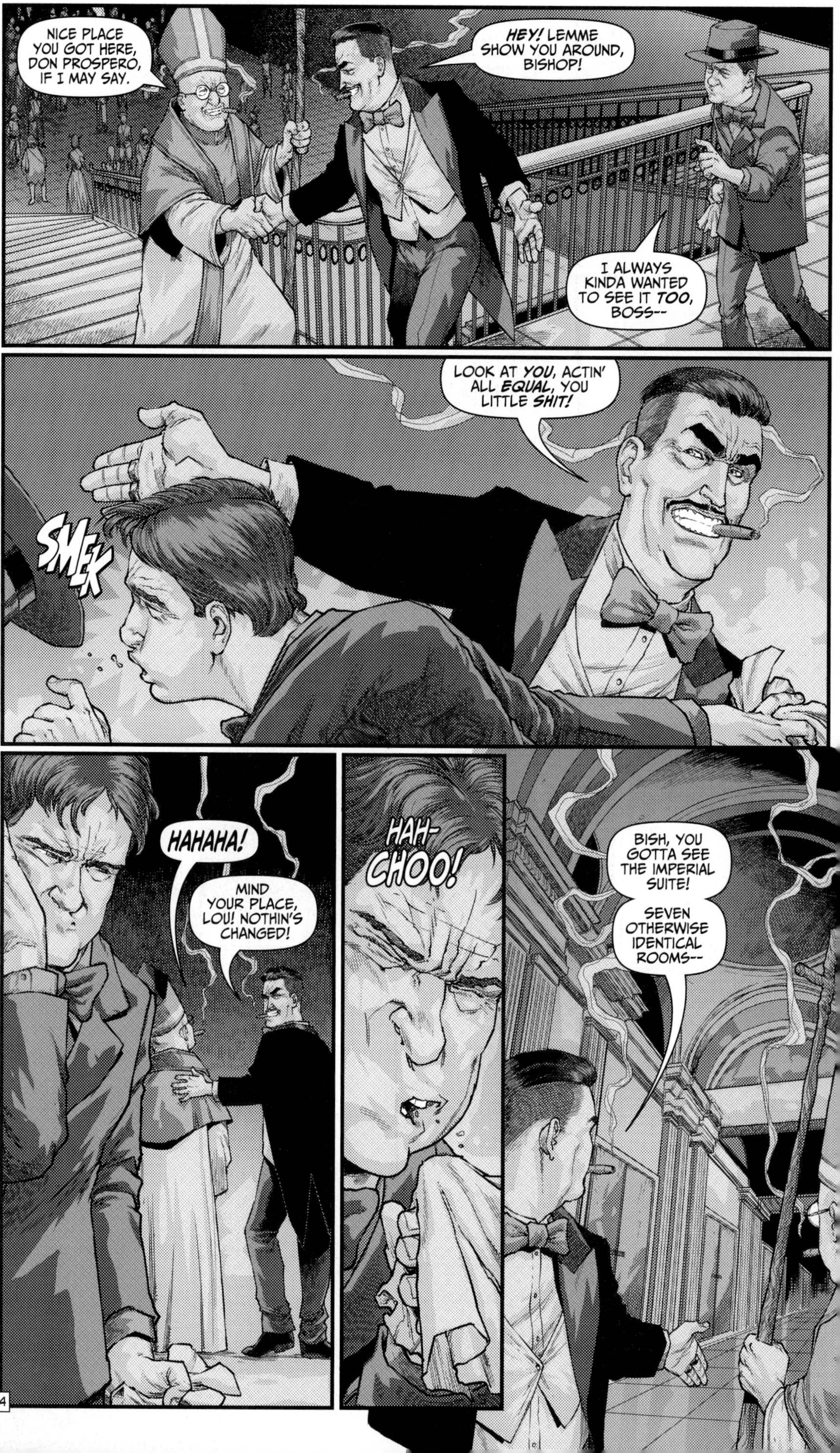
NICE PLACE YOU GOT HERE, DON PROSPERO, IF I MAY SAY.
HEY! LEMME SHOW YOU AROUND, BISHOP!
I ALWAYS KINDA WANTED TO SEE IT TOO, BOSS--
LOOK AT YOU, ACTIN' ALL EQUAL, YOU LITTLE SHIT!
SMEK
HAHAHA!
MIND YOUR PLACE, LOU! NOTHIN'S CHANGED!
HAH-CHOO!
BISH, YOU GOTTA SEE THE IMPERIAL SUITE!
SEVEN OTHERWISE IDENTICAL ROOMS--

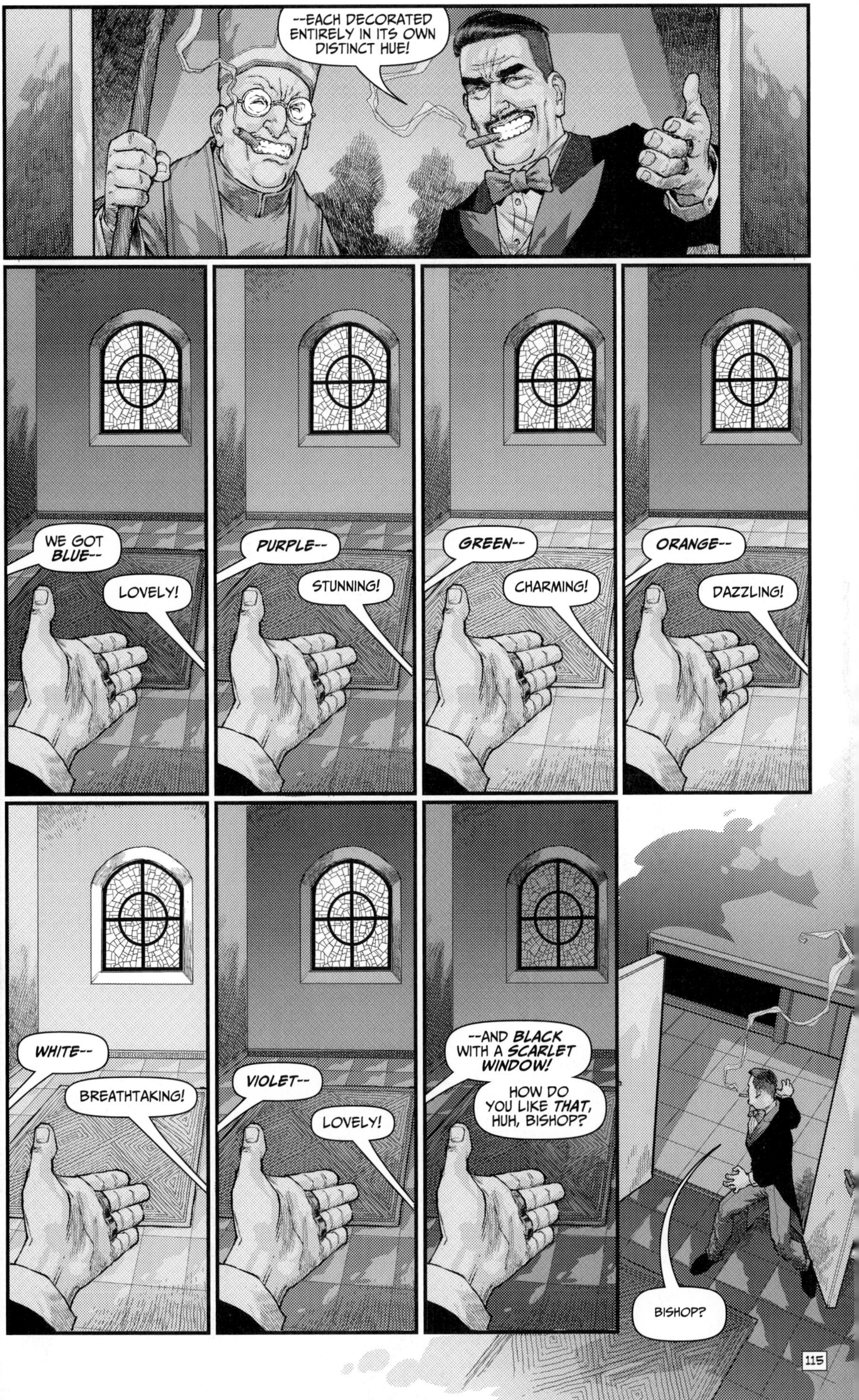
--EACH DECORATED ENTIRELY IN ITS OWN DISTINCT HUE!
WE GOT BLUE--
LOVELY!
PURPLE--
STUNNING!
GREEN--
CHARMING!
ORANGE--
DAZZLING!
WHITE--
BREATHTAKING!
VIOLET--
LOVELY!
--AND BLACK WITH A SCARLET WINDOW!
HOW DO YOU LIKE THAT, HUH, BISHOP?
BISHOP?

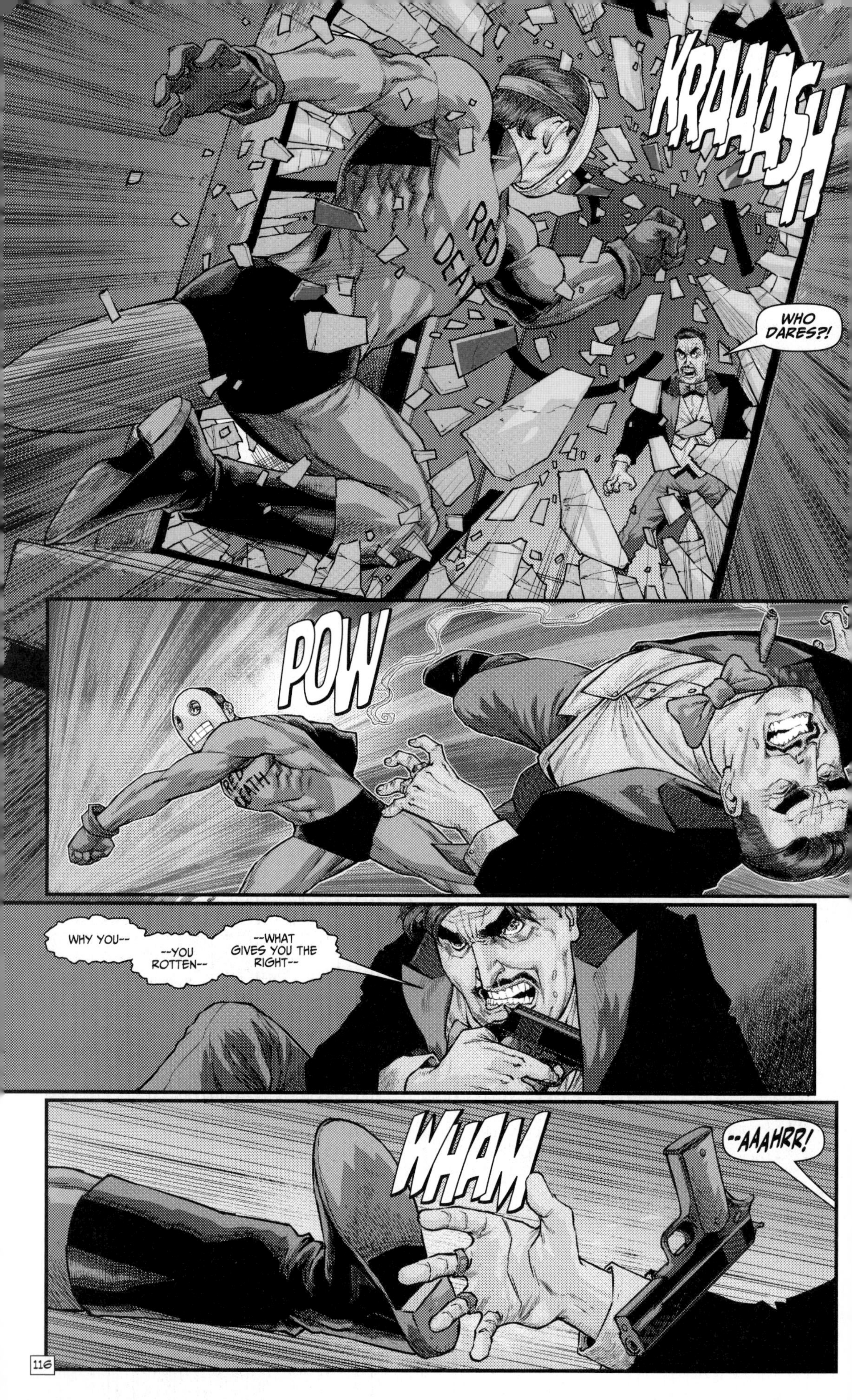
KRAAASH
WHO DARES?!
POW
RED DEATH
WHY YOU--
--YOU ROTTEN--
--WHAT GIVES YOU THE RIGHT--
WHAM
--AAAHRR!

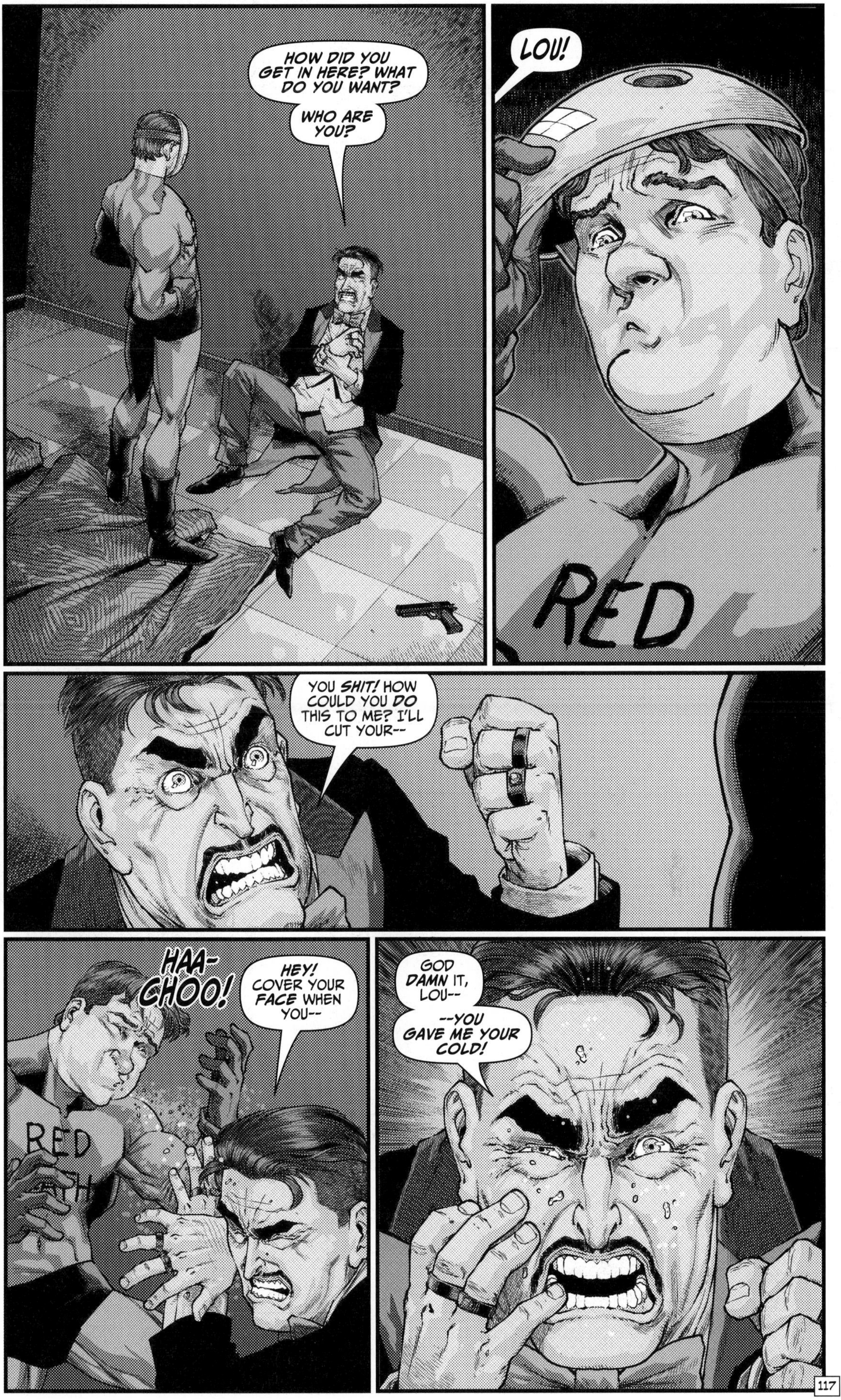
HOW DID YOU GET IN HERE? WHAT DO YOU WANT?
WHO ARE YOU?
LOU!
RED
YOU SHIT! HOW COULD YOU DO THIS TO ME? I'LL CUT YOUR--
HAA-CHOO!
HEY! COVER YOUR FACE WHEN YOU--
RED
GOD DAMN IT, LOU--
--YOU GAVE ME YOUR COLD!

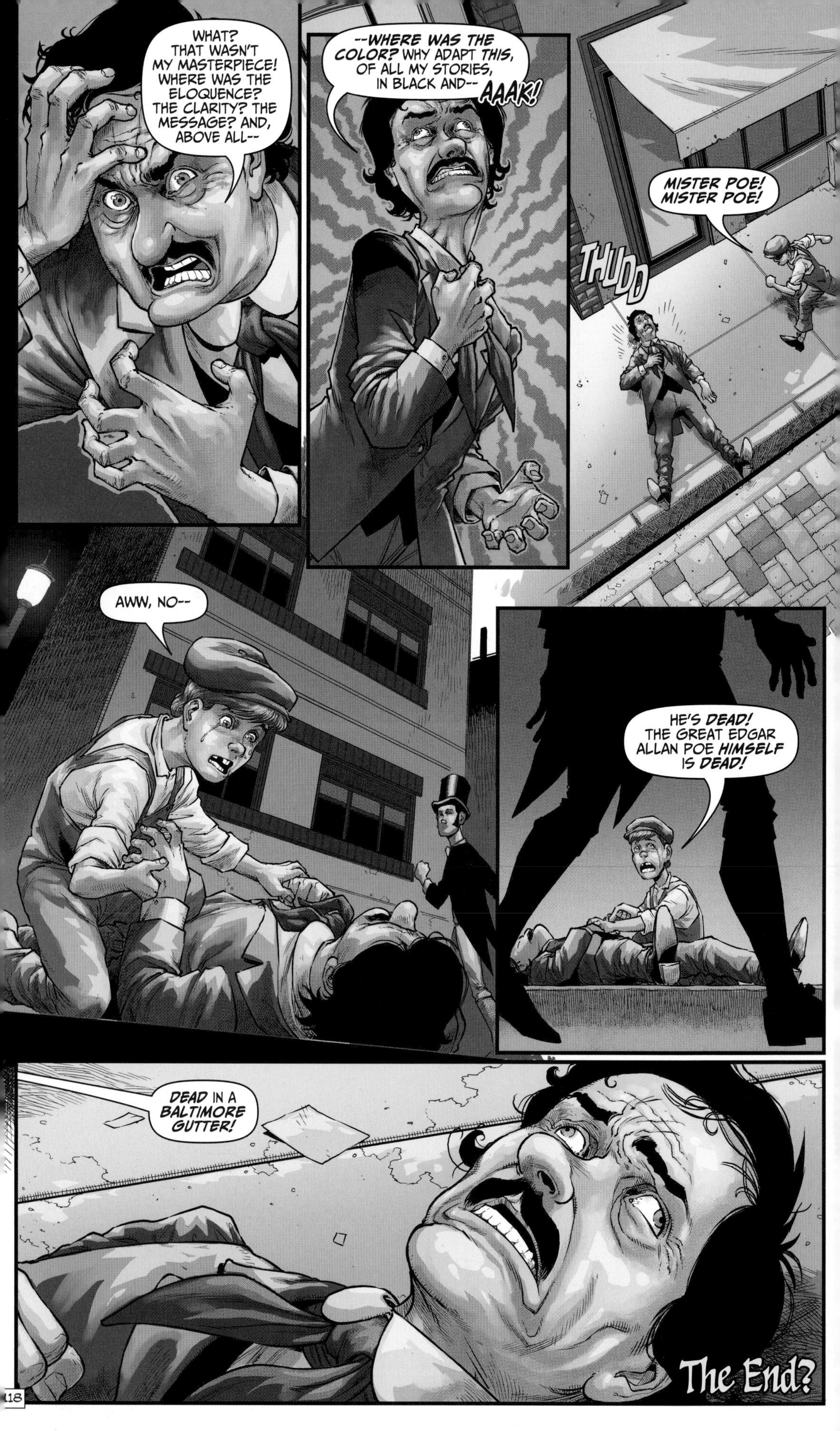
WHAT? THAT WASN'T MY MASTERPIECE! WHERE WAS THE ELOQUENCE? THE CLARITY? THE MESSAGE? AND, ABOVE ALL--
--WHERE WAS THE COLOR? WHY ADAPT THIS, OF ALL MY STORIES, IN BLACK AND-- AAAK!
MISTER POE! MISTER POE!
THUDD
AWW, NO--
HE'S DEAD! THE GREAT EDGAR ALLAN POE HIMSELF IS DEAD!
DEAD IN A BALTIMORE GUTTER!
The End?

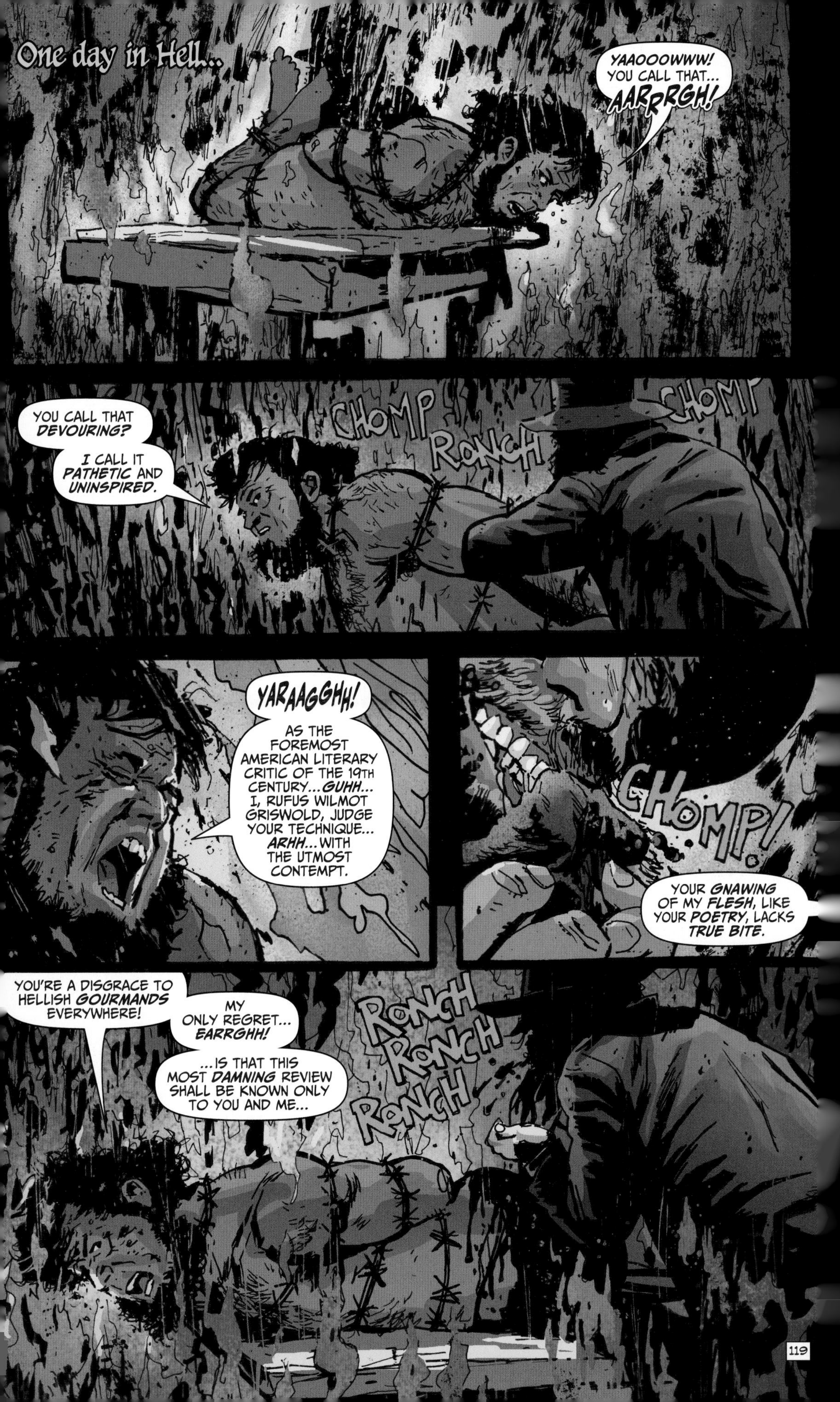

One day in Hell...
YAAOOOWWW! YOU CALL THAT... AARRRGH!
YOU CALL THAT DEVOURING?
I CALL IT PATHETIC AND UNINSPIRED.
CHOMP
RONCH
CHOMP
YARAAGGHH!
AS THE FOREMOST AMERICAN LITERARY CRITIC OF THE 19TH CENTURY...GUHH... I, RUFUS WILMOT GRISWOLD, JUDGE YOUR TECHNIQUE... ARHH...WITH THE UTMOST CONTEMPT.
CHOMP!
YOUR GNAWING OF MY FLESH, LIKE YOUR POETRY, LACKS TRUE BITE.
YOU'RE A DISGRACE TO HELLISH GOURMANDS EVERYWHERE!
MY ONLY REGRET... EARRGHH!
...IS THAT THIS MOST DAMNING REVIEW SHALL BE KNOWN ONLY TO YOU AND ME...
RONCH
RONCH
RONCH

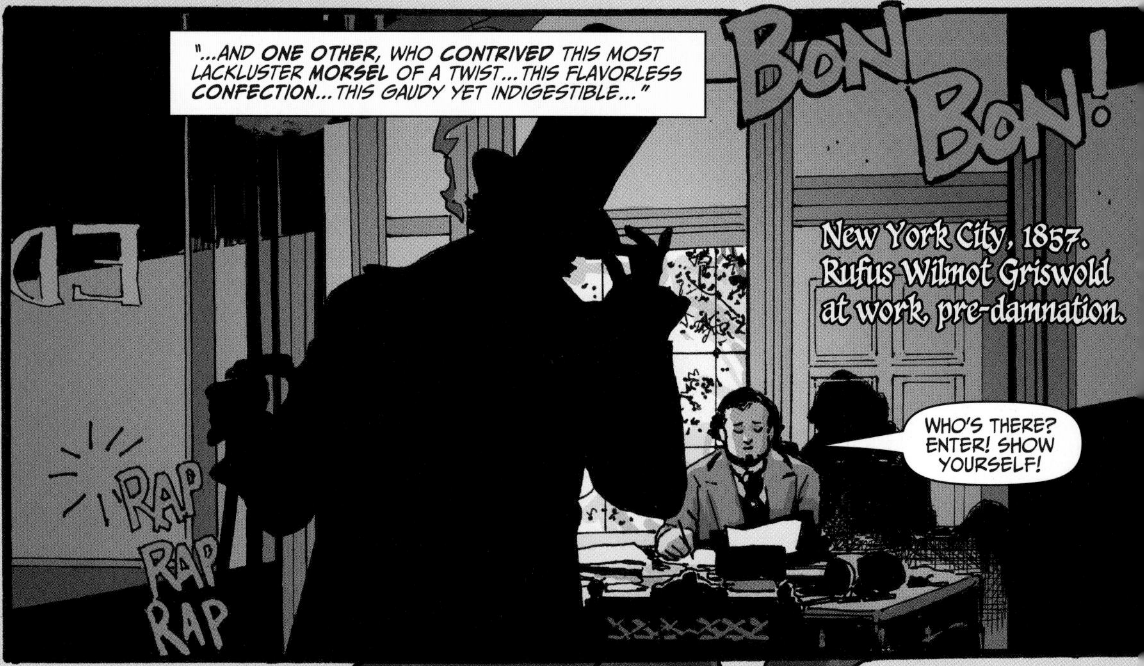
"...AND **ONE OTHER**, WHO **CONTRIVED** THIS MOST LACKLUSTER **MORSEL** OF A TWIST... THIS FLAVORLESS **CONFECTION**... THIS GAUDY YET INDIGESTIBLE..."
BON BON!
New York City, 1857. Rufus Wilmot Griswold at work, pre-damnation.
RAP RAP RAP
WHO'S THERE? ENTER! SHOW YOURSELF!

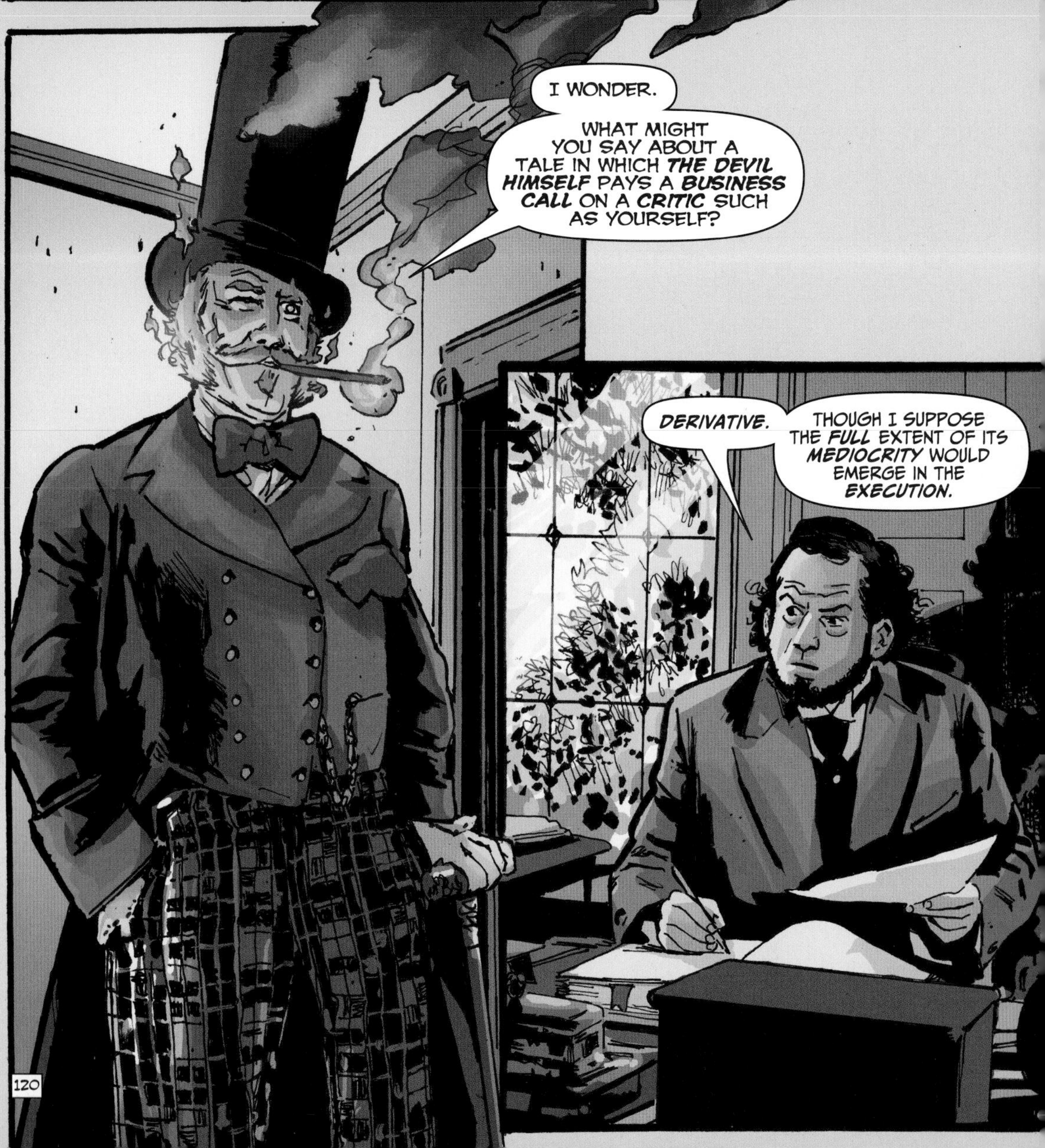
I WONDER.
WHAT MIGHT YOU SAY ABOUT A TALE IN WHICH **THE DEVIL HIMSELF** PAYS A **BUSINESS CALL** ON A **CRITIC** SUCH AS YOURSELF?
DERIVATIVE.
THOUGH I SUPPOSE THE ***FULL*** EXTENT OF ITS ***MEDIOCRITY*** WOULD EMERGE IN THE ***EXECUTION.***

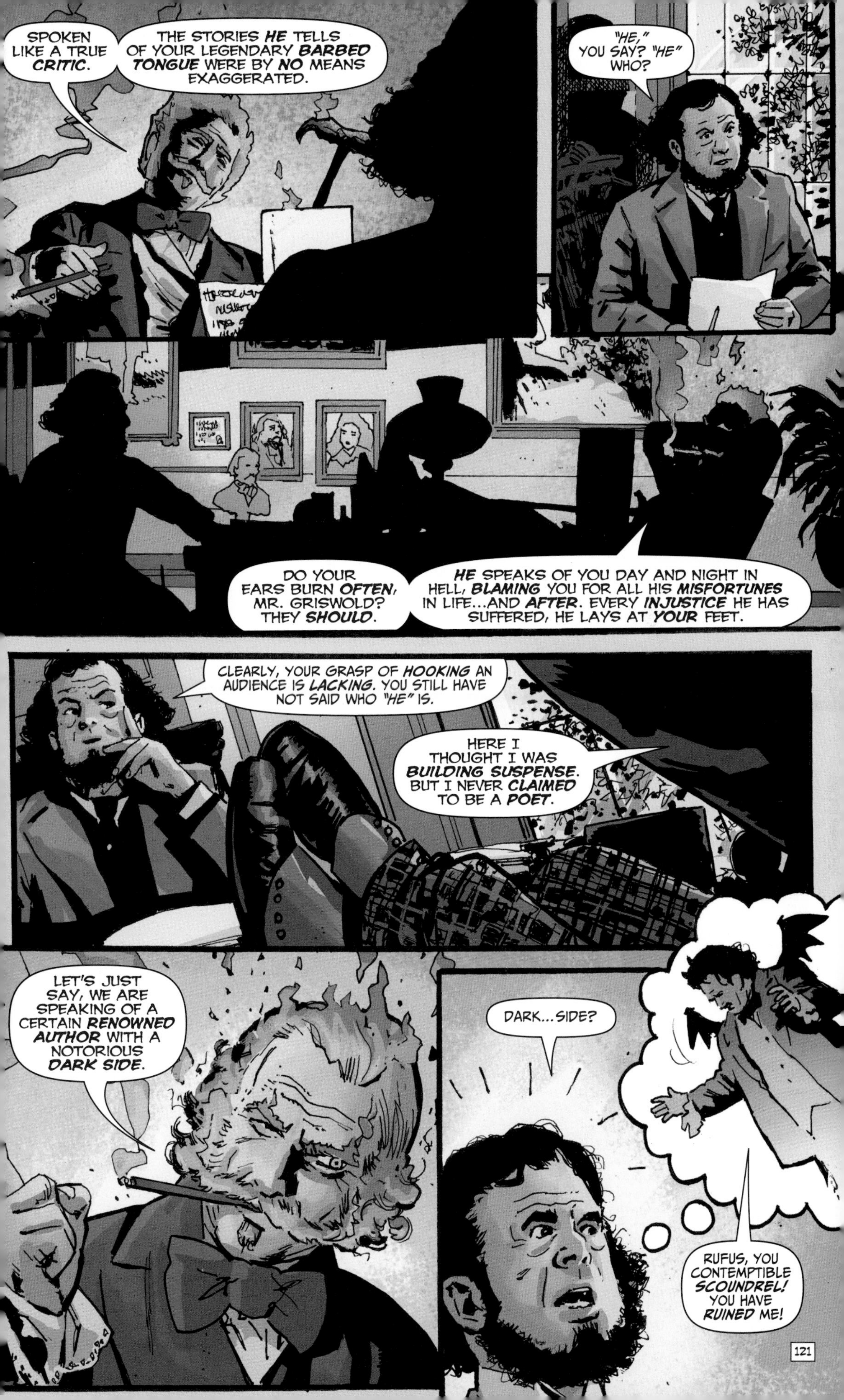
SPOKEN LIKE A TRUE CRITIC.
THE STORIES HE TELLS OF YOUR LEGENDARY BARBED TONGUE WERE BY NO MEANS EXAGGERATED.
"HE," YOU SAY? "HE" WHO?
DO YOUR EARS BURN OFTEN, MR. GRISWOLD? THEY SHOULD.
HE SPEAKS OF YOU DAY AND NIGHT IN HELL, BLAMING YOU FOR ALL HIS MISFORTUNES IN LIFE...AND AFTER. EVERY INJUSTICE HE HAS SUFFERED, HE LAYS AT YOUR FEET.
CLEARLY, YOUR GRASP OF HOOKING AN AUDIENCE IS LACKING. YOU STILL HAVE NOT SAID WHO "HE" IS.
HERE I THOUGHT I WAS BUILDING SUSPENSE. BUT I NEVER CLAIMED TO BE A POET.
LET'S JUST SAY, WE ARE SPEAKING OF A CERTAIN RENOWNED AUTHOR WITH A NOTORIOUS DARK SIDE.
DARK... SIDE?
RUFUS, YOU CONTEMPTIBLE SCOUNDREL! YOU HAVE RUINED ME!

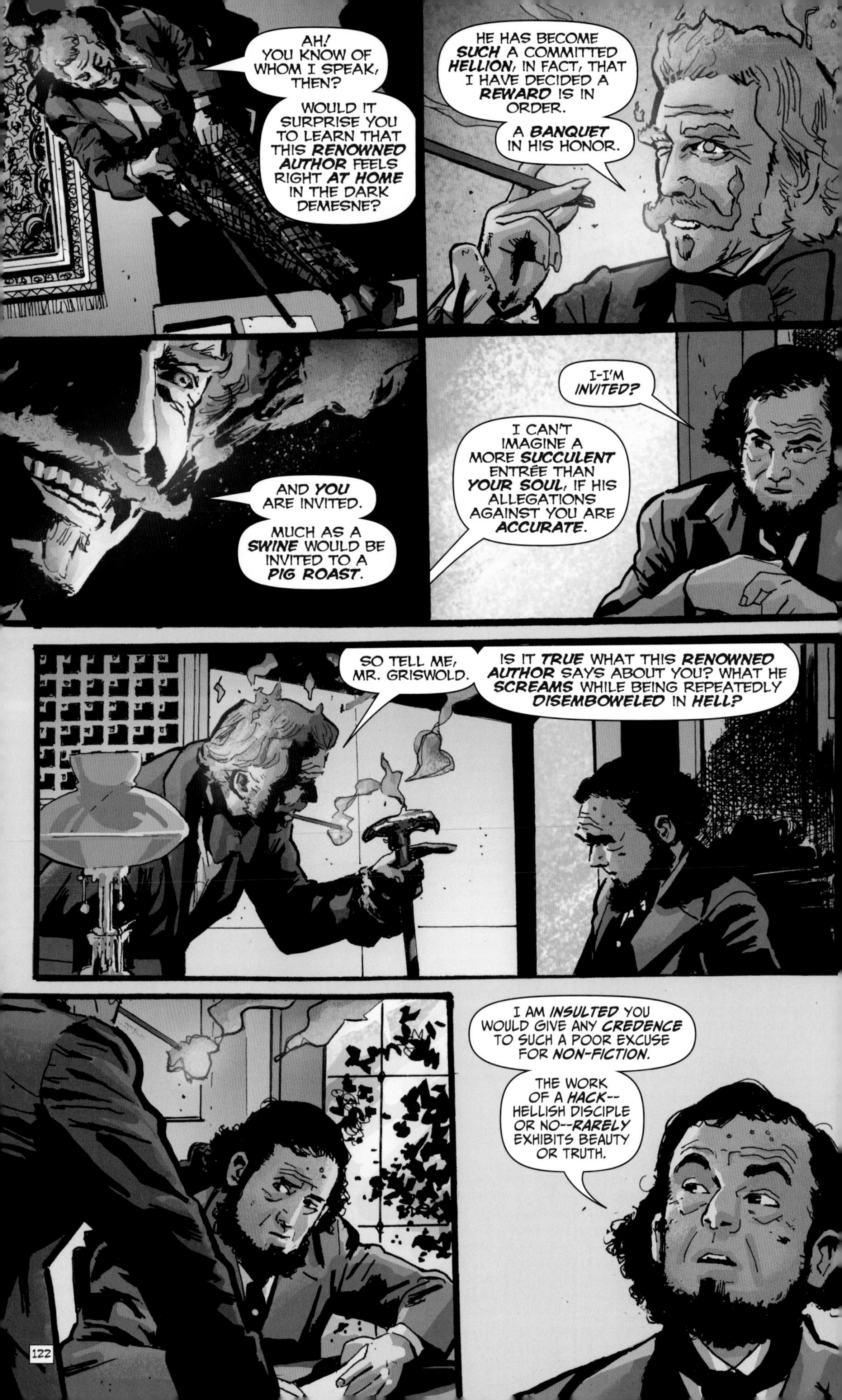
AH! YOU KNOW OF WHOM I SPEAK, THEN?
WOULD IT SURPRISE YOU TO LEARN THAT THIS RENOWNED AUTHOR FEELS RIGHT AT HOME IN THE DARK DEMESNE?
HE HAS BECOME SUCH A COMMITTED HELLION, IN FACT, THAT I HAVE DECIDED A REWARD IS IN ORDER.
A BANQUET IN HIS HONOR.
AND YOU ARE INVITED.
MUCH AS A SWINE WOULD BE INVITED TO A PIG ROAST.
I-I'M INVITED?
I CAN'T IMAGINE A MORE SUCCULENT ENTRÉE THAN YOUR SOUL, IF HIS ALLEGATIONS AGAINST YOU ARE ACCURATE.
SO TELL ME, MR. GRISWOLD.
IS IT TRUE WHAT THIS RENOWNED AUTHOR SAYS ABOUT YOU? WHAT HE SCREAMS WHILE BEING REPEATEDLY DISEMBOWELED IN HELL?
I AM INSULTED YOU WOULD GIVE ANY CREDENCE TO SUCH A POOR EXCUSE FOR NON-FICTION.
THE WORK OF A HACK--HELLISH DISCIPLE OR NO--RARELY EXHIBITS BEAUTY OR TRUTH.

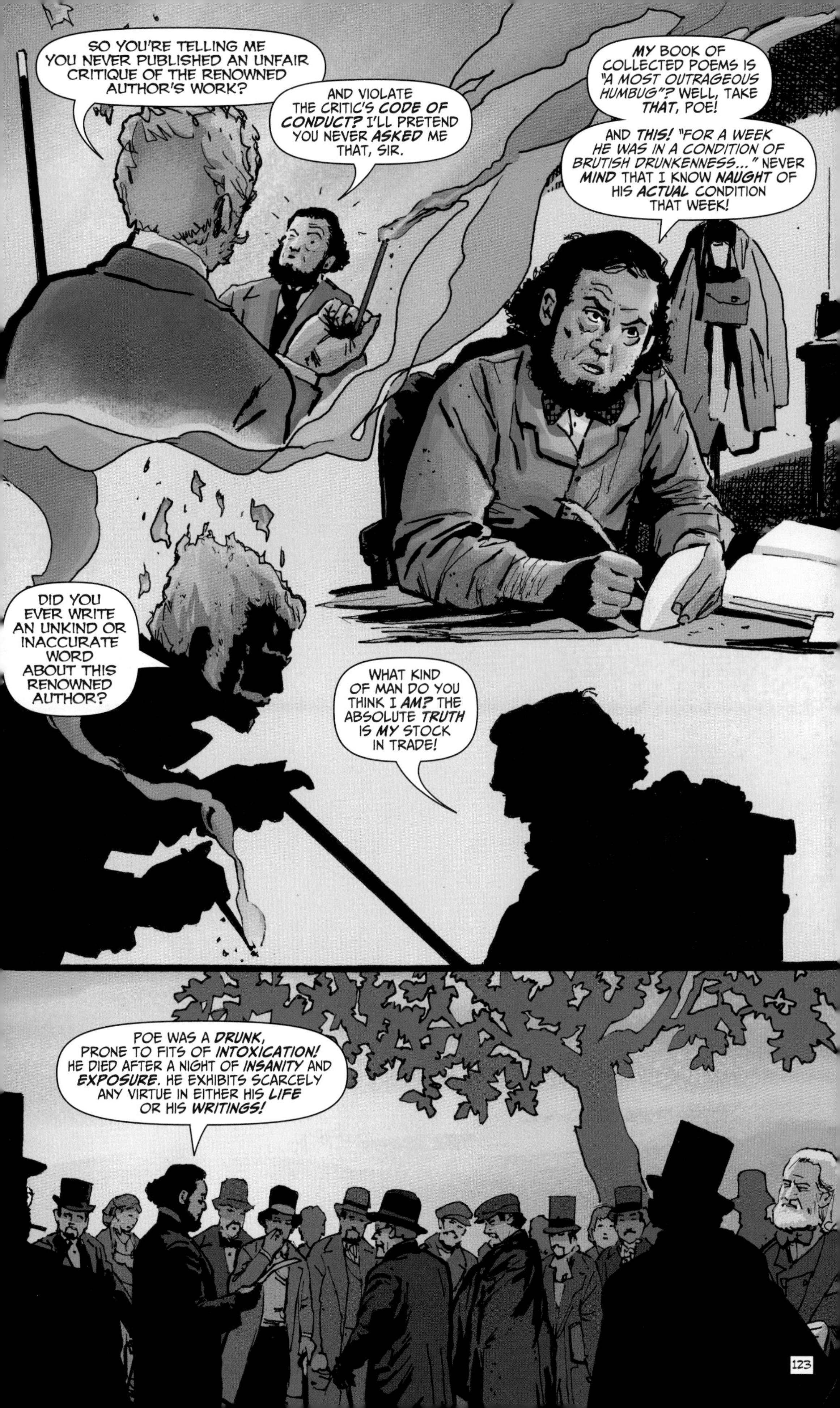
SO YOU'RE TELLING ME YOU NEVER PUBLISHED AN UNFAIR CRITIQUE OF THE RENOWNED AUTHOR'S WORK?
AND VIOLATE THE CRITIC'S CODE OF CONDUCT? I'LL PRETEND YOU NEVER ASKED ME THAT, SIR.
MY BOOK OF COLLECTED POEMS IS "A MOST OUTRAGEOUS HUMBUG"? WELL, TAKE THAT, POE!
AND THIS! "FOR A WEEK HE WAS IN A CONDITION OF BRUTISH DRUNKENNESS..." NEVER MIND THAT I KNOW NAUGHT OF HIS ACTUAL CONDITION THAT WEEK!
DID YOU EVER WRITE AN UNKIND OR INACCURATE WORD ABOUT THIS RENOWNED AUTHOR?
WHAT KIND OF MAN DO YOU THINK I AM? THE ABSOLUTE TRUTH IS MY STOCK IN TRADE!
POE WAS A DRUNK, PRONE TO FITS OF INTOXICATION! HE DIED AFTER A NIGHT OF INSANITY AND EXPOSURE. HE EXHIBITS SCARCELY ANY VIRTUE IN EITHER HIS LIFE OR HIS WRITINGS!

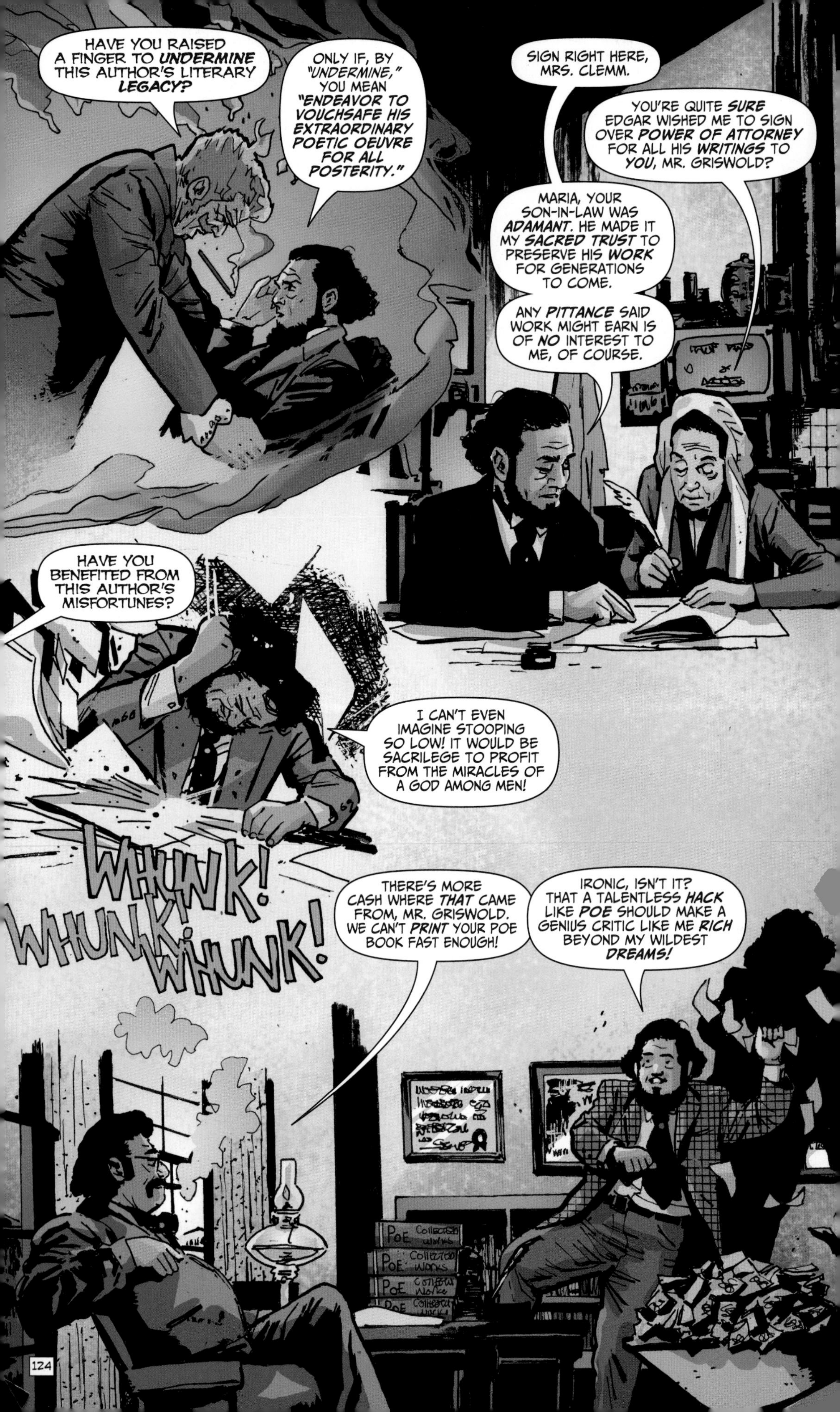
HAVE YOU RAISED A FINGER TO *UNDERMINE* THIS AUTHOR'S LITERARY *LEGACY?*
ONLY IF, BY *"UNDERMINE,"* YOU MEAN *"ENDEAVOR TO VOUCHSAFE HIS EXTRAORDINARY POETIC OEUVRE FOR ALL POSTERITY."*
SIGN RIGHT HERE, MRS. CLEMM.
YOU'RE QUITE *SURE* EDGAR WISHED ME TO SIGN OVER *POWER OF ATTORNEY* FOR ALL HIS *WRITINGS* TO *YOU*, MR. GRISWOLD?
MARIA, YOUR SON-IN-LAW WAS *ADAMANT*. HE MADE IT MY *SACRED TRUST* TO PRESERVE HIS *WORK* FOR GENERATIONS TO COME.
ANY *PITTANCE* SAID WORK MIGHT EARN IS OF *NO* INTEREST TO ME, OF COURSE.
HAVE YOU BENEFITED FROM THIS AUTHOR'S MISFORTUNES?
I CAN'T EVEN IMAGINE STOOPING SO LOW! IT WOULD BE SACRILEGE TO PROFIT FROM THE MIRACLES OF A GOD AMONG MEN!
WHUNK! WHUNK! WHUNK!
THERE'S MORE CASH WHERE *THAT* CAME FROM, MR. GRISWOLD. WE CAN'T *PRINT* YOUR POE BOOK FAST ENOUGH!
IRONIC, ISN'T IT? THAT A TALENTLESS *HACK* LIKE *POE* SHOULD MAKE A GENIUS CRITIC LIKE ME *RICH* BEYOND MY WILDEST *DREAMS!*
POE COLLECTED WORKS

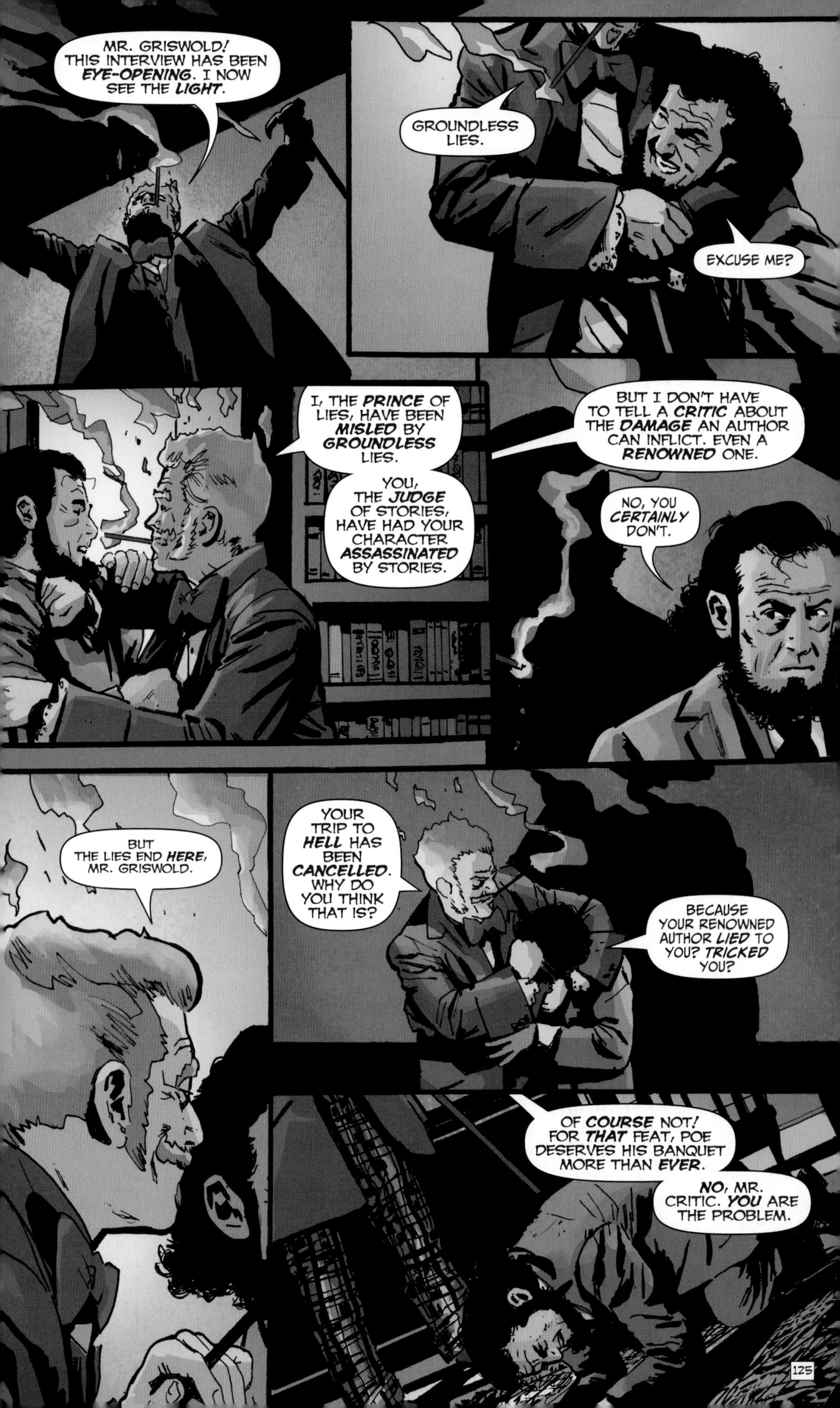
MR. GRISWOLD! THIS INTERVIEW HAS BEEN EYE-OPENING. I NOW SEE THE LIGHT.
GROUNDLESS LIES.
EXCUSE ME?
I, THE PRINCE OF LIES, HAVE BEEN MISLED BY GROUNDLESS LIES.
YOU, THE JUDGE OF STORIES, HAVE HAD YOUR CHARACTER ASSASSINATED BY STORIES.
BUT I DON'T HAVE TO TELL A CRITIC ABOUT THE DAMAGE AN AUTHOR CAN INFLICT. EVEN A RENOWNED ONE.
NO, YOU CERTAINLY DON'T.
BUT THE LIES END HERE, MR. GRISWOLD.
YOUR TRIP TO HELL HAS BEEN CANCELLED. WHY DO YOU THINK THAT IS?
BECAUSE YOUR RENOWNED AUTHOR LIED TO YOU? TRICKED YOU?
OF COURSE NOT! FOR THAT FEAT, POE DESERVES HIS BANQUET MORE THAN EVER.
NO, MR. CRITIC. YOU ARE THE PROBLEM.

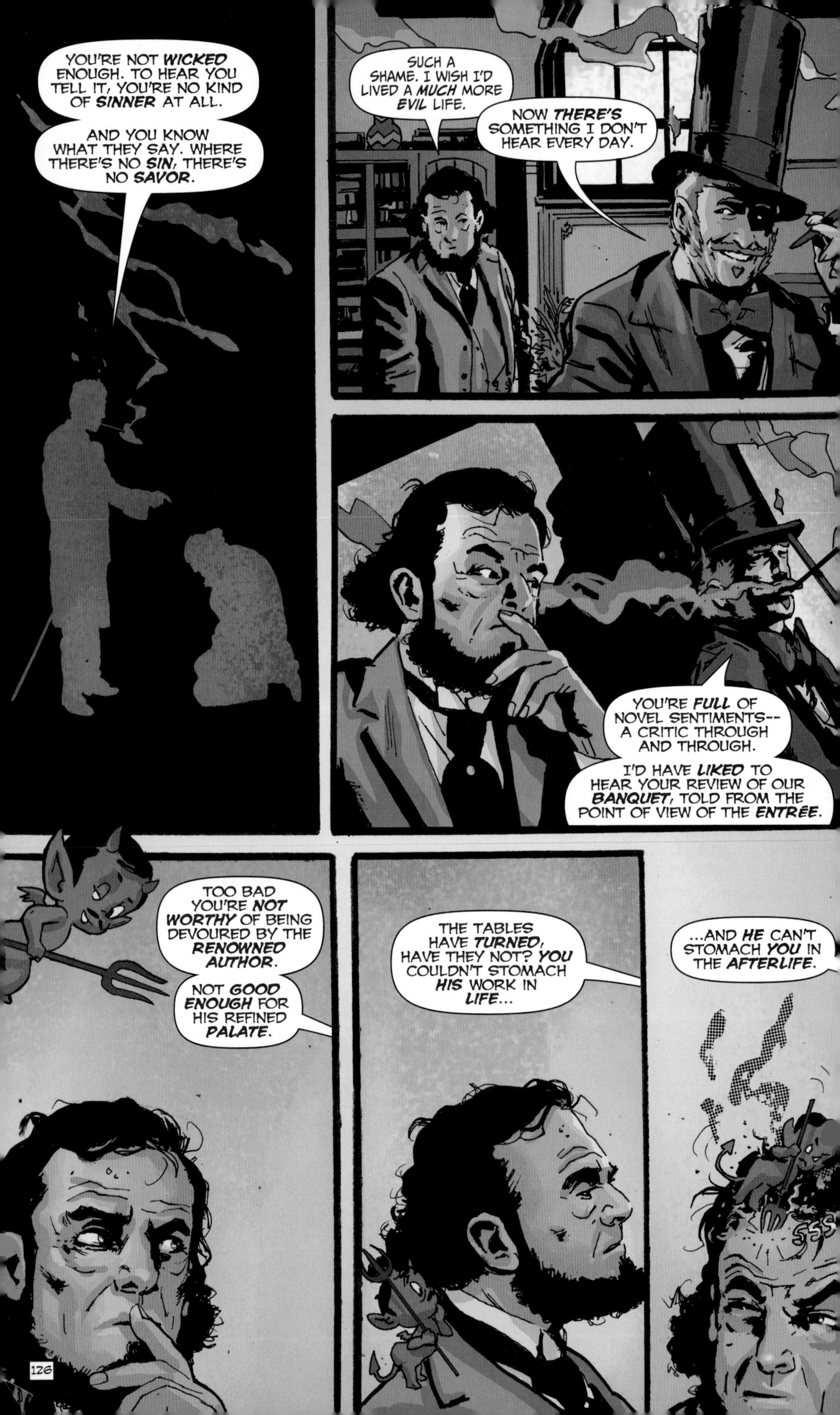
YOU'RE NOT *WICKED* ENOUGH. TO HEAR YOU TELL IT, YOU'RE NO KIND OF *SINNER* AT ALL.
AND YOU KNOW WHAT THEY SAY. WHERE THERE'S NO *SIN*, THERE'S NO *SAVOR*.
SUCH A SHAME. I WISH I'D LIVED A *MUCH* MORE *EVIL* LIFE.
NOW *THERE'S* SOMETHING I DON'T HEAR EVERY DAY.
YOU'RE *FULL* OF NOVEL SENTIMENTS-- A CRITIC THROUGH AND THROUGH.
I'D HAVE *LIKED* TO HEAR YOUR REVIEW OF OUR *BANQUET*, TOLD FROM THE POINT OF VIEW OF THE *ENTRÉE*.
TOO BAD YOU'RE *NOT WORTHY* OF BEING DEVOURED BY THE *RENOWNED AUTHOR*.
NOT *GOOD ENOUGH* FOR HIS REFINED *PALATE*.
THE TABLES HAVE *TURNED*, HAVE THEY NOT? *YOU* COULDN'T STOMACH *HIS* WORK IN *LIFE*...
...AND *HE* CAN'T STOMACH *YOU* IN THE *AFTERLIFE*.
SSS

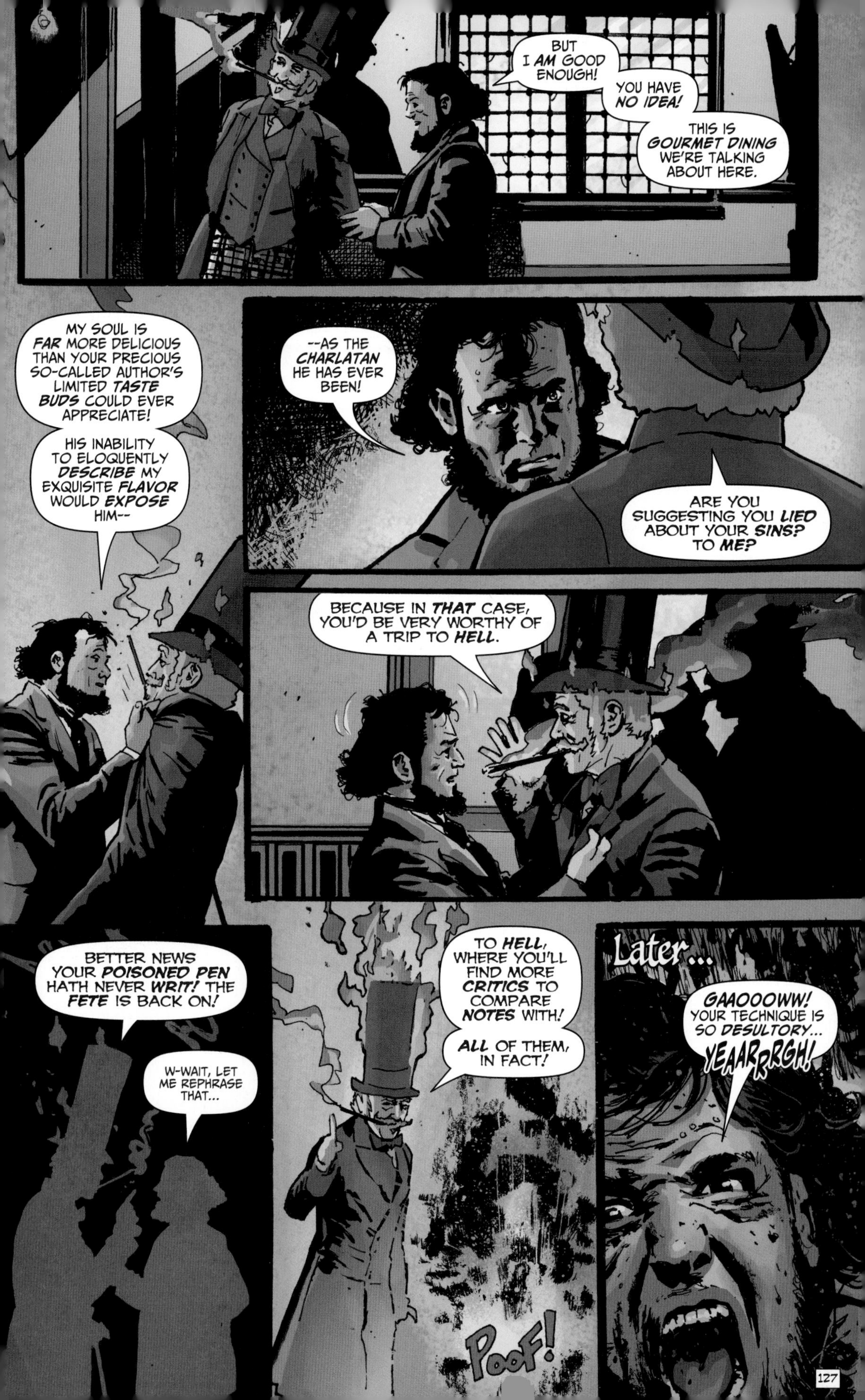
BUT I AM GOOD ENOUGH!
YOU HAVE NO IDEA!
THIS IS GOURMET DINING WE'RE TALKING ABOUT HERE.
MY SOUL IS FAR MORE DELICIOUS THAN YOUR PRECIOUS SO-CALLED AUTHOR'S LIMITED TASTE BUDS COULD EVER APPRECIATE!
HIS INABILITY TO ELOQUENTLY DESCRIBE MY EXQUISITE FLAVOR WOULD EXPOSE HIM--
--AS THE CHARLATAN HE HAS EVER BEEN!
ARE YOU SUGGESTING YOU LIED ABOUT YOUR SINS? TO ME?
BECAUSE IN THAT CASE, YOU'D BE VERY WORTHY OF A TRIP TO HELL.
BETTER NEWS YOUR POISONED PEN HATH NEVER WRIT! THE FETE IS BACK ON!
W-WAIT, LET ME REPHRASE THAT...
TO HELL, WHERE YOU'LL FIND MORE CRITICS TO COMPARE NOTES WITH!
ALL OF THEM, IN FACT!
POOF!
Later...
GAAOOOWW! YOUR TECHNIQUE IS SO DESULTORY...
YEAARRRGH!

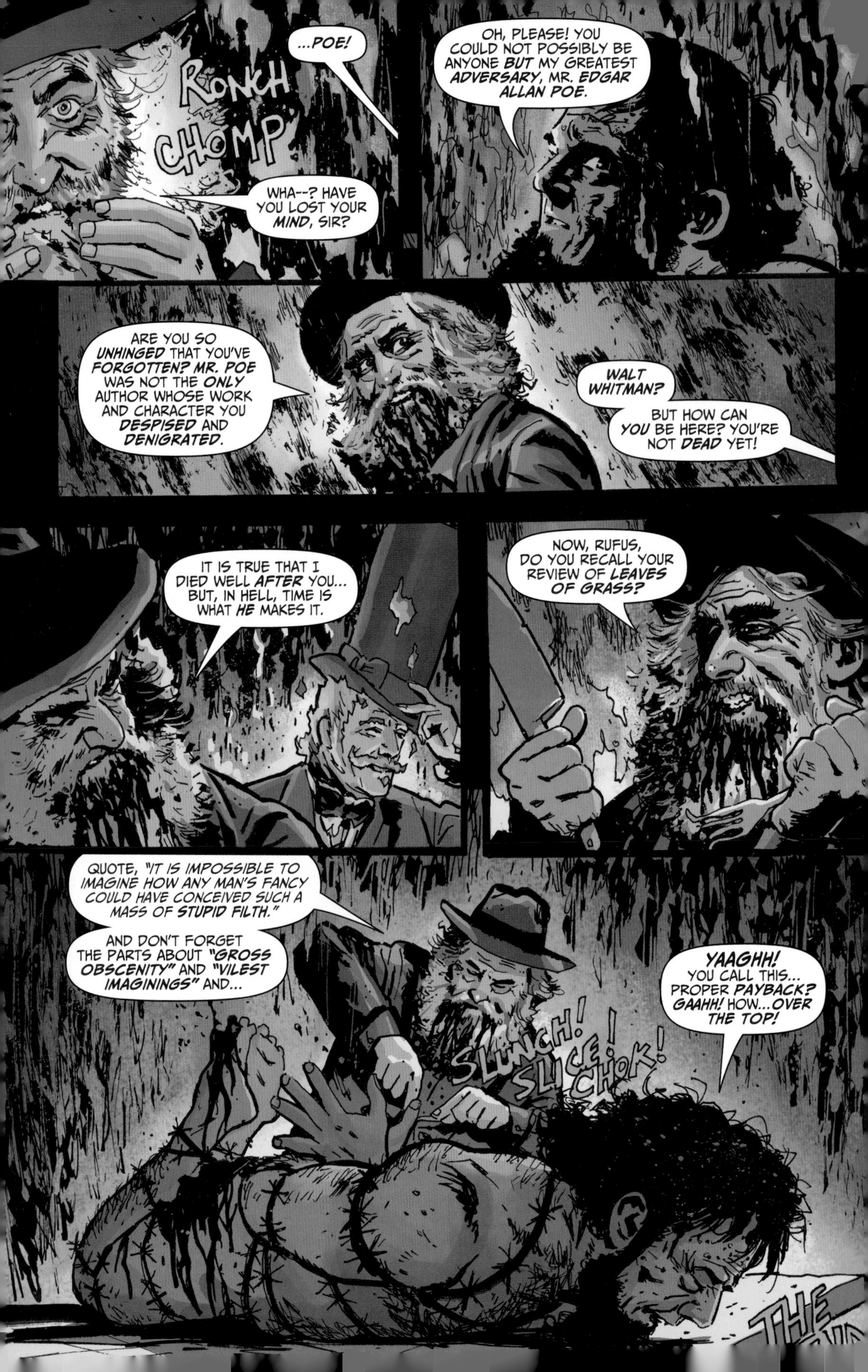

...POE!
RONCH
CHOMP
WHA--? HAVE YOU LOST YOUR *MIND*, SIR?
OH, PLEASE! YOU COULD NOT POSSIBLY BE ANYONE *BUT* MY GREATEST *ADVERSARY*, MR. *EDGAR ALLAN POE*.
ARE YOU SO *UNHINGED* THAT YOU'VE *FORGOTTEN? MR. POE* WAS NOT THE *ONLY* AUTHOR WHOSE WORK AND CHARACTER YOU *DESPISED* AND *DENIGRATED*.
WALT WHITMAN?
BUT HOW CAN *YOU* BE HERE? YOU'RE NOT *DEAD* YET!
IT IS TRUE THAT I DIED WELL *AFTER* YOU... BUT, IN HELL, TIME IS WHAT *HE* MAKES IT.
NOW, RUFUS, DO YOU RECALL YOUR REVIEW OF *LEAVES OF GRASS?*
QUOTE, "IT IS IMPOSSIBLE TO IMAGINE HOW ANY MAN'S FANCY COULD HAVE CONCEIVED SUCH A MASS OF ***STUPID FILTH."***
AND DON'T FORGET THE PARTS ABOUT ***"GROSS OBSCENITY"*** AND ***"VILEST IMAGININGS"*** AND...
SLUNCH!
SLICE!
CHOK!
YAAGHH! YOU CALL THIS... PROPER ***PAYBACK?*** ***GAAHH!*** HOW...***OVER THE TOP!***
THE

EDGAR ALLAN POE'S SNIFTER OF BLOOD #1 COVER by Jill Thompson

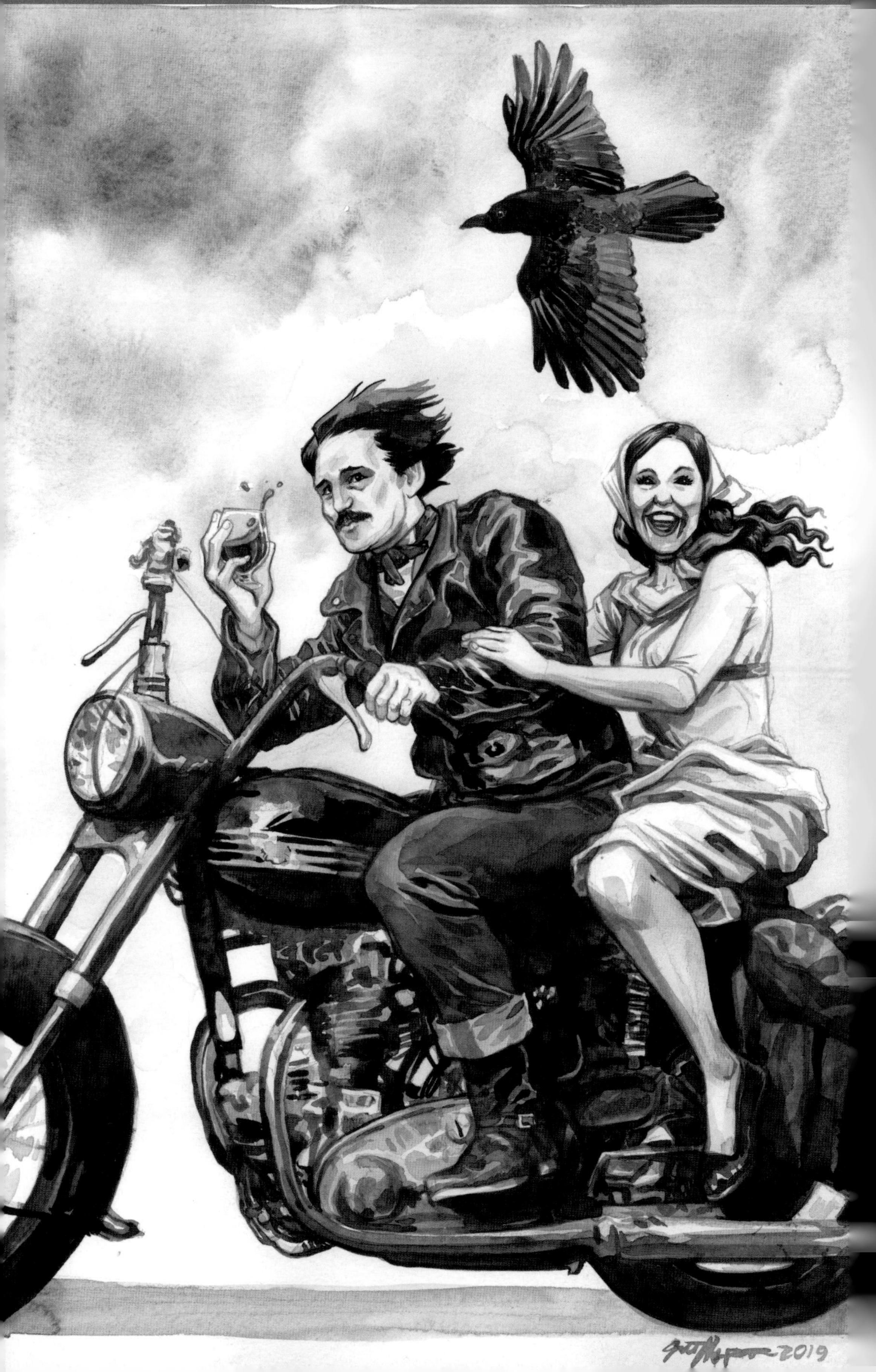

EDGAR ALLAN POE'S SNIFTER OF BLOOD #2 COVER by Ryan Kelly & Andy Troy

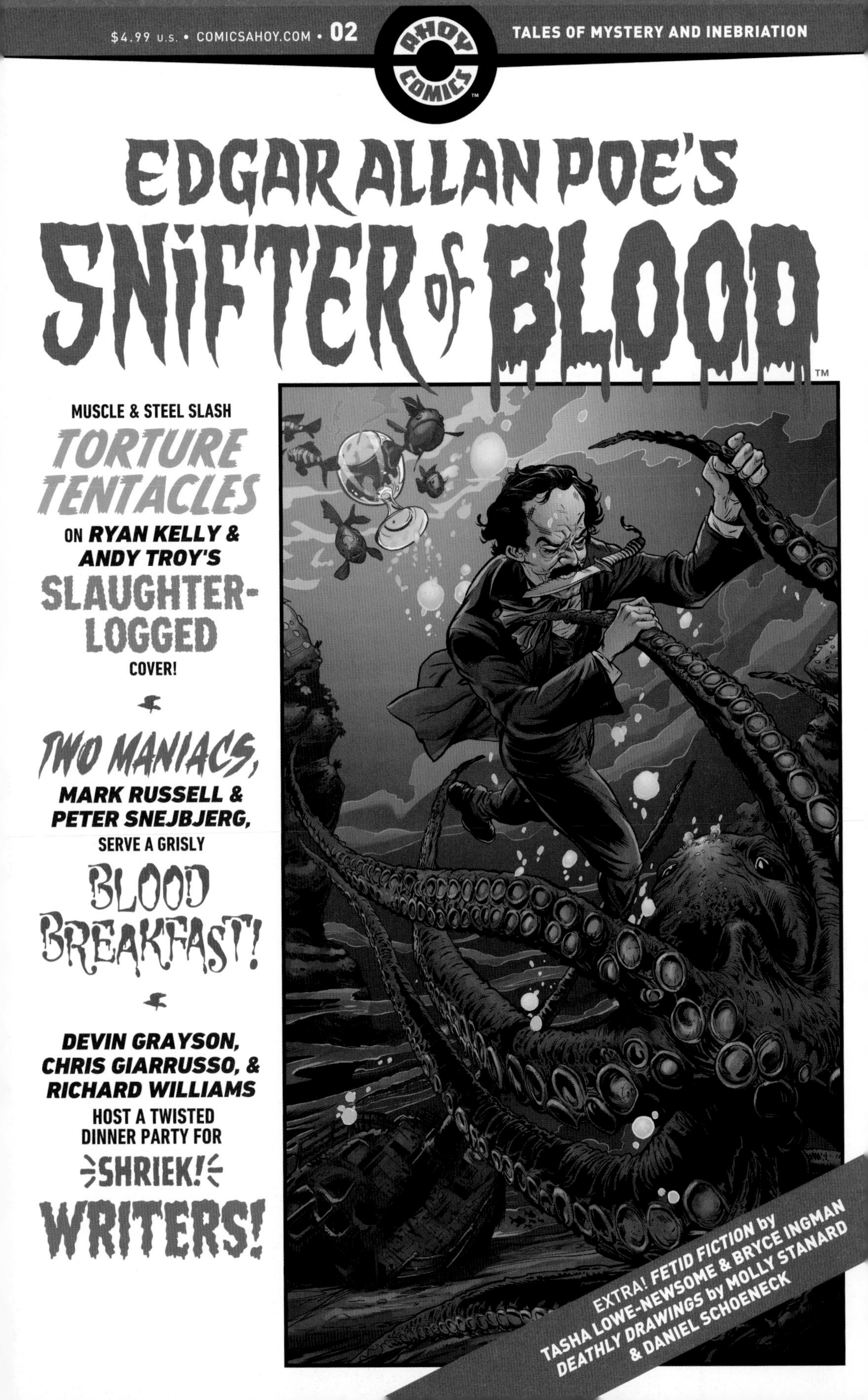
$4.99 U.S. • COMICSAHOY.COM • 02
AHOY COMICS
TALES OF MYSTERY AND INEBRIATION
EDGAR ALLAN POE'S
SNIFTER of BLOOD
MUSCLE & STEEL SLASH
TORTURE TENTACLES
ON RYAN KELLY & ANDY TROY'S
SLAUGHTER-LOGGED
COVER!
TWO MANIACS,
MARK RUSSELL & PETER SNEJBJERG,
SERVE A GRISLY
BLOOD BREAKFAST!
DEVIN GRAYSON, CHRIS GIARRUSSO, & RICHARD WILLIAMS
HOST A TWISTED DINNER PARTY FOR
SHRIEK! WRITERS!
EXTRA! FETID FICTION by
TASHA LOWE-NEWSOME & BRYCE INGMAN
DEATHLY DRAWINGS by MOLLY STANARD
& DANIEL SCHOENECK

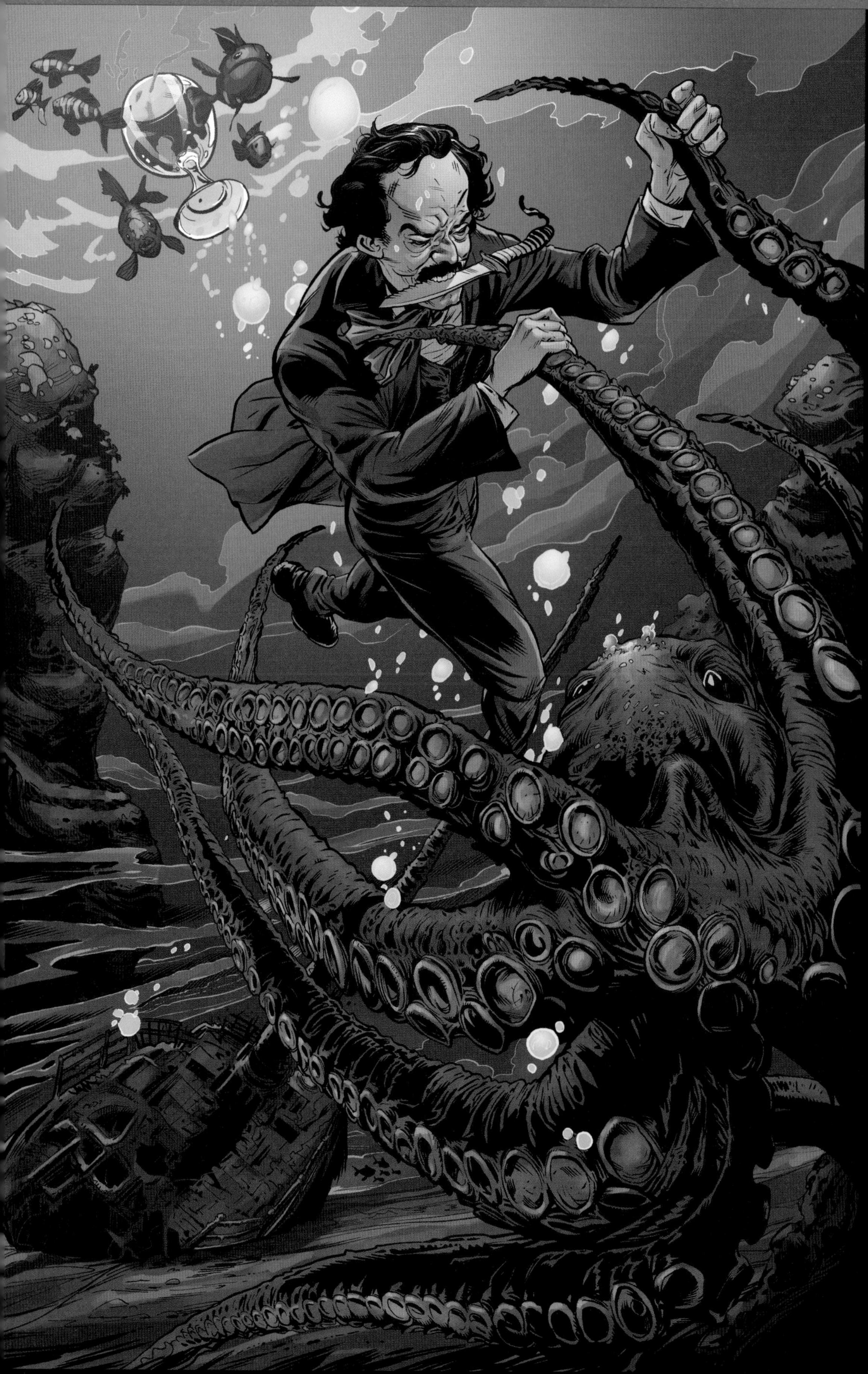

EDGAR ALLAN POE'S SNIFTER OF BLOOD #3 COVER by Jon Proctor & Andy Troy

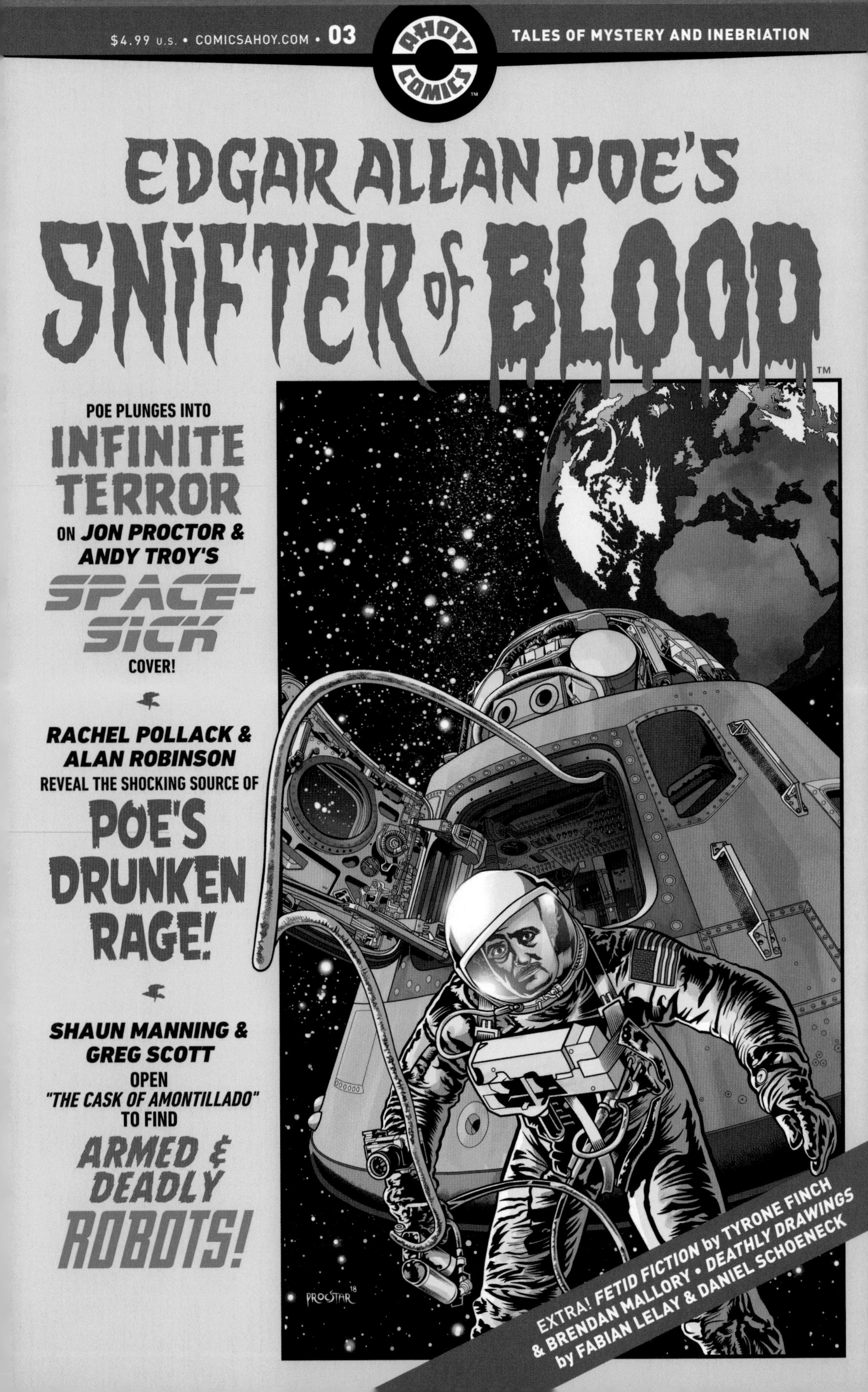
$4.99 U.S. • COMICSAHOY.COM • 03
AHOY COMICS
TALES OF MYSTERY AND INEBRIATION
EDGAR ALLAN POE'S
SNIFTER of BLOOD
POE PLUNGES INTO INFINITE TERROR ON JON PROCTOR & ANDY TROY'S SPACE-SICK COVER!
RACHEL POLLACK & ALAN ROBINSON REVEAL THE SHOCKING SOURCE OF POE'S DRUNKEN RAGE!
SHAUN MANNING & GREG SCOTT OPEN "THE CASK OF AMONTILLADO" TO FIND ARMED & DEADLY ROBOTS!
PROCSTAR 18
EXTRA! FETID FICTION by TYRONE FINCH & BRENDAN MALLORY • DEATHLY DRAWINGS by FABIAN LELAY & DANIEL SCHOENECK

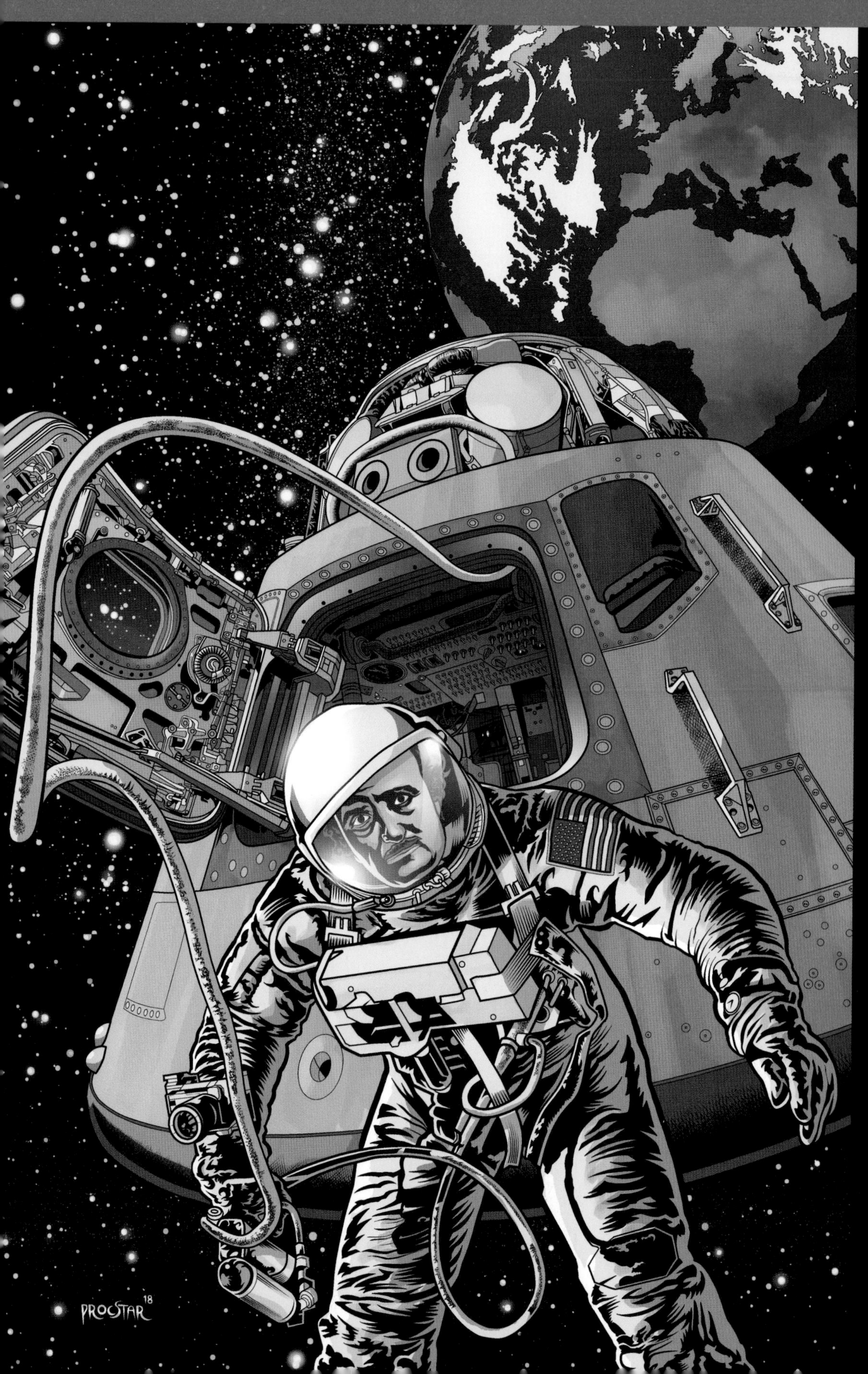
PROCSTAR 18

EDGAR ALLAN POE'S SNIFTER OF BLOOD #4 COVER by Alan Robinson

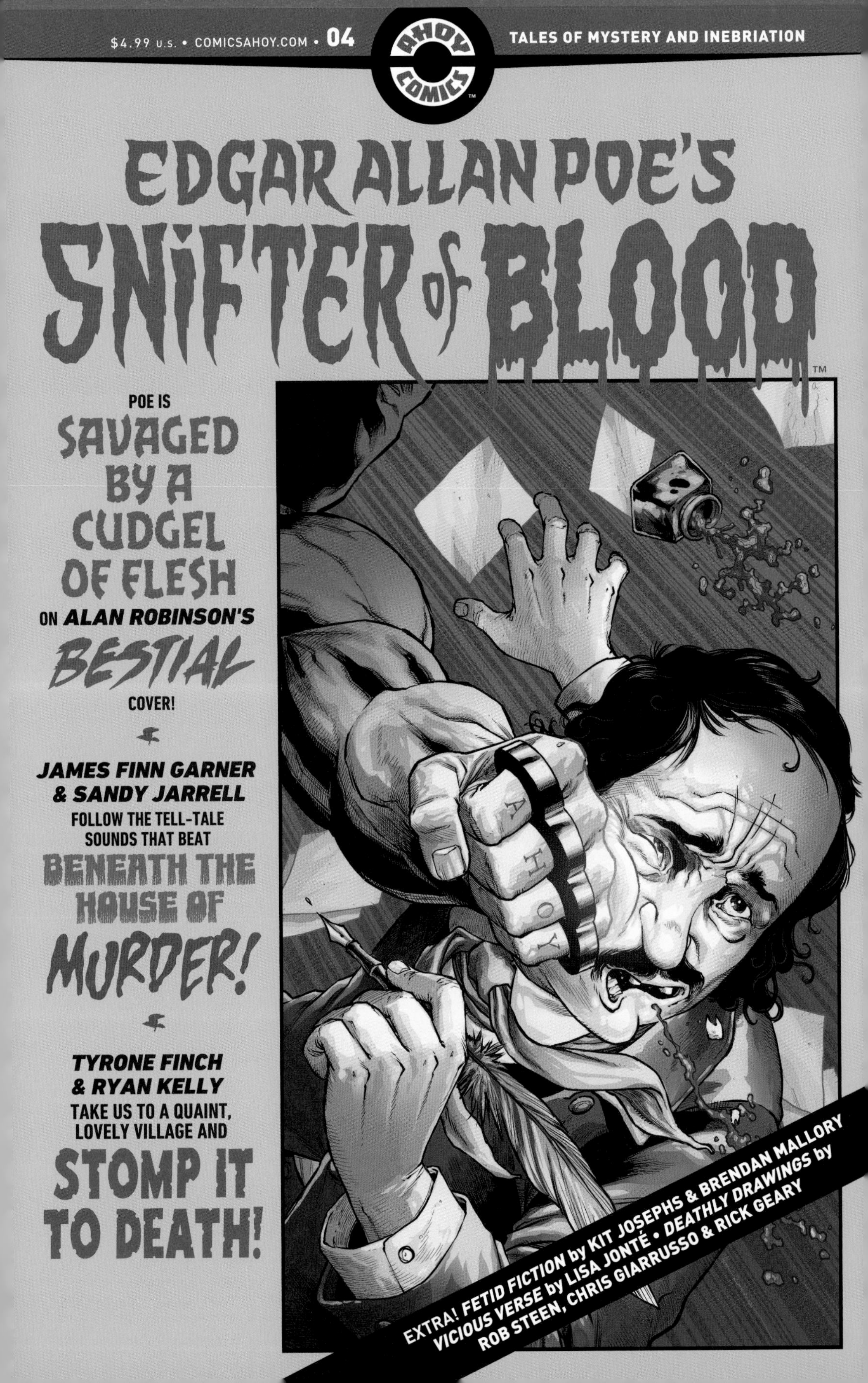
$4.99 U.S. • COMICSAHOY.COM • 04
AHOY COMICS
TALES OF MYSTERY AND INEBRIATION
EDGAR ALLAN POE'S
SNIFTER of BLOOD
POE IS SAVAGED BY A CUDGEL OF FLESH ON ALAN ROBINSON'S BESTIAL COVER!
JAMES FINN GARNER & SANDY JARRELL
FOLLOW THE TELL-TALE SOUNDS THAT BEAT
BENEATH THE HOUSE OF MURDER!
TYRONE FINCH & RYAN KELLY
TAKE US TO A QUAINT, LOVELY VILLAGE AND
STOMP IT TO DEATH!
AHOY
EXTRA! FETID FICTION by KIT JOSEPHS & BRENDAN MALLORY
VICIOUS VERSE by LISA JONTÉ • DEATHLY DRAWINGS by
ROB STEEN, CHRIS GIARRUSSO & RICK GEARY

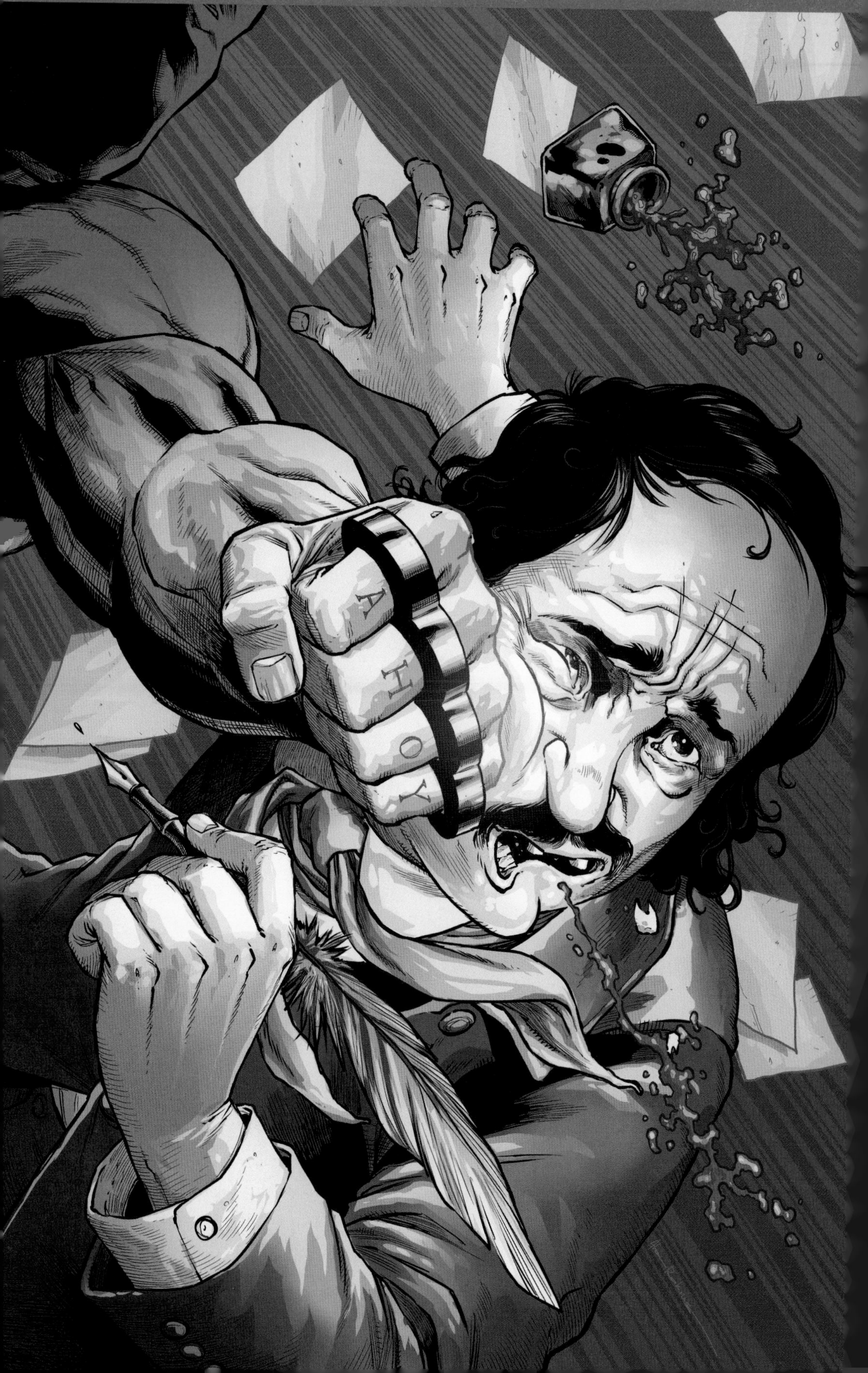
AHOY

EDGAR ALLAN POE'S SNIFTER OF BLOOD #5 COVER by Alan Robinson

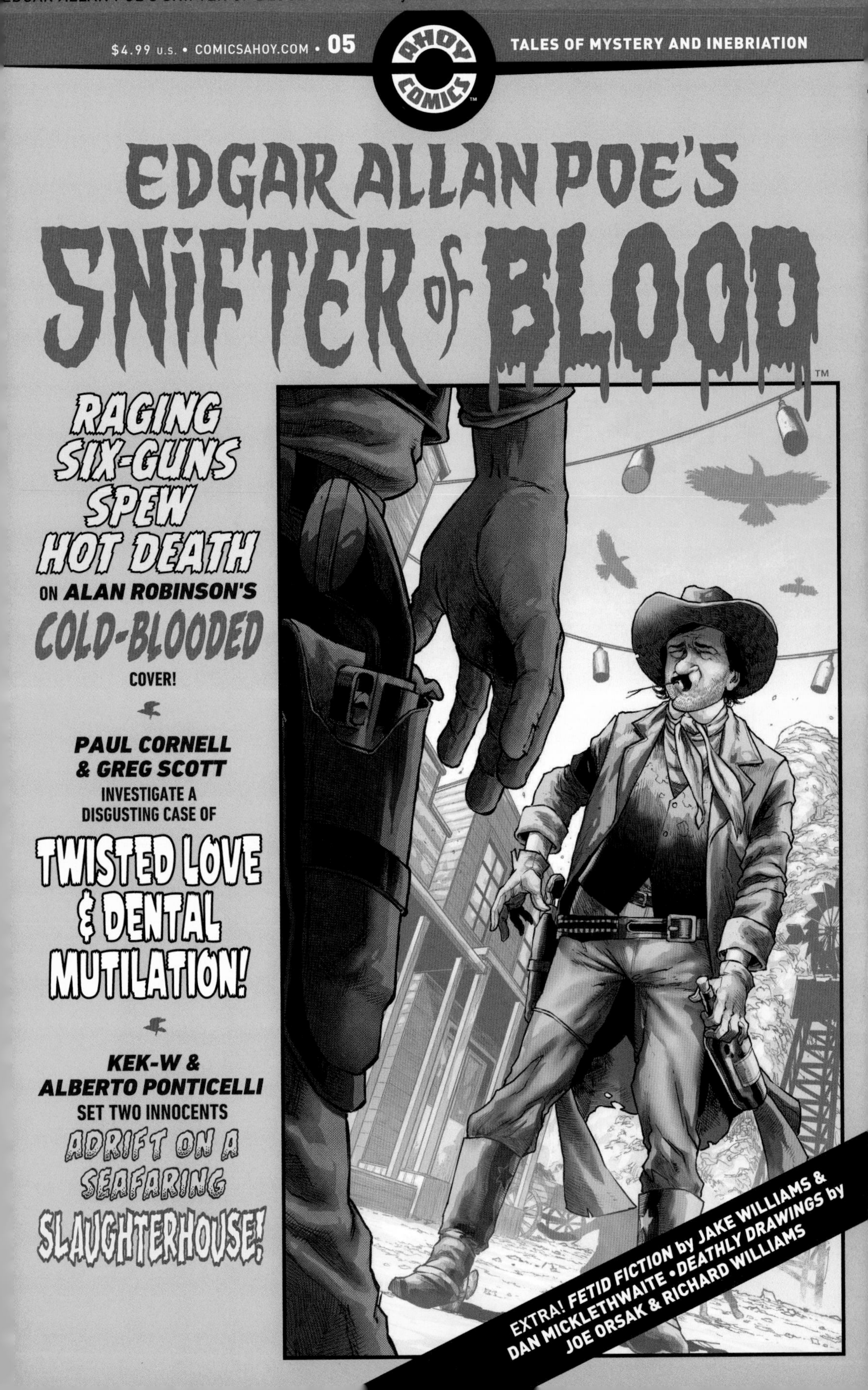
$4.99 U.S. • COMICSAHOY.COM • 05
AHOY COMICS
TALES OF MYSTERY AND INEBRIATION
EDGAR ALLAN POE'S
SNIFTER OF BLOOD
RAGING SIX-GUNS SPEW HOT DEATH ON ALAN ROBINSON'S COLD-BLOODED COVER!
PAUL CORNELL & GREG SCOTT INVESTIGATE A DISGUSTING CASE OF TWISTED LOVE & DENTAL MUTILATION!
KEK-W & ALBERTO PONTICELLI SET TWO INNOCENTS ADRIFT ON A SEAFARING SLAUGHTERHOUSE!
EXTRA! FETID FICTION by JAKE WILLIAMS & DAN MICKLETHWAITE • DEATHLY DRAWINGS by JOE ORSAK & RICHARD WILLIAMS

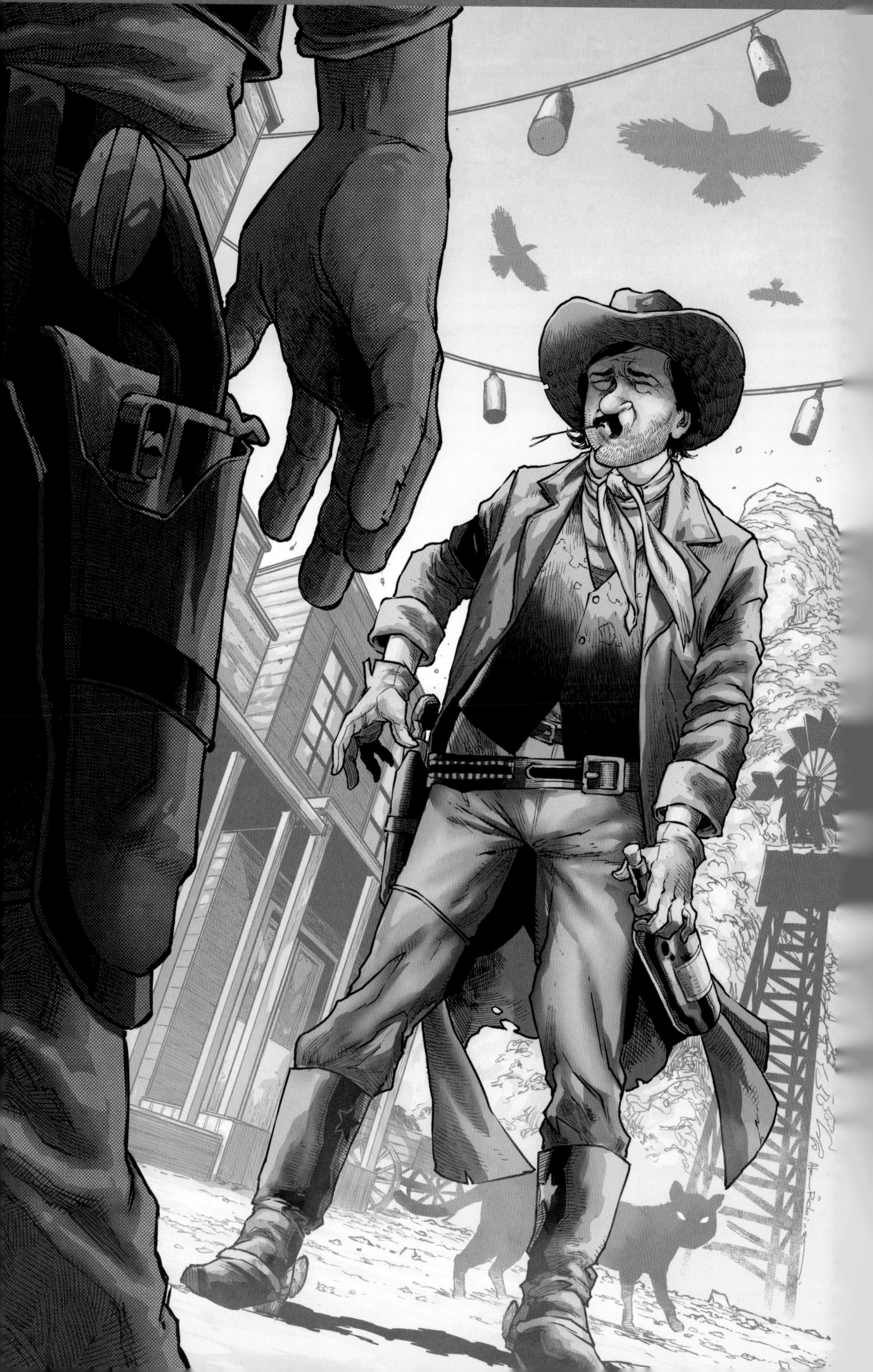

EDGAR ALLAN POE'S SNIFTER OF BLOOD #6 COVER by Alan Robinson

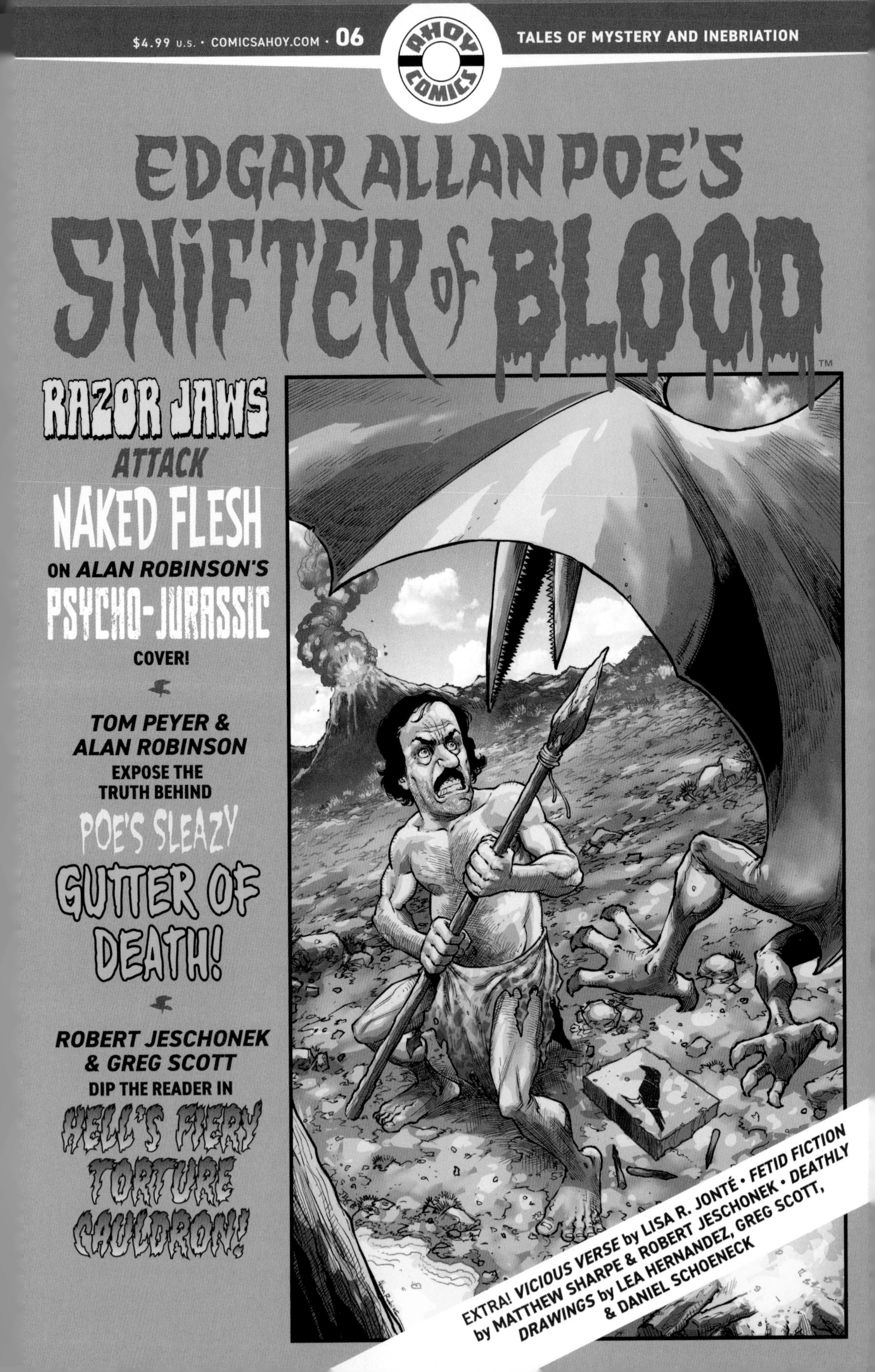

$4.99 U.S. • COMICSAHOY.COM • 06
AHOY COMICS
TALES OF MYSTERY AND INEBRIATION
EDGAR ALLAN POE'S SNIFTER OF BLOOD™
RAZOR JAWS ATTACK NAKED FLESH ON ALAN ROBINSON'S PSYCHO-JURASSIC COVER!
TOM PEYER & ALAN ROBINSON EXPOSE THE TRUTH BEHIND POE'S SLEAZY GUTTER OF DEATH!
ROBERT JESCHONEK & GREG SCOTT DIP THE READER IN HELL'S FIERY TORTURE CAULDRON!
EXTRA! VICIOUS VERSE by LISA R. JONTÉ • FETID FICTION by MATTHEW SHARPE & ROBERT JESCHONEK • DEATHLY DRAWINGS by LEA HERNANDEZ, GREG SCOTT, & DANIEL SCHOENECK

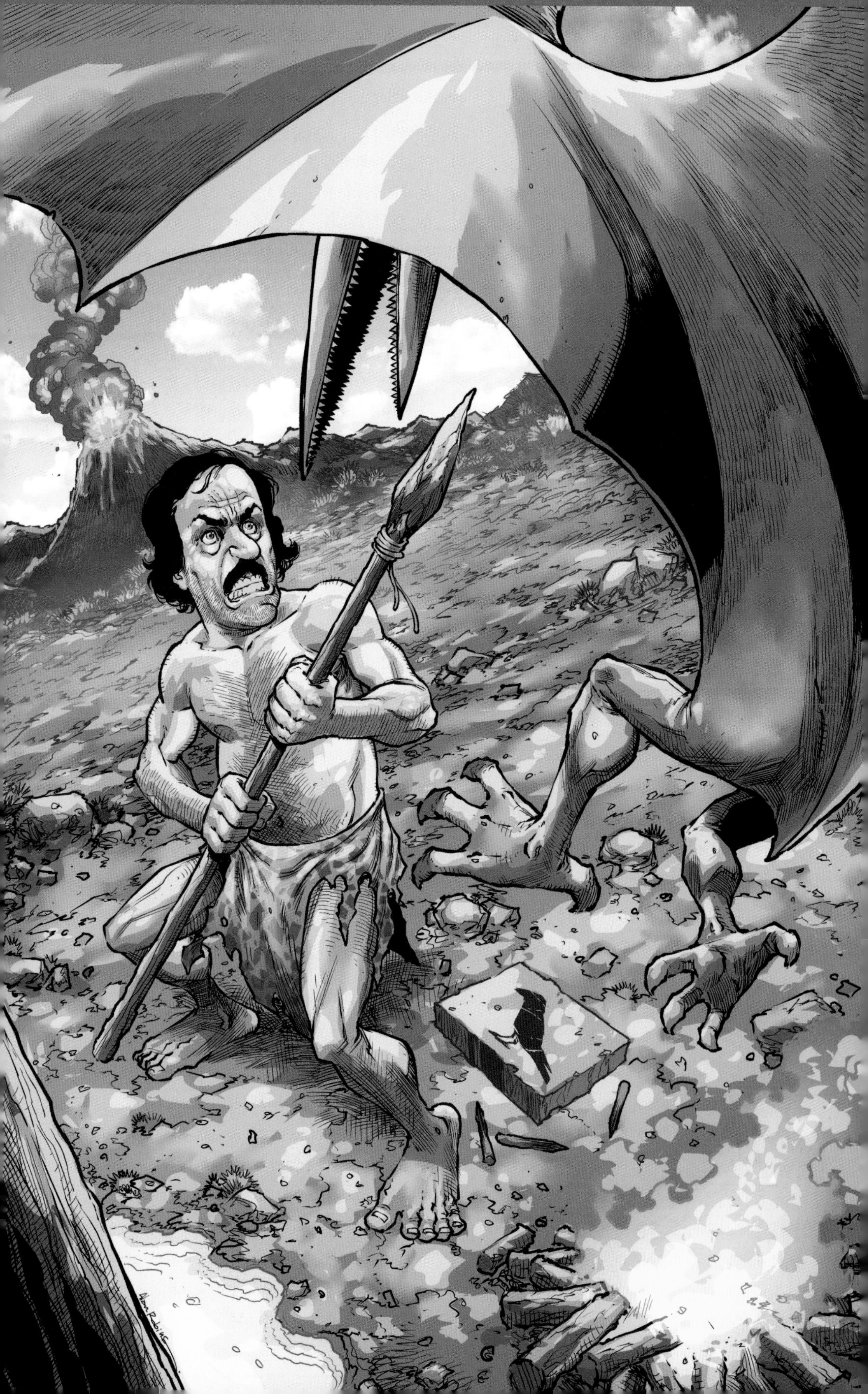

"TO HELL COMES A GUEST," Pages 3-6 pencil layouts by Peter Snejbjerg

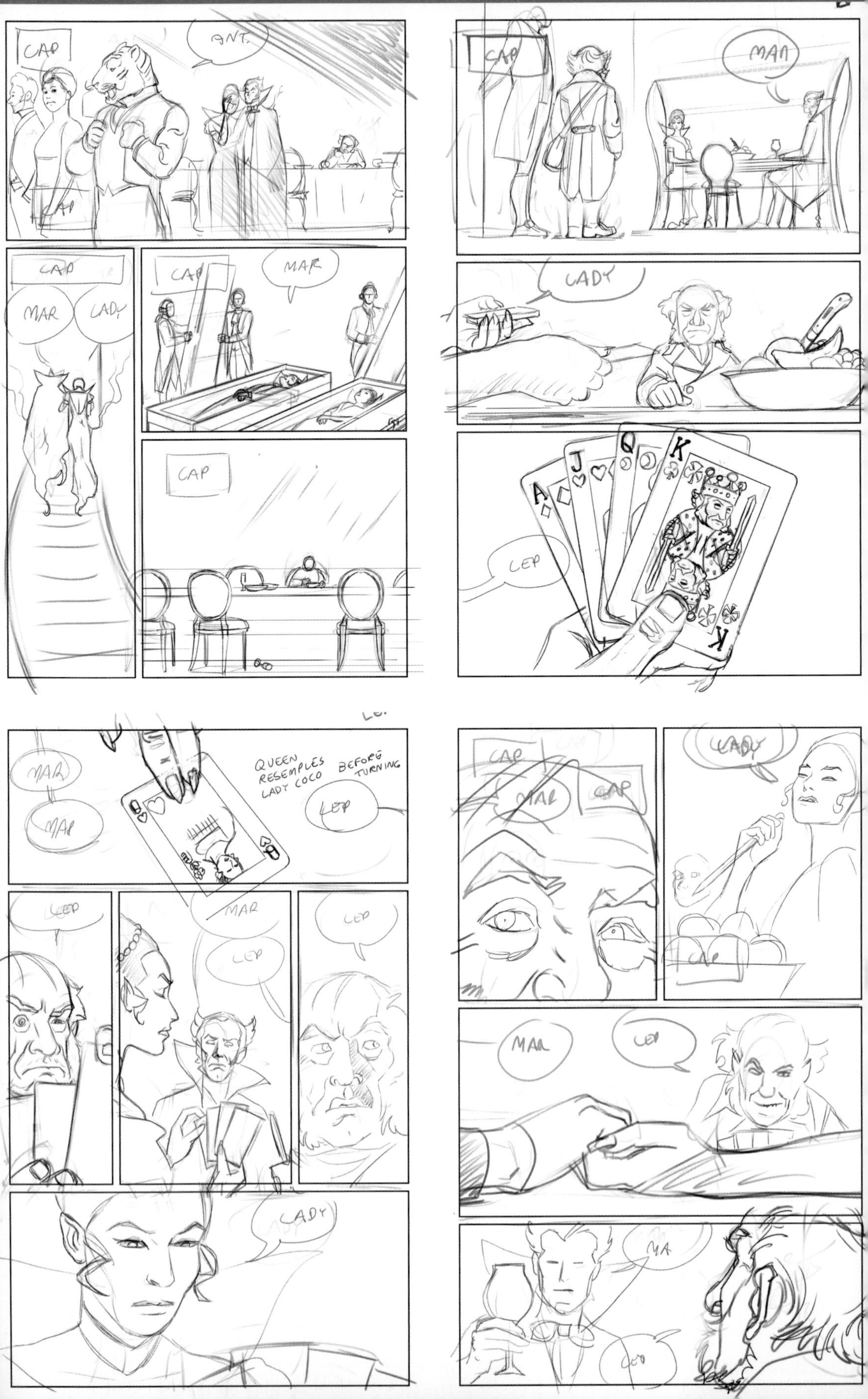

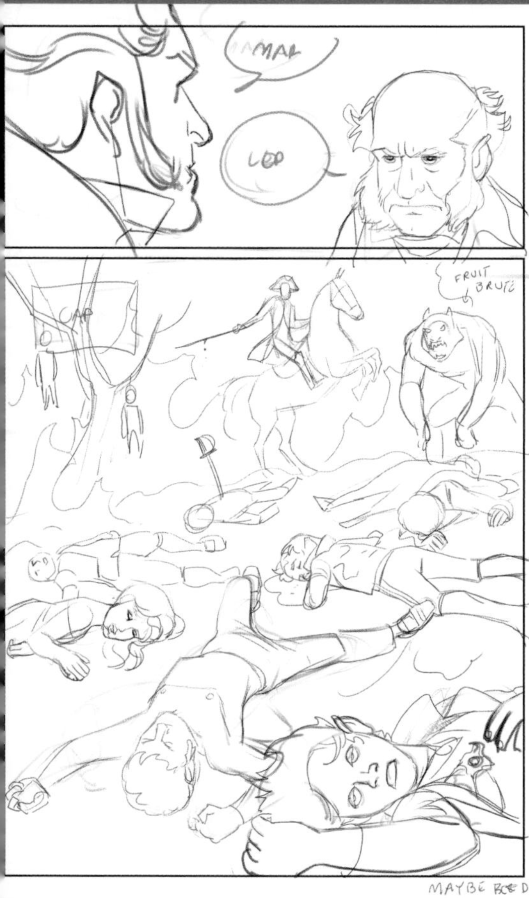
MAR
LEP
CAP
FRUIT BRUTE
MAYBE BED

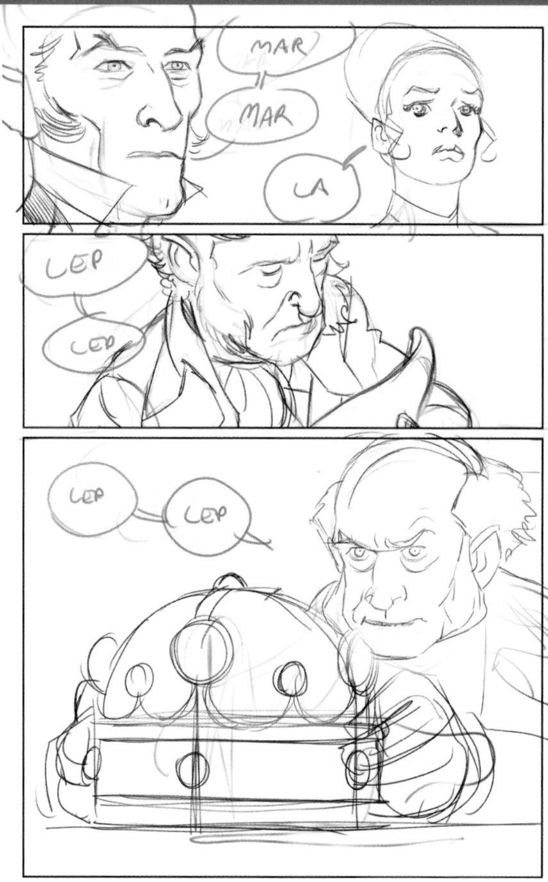
MAR
MAR
LA
LEP
LEP
LEP
LEP

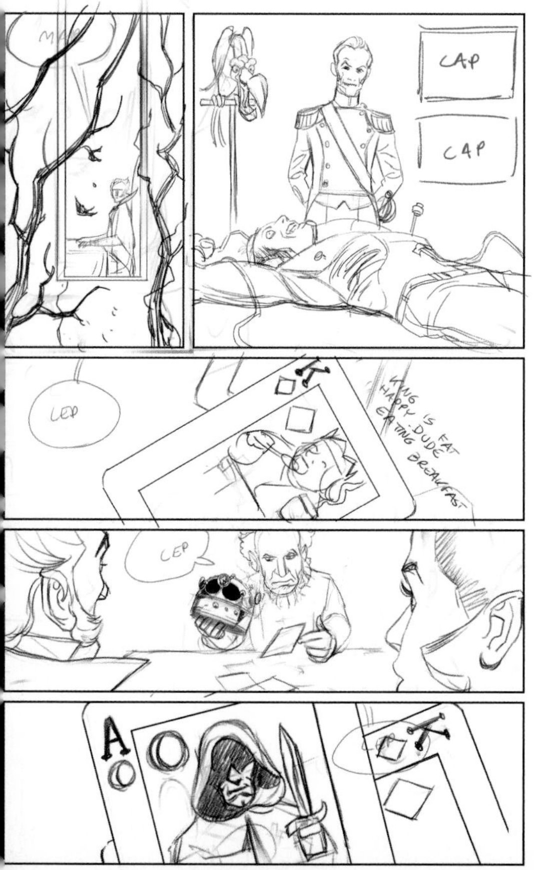
CAP
CAP
LEP
KING IS FAT HAPPY DUDE EATING BREAKFAST
LEP

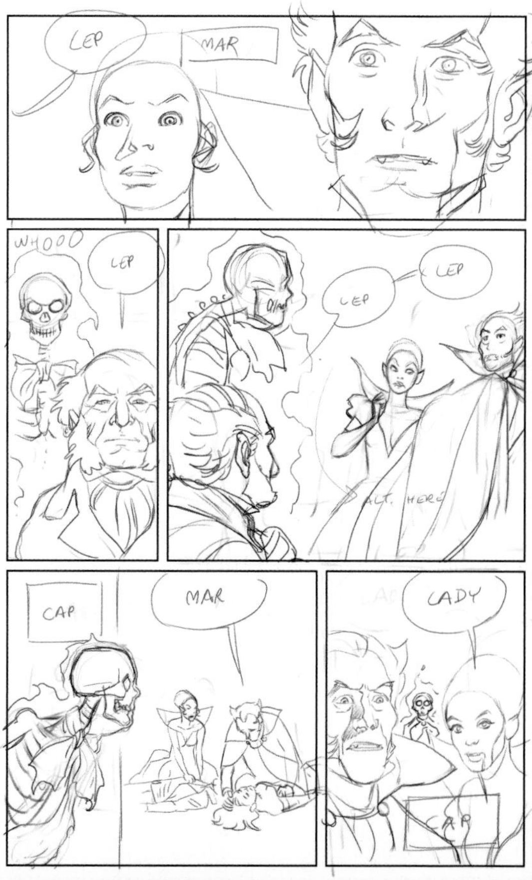
LEP
MAR
WHOOO
LEP
LEP
LEP
ALT. HERE
CAP
MAR
LADY
CAP

JULIE BARCLAY is a comic book colorist with a penchant for cats. Her work has appeared in Action Lab's *Hero Cats of Stellar City* and its *Midnight* and *World Tour* spinoffs as well as a suitably cat-based tale for AHOY's *EDGAR ALLAN POE'S SNIFTER OF TERROR*.

RUSS BRAUN has been drawing comics for almost 30 years, with time away for a seven-year stint with Walt Disney Feature Animation. Known for his expressive character work and storytelling on everything from *Batman*, *Swamp Thing*, *Fables* and *Jack of Fables*, Braun is perhaps best known for his frequent collaborations with Garth Ennis.

OLE COMOLL has been a full-time illustrator since 1997. He is also a member of Denmark's influential Drawing Room Gimle. Comoll has drawn comic books, book illustrations, educational illustrations, storyboards and more. He lives and works in Copenhagen, and has directed "graphic facilitation" workshops at business meetings and conferences across Denmark and internationally.

PAUL CORNELL is a writer of science fiction and fantasy in prose, comics and TV, one of only two people to be Hugo Award-nominated for all three media. He's written *Doctor Who* for the BBC, *Action Comics* for DC, and *Wolverine* for Marvel. He's won the BSFA Award for his short fiction, an Eagle Award for his comics, and shares in a Writer's Guild Award for his television. He lives in Gloucestershire with his wife and son.

TYRONE FINCH hails from Cleveland, Ohio. What? That's not enough? Okay, his favorite color is blue, he's not fond of green olives and he doesn't understand maraschino cherries. He loves Earth, Wind and Fire and he will make you love them too. Finch likes to write all kinds of stuff. TV stuff. Movie stuff. Short story stuff. Shopping list stuff. For more info on the stuff he likes to write, catch him on the street and ask him. He's the guy wearing the yellow Walkman and singing "On Your Face" at the top of his lungs. (Yeah, he's off-key, but at least he's loud.)

JAMES FINN GARNER grew up in the company town of Dearborn, Michigan. After graduating from the University of Michigan, he moved to Chicago and worked as a house painter, baker, warehouse clerk, public relations whipping boy, and editor of real estate appraisal publications. Seeking a creative outlet, he began to take improvisational comedy classes. His most infamous project—the performance art comedy troupe JazzPoetry…TRUTH!—was labeled "out-and-out painful in its sheer stupidity" by the *Chicago Tribune* and "one of the funniest things I have ever seen" by one of the founders of The Second City.

Garner's first book, *Politically Correct Bedtime Stories*, has sold more than 2.5 million copies in the U.S., has been translated into 20 languages, and spawned sequel books, computer games, TV pilots, and stage productions. His other books include *Apocalypse WOW!: A Memoir for the End of Time*, *Recut Madness*, *Tea Party Fairy Tales*, and the clown noir mystery series starring Rex Koko, Private Clown. His fiction and satire have also appeared in *Playboy*, *The New York Times*, *The Wall Street Journal*, and other publications. He currently lives in Chicago with his wife and two grown children.

CHRIS GIARRUSSO is a writer and artist best known for creating the *G-Man* graphic novel series for young readers at Image Comics and the *Mini Marvels* strips at Marvel Comics. His work has been published by Andrews McMeel, Scholastic, Marvel, Image, IDW, Valiant, Lion Forge, and several independent publishers. Find Chris at ChrisGiarrusso.com.

DEVIN GRAYSON started her writing career in Gotham City and became the first female to create, launch and write a new, ongoing Batman title, *Batman: Gotham Knights*. Since then, Devin has published novels and short stories, worked on video game scripts and essays, consulted for entertainment industry luminaries looking to expand their brands into graphic novels and comics, and taught and guest-lectured at conventions, universities, and seminars around the world. Additional career highlights include two *Black Widow* miniseries, *Doctor Strange: The Fate of Dreams*, and *USER*—a highly personal three-part, creator-owned Image series about gender identity and online role-playing.

SANDY JARRELL first learned to fear the terrible beating of "The Tell-Tale Heart" as a small child, when gifted a book-on-record version of the story. He lives with his wife, two kids and two dogs in their home in North Carolina, where's he's still sometimes rattled by sounds from under the floorboards.

ROBERT JESCHONEK is an award-winning author whose envelope-pushing fiction has made waves around the world. He has an eye for the unusual, which he puts to work in freaky-cool novels like *A Pinstriped Finger's My Only Friend* (starring a pinky finger with a mind of its own) and *Day 9* (narrated by a Spanish cathedral and an Amish serial killer). His stories have appeared in *Pulphouse, Fiction River, Galaxy's Edge, Tales from the Canyons of the Damned, Boundary Shock Quarterly*, and many other publications. He has also written official Doctor Who and Star Trek fiction and Batman and Justice Society comics for DC Comics. He regularly writes for the *Fractured Scary Tales* comic series, and his graphic novel, *Hell's Treasure*, is in the works. Hugo and Nebula Award-winning author Mike Resnick calls him "a towering talent."

KEK-W writes *Fall of Deadworld* (featuring Judge Death and the Dark Judges), *The Order, Indigo Prime* and *Black Max* for 2000AD and Rebellion. Past credits include *Cap'n Dinosaur* for Image Comics and *Commando* for DC Thompson. His work has appeared in *New Scientist, Wire, Dazed & Confused, Bizarre* and *Tattoo*, among others. He is the award-avoiding creator of Conspiracy Theory Dog, Heavy Metal Genie and Ted, the Talking Atomic Submarine—characters beloved by dozens around the globe. Kek lives and works in Yeovil, Somerset, deep in the dark, witch-haunted heart of the UK's rural West Country. Also available on VHS and Betamax.

RYAN KELLY is perhaps best known for the twelve-issue run of *Local* with writer, Brian Wood for Oni Press. Always a Mid-Westerner, Kelly received his art training at the Minneapolis College of Art and Design from which he graduated in 1998. There he studied under comic book artist, Peter Gross, with whom he worked on *The Books of Magic* and *Lucifer* for Vertigo. Ryan is on the MCAD staff, teaching classes for younger students and the occasional inking class as well. He has guest inked on *American Virgin* and drew the graphic novel *Giant Robot Warriors* as well as another Brian Wood project, Vertigo's *Northlanders*. Kelly has had various Minneapolis area exhibitions of his paintings. He has also done illustrations for *Rolling Stone* and *Time*, among others.

LEE LOUGHRIDGE is a color artist who has created award-winning work for Marvel, DC, Dark Horse and Image Comics throughout his 25-year career.

SHAUN MANNING is the creator and writer of *Interesting Drug* for BOOM! Studios' Archaia imprint and *Hell, Nebraska* on Comixology. His work has appeared in *Dark Horse Presents, Top Shelf 2.0, Hope: New Orleans*, and *The Looking Glass Wars: Hatter M*, as well as in several literary magazines, on stage, and on BBC Radio 4. Shaun took home first prize for a reading from his comedy novella

Pizza Good Times in Edinburgh, Scotland; the trophy was a bottle of whiskey.

DEAN MOTTER, artist/writer and designer, is best known for the comics sensation *Mister X* (now in its 35th year). He has created works for *Superman, Batman* (most notably the award-winning "film noir" graphic novel, *Batman: Nine Lives*), *The Shadow, The Spirit, Mad Max: Fury Road, Spongebob Squarepants*, and *Wolverine*. His Vertigo series *Terminal City* was nominated for both Eisner and Kurtzman Awards. He is also known for the acclaimed graphic novel, *The Prisoner: Shattered Visage*, based on the '60s British TV series. Motter has also designed several award-winning album covers and book jackets.

In the '90s Dean served on staff at both DC Comics and Byron Preiss Visual Publications as editorial art director, supervising graphic novel projects such as the works of Ray Bradbury, Raymond Chandler and Harlan Ellison as well as *The Hitchhiker's Guide to the Galaxy*. Motter has worked with the David S. Wyman Institute for Holocaust Studies and the Los Angeles Museum of the Holocaust illustrating the comic book accounts, *The Book Hitler Didn't Want You to Read*, and *Karski's Mission: To Stop the Holocaust*. Though he has spent most of his professional life in Toronto and Manhattan, he now resides and works tirelessly in Dixie.

TOM PEYER is cofounder and editor-in-chief of AHOY Comics. His recent writing projects include *THE WRONG EARTH, DRAGONFLY & DRAGONFLYMAN, PENULTIMAN, HASHTAG: DANGER*, and *HIGH HEAVEN*. In the before-time he wrote *Hourman* and *Legion of Super-Heroes* for DC Comics and was one of the original editors at Vertigo.

RACHEL POLLACK is the author of 41 books, including two award-winning novels, *Unquenchable Fire* and *Godmother Night*. Her comics work includes *Doom Patrol, The New Gods, Tomahawk, The Geek*, and *Time Breakers*. She has also written a series of books about Tarot cards that have sold all over the world, and is the creator of *The Shining Tribe Tarot*, designed and drawn by Rachel herself. Rachel has taught, lectured, and presented her work on four continents.

ALBERTO PONTICELLI developed a passion for illustration at a young age and pursued his dream of being a comic book artist through a self-publishing collaborative, Shok Studios, in his native Italy. His work was quickly recognized and reprinted by Dark Horse, launching his career in American comics. Since, Ponticelli has done work for Marvel, DC, Image and IDW as well as his award-winning graphic novel *Blatta* for Leopoldo Bloom Editore.

JON PROCTOR received his BFA from the Savannah College of Art and Design in 1997 and has since called the city home. In his early career, he worked primarily in the comic book industry. In addition to credits at Marvel and DC Comics, among others, Jon co-created the *Black Diamond* series with Larry Young at AIT/Planet Lar and more recently co-created *Gun Theory* with writer Daniel Way for Dark Horse. Jon has otherwise amassed an impressive client list for his illustration work in both editorial and commercial environments including *The Wall Street Journal*, Nike, Adidas, Amazon, and Cartoon Network. He has also worked for both mainstream and educational publishing houses, as well as local and regional press imprints. Away from the worktable, Jon enjoys travel both near and far—from trips to the local farmer's market to travels abroad.

ALAN ROBINSON has been drawing comics professionally for more than ten years, working for IDW Publishing, Dark Horse, and Beyond Reality Media, on titles such as *Back to the Future*, *V-Wars*, *Star Wars*, *Warden*, *Terminator*, and *Secret Battles of Genghis Khan*. He lives in Concepcion, Chile, with his wife Jessica and their lovely kids Matilda and Agustin.

MARK RUSSELL is the author of not one, but two, books about the Bible: *God Is Disappointed in You* and *Apocrypha Now*. In addition, he is the writer behind AHOY's *SECOND COMING*, *BILLIONAIRE ISLAND* and "The Monster Serials" in *EDGAR ALLAN POE'S SNIFTER OF TERROR*, as well as various DC comic books including *Prez*, *The Flintstones*, and *Exit Stage Left: The Snagglepuss Chronicles*. He lives in obscurity with his family in Portland, Oregon.

GREG SCOTT is a comic book artist who pencils and inks his own work. He has drawn such titles as *X-Files*, *Black Hood*, *Steve McQueen*, and *Area 51*. He broke into comics through espionage: learning the time of day Marvel editors went outside for a cigarette break, he passed them art samples and was quickly given an assignment.

PETER SNEJBJERG draws drawings for a living and has done so for many years. He has worked for a number of American and international comic book publishers. He lives in Copenhagen, Denmark.

MADELINE SEELY is a multimedia artist and musician currently living and working in New York City. After receiving her BFA in painting from the Maryland Institute College of Art, she decided to pursue pretty much any creative outlet other than painting. Whether she's making heavy electronic music, weird videos, experimenting with new vehicles for eating hummus, or coloring for comic books, she's having fun and learning along the way.

FELIPE SOBREIRO is a Brazilian artist and colorist. He has worked for all major comic book publishers, including Marvel, DC, Image, Dark Horse, IDW, Heavy Metal and others.

ROB STEEN is the illustrator of *Flanimals*, the best-selling series of children's books written by Ricky Gervais, and *Erf*, a children's book written by Garth Ennis.

JILL THOMPSON is a ten-time Eisner Award-winning comic book creator whose career spans decades. A graduate of The American Academy of Art, Jill was one of the first female creators to come to prominence in the comics industry. She is best known for her work on her own creations, *Scary Godmother* and *Magic Trixie*, as well as *The Little Endless Storybook*, and *Wonder Woman: The True Amazon*.

She has worked for nearly every major comic book company and has collaborated with such noted writers as Neil Gaiman, Grant Morrison, Mark Millar, WWE Legend Mick Foley and many more. In her off time, Jill designs wrestling gear for WWE superstar Daniel Bryan. She is a Spartan Race competitor, an avid cook and baker and a practitioner of longsword in the Chicago Swordplay Guild. Jill also teaches the Art of Comic Book storytelling at The International School of Comics.

ANDY TROY has colored for Marvel Comics, DC Comics, Extreme Studios, and others, working on such characters as *Spawn*, *Batman*, *Captain America*, and *Iron Fist*. He lives and works in Huntsville, AL, where he used to play in the metal band Diamond White.

RICHARD WILLIAMS' illustration work has appeared in many national magazines, most notably *MAD*, for which he was the cover artist during the 1980s. He has also illustrated children's books (*The Legend of the Christmas Rose*, *Lewis and Clark: Explorers of the American West*) and painted covers for many young adult books such as *Encyclopedia Brown*. His paintings have been purchased by Steven Spielberg, George Lucas, and Howard Stern and are in the collections of the Society of Illustrators and the Library of Congress.